LANDRY

THE MAN INSIDE...

LANDRY

Bob St. John

WORD BOOKS
PUBLISHER

My friend, FORREST CARTER,

who died in the summer of 1979, once told me
if during his lifetime a man had two friends,
people who loved and cared for him equally
during the best and worst of times, then that
man should consider himself fortunate. I am
indeed fortunate, for I have more. This is
to them for caring, for being there.

Acknowledgments

It would take another chapter to thank all the people to whom I am indebted for help on this project. Space does not allow me to mention everyone but please understand that I appreciate your help. Particularly I would like to express my gratitude to Katherine St. John, who proofed and typed the original manuscript; to Harless Wade, Linda Little and John Anders, not only for helping gather material but in contributing to its order; to Dick Nolan who so graciously gave of his time; to Henry and Iris Stowers; to Frank Luksa, Doug Todd, Carlton Stowers and Tex Schramm; to Mr. and Mrs. Don Albrecht, Viola Bourgeois and, of course, especially to Tom and Alicia Landry.

Preface

During the years I was a sportswriter and sports columnist for the Dallas Morning News I was in what seemed, at times, almost constant contact with the personalities who are big time sport. I visited with and got to know the brightest of stars, the near-stars, the movers, the strategists, and those who tried but failed on the gamut, the panorama of sport. But I never met anyone who intrigued me more or for whom I had more respect than Thomas Wade Landry. Certainly, I disagreed at times with things he did or said, decisions he made, but I'm sure he also didn't agree with some of the things I wrote during the eleven years I covered professional football in general and the Dallas Cowboys in particular. But no matter whether the times were good or bad Tom Landry remained a great constant.

His public face seems but one. Yet, I have seen and talked with him when he was philosophical, candid, reflective, angry and when he eased the great control he has over his emotions. I have jogged, fished, worked out with him and we have discussed not just football but everything from religion and politics to the theater. When the limelight is dim he can become guarded about his personal life and, outside of his immediate family and a few close friends I don't think anybody has come to know him very well. But through scenes, observations, conversations and his reactions and relationships with others, I believe this book will be the closest you'll ever get to knowing him.

BOB ST. JOHN

Dallas, Texas
Fall, 1979

An Overview

Chapter 1. The pomp and circumstance of the Super Bowl and a setback at the brink of history

Chapter 2. Beginnings in Mission, Texas, and the winds of World War II

Chapter 3. Landry's coolness and presence of mind in battle

Chapter 4. Austin and the University of Texas following the war years

Chapter 5. The beginning of a New York adventure

Chapter 6. Tom Landry, resident genius of the New York Giants during their heyday

Chapter 7. A confrontation at Dallas that changed the direction of Landry's life

Chapter 8. Landry becomes head coach of the expansion team, the Dallas Cowboys, put together with barbed wire and chewing gum, and the relationship with Don (call me Dandy) Meredith

Chapter 9. Landry's exciting but frustrating encounters with the Green Bay Packers as the Cowboys come of age

Chapter 10. Reflections on the Kennedy assassination, conditions in the 1960s, and the disastrous encounters with Cleveland

Chapter 11. Landry does some soul-searching, changes his strategy, and discovers the Super Bowl

Chapter 12. The Cowboys go all the way in spite of criticism and a quarterback quandary

Chapter 13. The Duane Thomas enigma and disappointing setbacks

Chapter 14. Landry's "most enjoyable" year

Chapter 15. Finding the right players for another Super Bowl championship

Chapter 16. Landry at home with his family and a look at the future

A PROLOGUE

*The man's head, bent low, was resting in his hands for what seemed
a very long time. There was really no gauge of seconds or minutes because it was one of those times when the clock stops. I sat across the aisle
from him on the charter flight, a row back, and watched him and knew
the best I could what a terrible weight he was feeling. The dream . . .
oh, not really a dream but a reality for which the man, Tom Landry,
had worked, planned for—had blown up in his face, leaving the entire
Dallas Cowboy organization in ashes, both real and imagined. The
heavily favored Cowboys had gone to Cleveland to play the Browns for
the 1968 Eastern Conference championship, a game which appeared to
most only a formality to get the Cowboys back into the NFL championship contest.*

*Certainly, this was Landry's best team, better and more mature than
the ones which, the two previous years, had gone all the way to the NFL
championship before losing to the veteran teams of Vince Lombardi in
the twilight hours. It was to be the year, the time, the place, to end the
frustration of the Packer games, the narrow misses. But when the moment came, the machine malfunctioned and Landry's blueprint for a
championship crumpled before his very eyes in what must have seemed
an infinity of disappointments and frustrations.*

*The shock, reality if you will, of unexpected failure was thick, stifling.
Until that time the organization had progressed, although sometimes
very painfully, from an expansion team of castoffs, unwanteds, to contenders in 1968 when it all seemed to be there. But it had not been, and
inside the charter that evening it was like being in a hearse, dead quiet,
even for those who had tried to blunt feelings with a few beers.*

*Landry had not chosen that route, and when he raised his head, turn-
ing slightly, he looked like a defrocked priest. His eyes were glassy,
faded watercolors. When a proud man, a man with such great control,
is hit so hard by something it goes very deep. Landry since has said that
there have been times when he felt worse about losing—but that time
was the lowest I have seen him, with the hurt showing through.*

9

The jet landed at Love Field and the slow procession off the plane and into the terminal began. Players and coaches filed off, walking slowly with their heads down, dragging the weight of what had happened. It was as if they walked down some psychological tunnel of no purpose, of what seemed hopelessness. It was then, I think, that I told myself once again what, on the surface, is a truism: football is a game, sport is recreation or business, no more and no less. Certainly, it is neither life nor death. And it was then, too, that as I watched the people file from the plane I realized something else: sport becomes much more when a person puts such a big part of his life, his hopes into it.

I shrugged, started to walk into the terminal and looked back. Suddenly Tom Landry came off the plane, his wife Alicia beside him. His head was high, his eyes were clear and he seemed almost to be marching to a beat that only he heard. Soon others started watching him. He looked neither right nor left but marched straight through the terminal. It made everybody feel better. Landry was already back from where he had been and was ready for another step, another tomorrow.

I have seen championships won and lost by the Dallas Cowboys. I have seen coaches and players come and go, but the scene in the terminal that evening, as much as anything I know, is Tom Landry.

LANDRY

Landry at the University of Texas.

1

THE BAHIA MAR is one of those southern Florida hotels you see in travel posters with the ocean shown too blue and the beach too clean. Such places are pictured with tan, healthy, vibrant young people basking in the sun, riding the Big Wave, or embracing beneath swaying palms with the moon, of course, big and round and yellow. People depicted in the posters are living the good life, as we imagine it to be.

Generally speaking, the posters are wrong, out of focus. The young usually are not at the big hotels. Rather, you find the older people who have the money to spend for long Miami vacations or have come to the area to retire. They seek the sun as though it were the Fountain of Youth.

This tends to change during special events, however. There is no more special time in the life and legend of this decade than the Super Bowl. People from all walks of life beg, borrow, steal or mortgage to come from all over the country to be a part of the fine madness surrounding the biggest sporting event of any year. The elderly stand back and watch, perhaps wondering a bit about all the fuss. When it is over, they come out again, sitting quietly at their tables in the restaurants and taking slow walks along the beach.

Very early on the Monday after Super Bowl XIII in 1979, a man who must have been in his 70s moved along the shoreline near the Bahia Mar. He was bent, limping but moving along at a good pace. The beach was almost deserted and so when he passed he spoke to me and we both stopped. I wore a blue baseball cap with a "D" on it and so he assumed I was from Dallas and, perhaps, a coach or official with the Cowboys.

"So now it's over and Pittsburgh has beaten the Cowboys," he said. "I watched portions of the game on television." I responded, properly I hoped, to what he was saying and, finally, he asked, "Your Tom Landry, is he really like what you see on television? He seems such a serious man. Is he truly so devoid of emotion?"

"Not really," I said. "Perhaps the camera didn't catch him at the right times. Perhaps some know they are being watched and act animated. Landry doesn't do that. But I have seen him very animated on the sidelines. He will pace, sometimes yell at an official or throw up his hands and spin around . . . you know, like a puppet suddenly jerked."

"Oh. Well, I just see him very . . . unemotional. So, what is he really like? Is he really so staid?"

"He is and he isn't. He's what you see and what you do not see. It would take a long time for me to explain."

"I see. I think I understand." The old man said good-by and walked on down the beach, stopping ever so briefly to check the remnants of a sand castle, built by the young and washed away during the night.

The sun came out briefly that morning. Early risers, bleary eyed, had begun to gather in the lobby, hoping to get a final glimpse of Tom Landry or one of the Dallas Cowboys. The golf hats, with "Dallas Cowboys" written on them, were worth about $3 and were being sold in the shop just off the lobby for as much as $15. Prices on about everything in the Fort Lauderdale area were marked up accordingly during the Super Bowl. The T-shirts with the Cowboys, SB XIII emblem were gone but the lady in the shop said she'd try to have more by midafternoon. The T-shirts were selling for $10 and $12.

People around the lobby and just outside didn't seem to know what to do. Dallas had lost to Pittsburgh in the most exciting of Super Bowl games and now the party, the game, and the season were over and they must go back home, back to the nine-to-five routine. They seemed like people who had been in a long conversation which had been interesting but run its course. There was nothing else to say but they wanted something to be said.

14

In Tex Schramm's suite on the top floor of the Bahia Mar, which had been the Super Bowl home in Fort Lauderdale for the Cowboys, a small group of newspapermen waited for an early morning press conference with Tom Landry. Suddenly, Billy Carter, the wayward brother of the President, came through the door with a small entourage. He looked around and saw the bar. Walking over, he found a bottle of gin and filled a glass three-fourths full. He splashed a little water into the glass, symbolically I suppose, and then started sipping. He asked if anybody knew where Clint Murchison's suite was and, when told, walked out, the entourage on his coattails.

The team party the night before had been like an Irish wake. The Irish attempt to celebrate death with drink and positive talk, but just below the surface they feel for the friend or the relative who has died.

It had been that way at the Cowboy team party Sunday night. There was nothing to celebrate and, perhaps, if everybody talked loud enough, laughed hard enough, and the music were strong enough it would drown out the very bitter 35–31 loss to the Steelers. The party cost the team an estimated $80,000. The giant tent, set up near the hotel, cost $25,000, but was well equipped with carpeting, lighting, decorations and a paging system. Outside hung two Texas flags, and three groups entertained, playing and singing mostly hard rock, although there was some calypso and an attempt at country and western. Ordinarily, Willie Nelson, a big fan of the Cowboys and a long-time admirer of Tom Landry (although they would have difficulty understanding one another), entertains for the team after a Super Bowl game, win or lose. But the black players opted for a change in music style and got it. It never was clear if the groups entertaining in Fort Lauderdale were admirers of Tom Landry or not.

Tom and Alicia appeared at the party about an hour after it had started, after the predinner drinks had disappeared or melted in ice. They moved around a number of tables, speaking to people, saying quiet hellos. They sat at their table long enough to finish their meal, then got up and left, cordially but without nonsense. The previous year after the Cowboys had beaten Denver in the Super Bowl, the Landrys had stayed at the team party until the early morning hours. But for Landry that is the difference between victory and defeat. He does not talk or laugh loud enough and the music is not strong enough to drown it out.

When the Landrys left the party I told someone at my table, "He's going to look at game films."

Just before the press conference that Monday morning, Frank Luksa of the Dallas *Times-Herald* said, "Tom probably was up half the night looking at films."

15

"No," said Landry, sitting down on a couch, surrounded by writers, "I didn't see the films last night. They weren't ready. I saw them this morning."

Landry has a face which hides things well. Sometimes it almost seems to have been chiseled in stone, with deep-set, pale eyes which become almost like slits when he smiles or is deep in concentration, and a chin which juts out, lending itself to caricatures. His head has been bald on top since I have known him and I thought, sitting there, that his only obvious concession to the aging process in the last dozen years is that the hair on his neck and his neatly trimmed sideburns show more gray each year. He still has the body of an athlete, although I know old athletic injuries, especially to a knee, at times pain him.

That morning his eyes were clear, his face only slightly drawn, vague signs of lack of sleep which, on most other men of 54, would have shown much more clearly. But although he was outwardly in control and very calm, he was upset, more so than we could see, more so than we imagined, although we would find out. Landry would display very human bitterness about some key decisions made by the referees, particularly on a pass interference call Fred Swearingen made on Benny Barnes. But Landry would do so with more diplomacy than most. Tom Landry knows very well how to bite the bullet.

Just before the reporters began asking questions Landry was told that he'd missed Billy Carter, who had just walked out.

"I'm glad he wasn't running the country this morning," said Landry.

The reporters in the room who regularly write about the Cowboys wanted to know about the call on Barnes. Landry frankly said Swearingen had made a mistake and that he felt the error had taken something away from what would have been an even more exciting game.

"It's just a shame," said Landry, "that a play like that has to take something off the game. Not that we would have won or lost if it hadn't happened but you focus down on one play, like the play Jack Fette called in our first Super Bowl game here against Baltimore and the lack of officiating . . . against a fiercely aggressive Steeler team three years ago. The officials had a prominent part and it's just too bad it happens in such a big game."

I thought of the January 1971 game in the Orange Bowl when Dallas had control. They were moving for what probably would have been the decisive points as Duane Thomas fumbled on first down at the Colt one-yard line. Fette mistakenly gave the ball to Baltimore when films clearly showed it bounced into the arms of Cowboy center Dave Manders, who simply recovered it. Instead of seven points, three at the least, Dallas had nothing. Baltimore won, 16–13. And in the Super Bowl game of 1976 the Steelers came into the game as the most penalized team in the NFL and yet not one penalty was called against Pittsburgh, which beat Dallas 21–17. There did seem to be some overly aggressive tactics by the Steeler defensive backs, but that year Pittsburgh was clearly the better team.

Yet, these incidents had been buried, almost forgotten, until the call by Swearingen and then they had come back to haunt Landry. Now he was having his say about them, speaking unemotionally, matter-of-factly, but speaking out just the same. He did not say the call against Barnes cost Dallas the game. He didn't say it, although there was that possibility. Yet, frankly, as in 1976, the Steelers just appeared to have the best team.

But there at the press conference I kept thinking how Landry and the Cowboys again had missed the brass ring, of how they had come to the brink of the cup of history and just missed it . . . of how, when you just miss like that, fairly or unfairly, it's often like missing by a mile.

"I am upset," Landry continued, "not so much for myself as for the players who had worked so hard. But, sure, I'm upset because this game was the culmination of a decade in which we have been to the Super Bowl five times. We could have been the first team to win three Super Bowls and it would have been a great climax to an era. But we didn't."

For a while, the past was there again. Most insiders around the league will tell you Landry and Don Shula are the best coaches and yet, once again, history had slipped through Landry's hands. Dallas had almost beaten Green Bay in the NFL title game of 1966 and, in the Ice Bowl game against the Packers in 1967. Had Dallas won that Ice Bowl game in Green Bay it might have been Landry everyone was talking about, immortalizing, instead of Vince Lombardi.

And truly, it is most amazing when you consider that Landry brought five teams to the Super Bowl in the 1970s, in nine years, something which has not heretofore been equaled nor probably ever will be. It is even more amazing when you consider the NFL Super Bowl champion teams of 1972 and 1978 had only three carry-over starters—Roger Staubach, Cliff Harris and Jethro Pugh. So the Cowboys won two Super Bowl titles in six years with virtually different teams.

But history, as it will, sometimes ignores such things and sees only the final victory. So the team of the 1960s was Vince Lombardi's Green Bay Packers and the team of the 1970s was Chuck Noll's Pittsburgh Steelers, the first team, the first coach to take three Super Bowl titles.

I thought about the nature of things, the nature of people, of games, of history and interrupted Landry in his analysis of the game long enough to ask him how he felt the Cowboys would be remembered in the '70s, how he would be remembered.

He reflected briefly and then said, "I suppose . . . as the runnerup." When he said this everybody in the room became quiet for a while, feeling much as the people standing around the hotel lobby that morning. There was nothing else to say but they wanted something else to be said.

Just about everyone had favored the Steelers to win Super Bowl XIII. They had the best record in the NFL, 14–2 compared to 12–4 for Dallas, and had come through a tougher schedule, featuring the AFC Central Division. The defense had been superb, allowing a league low of just 195 points. Terry Bradshaw was having a magnificent season, realizing all the promise he'd always shown. And there are no better receivers in the league than the very acrobatic Lynn Swann and James Stallworth. Pittsburgh had a slight edge in a number of categories against Dallas and just appeared to be, and as it turned out was, the better team. And the Steelers had destroyed fine teams in the play-offs—Denver, 33–10, and Houston, 34–5.

The 1978 season for Dallas had taken the shape of so many others. It had been a year in which the Cowboys had been hot and cold before sitting down to steak for the NFC Eastern Division title and the play-offs. With the retirement of Ralph Neely and the slow rehabilitation of Rayfield Wright's knee, the offensive line had problems for much of the early part of the season. Harvey Martin also was idled or played with an injured knee and Tony Dorsett was guilty of a rash of fumbles.

Landry also had credited some of the early problems to an easy 38–0 opening victory over Baltimore in what many at that time had judged to be a preview of the Super Bowl game. But the Colts were playing without Bert Jones and had other problems. They were not nearly the team they had been or were supposed to be. Landry believed the victory made the Cowboys think they were better than they actually were, giving them a feeling of false security which culminated in a 6–4 record with six games remaining in the new format of sixteen instead of fourteen regular season games. As had been traditional, fans were asking the ageless question, "What's wrong with the Cowboys?" I had seen Landry's team make the Super Bowl after having 5–4 and 4–3 records, and make the play-offs with 4–3 and 5–3 beginnings. Cliff Harris had played on all those teams and we agreed that Landry, with the 6–4 record, had the NFC right where he wanted it.

Dallas won its final six games, taking the division over Philadelphia by three full games. There had been no great upheavals or problems during the season, the headliner being when Landry, figuratively, slapped Tony Dorsett on the hand for missing a Saturday morning practice before a home game against Philadelphia. Practices the day before a game are for limbering up but Dorsett failed to show up, saying he didn't hear his alarm clock and overslept. Landry said, all right, fined Dorsett, and took him out of the starting lineup. But Tony played much of the game and was back in as a starter the rest of the season. He finished with 1,325 yards rushing, Staubach led the NFL in passing for the third time and Randy White, Charlie Waters and Cliff Harris all made All-Pro and led the defensive unit to championship form.

In the first play-off game Dallas had encountered problems beating Atlanta, a wildcard team, 27–20, eventually relying on some trickery and backup quarterback Danny White, who replaced Roger Staubach when he was knocked out in the first half. As usual, the insiders believed the powerful Los Angeles Rams, 34–10 play-off winners over Minnesota and a team which had beaten Pittsburgh 10–7 during regular season, would handle the Cowboys in the NFC title game in the Los Angeles Coliseum.

When you talk about talent and material, the Rams are the equal of any team in the league and probably stand alongside Pittsburgh and, perhaps, New England as having the best overall talent. Dallas is close to this group and has superior talent in key positions but, as New Orleans Saints' coach Dick Nolan, a former Landry aide, pointed out, "Tom's system can take care of some players who don't have the great talent and ability."

Certainly, the Los Angeles defense is as good as any there is and I had asked Landry a week before that game if calling the plays against such a defense presented a special challenge to him. He smiled and said, "It's always a challenge." But against a defense such as the Rams it's very special, I suggested. He smiled, nodded what I interpreted as a confirmation, or the closest I'd get to one.

Actually, the way it turned out Landry called a conservative game because his defense was in control and very much outplayed the Ram offense. The Rams of Chuck Knox ran a simple offense and the Rams of his successor, Ray Malavasi, did the same. Landry has long had their number.

"Landry's offense is so complicated it takes a book to explain it," said Pittsburgh All-Pro linebacker Jack Ham, commenting on the Dallas–Los Angeles NFC title game. "You could put the Los Angeles offense on a postcard."

The 28–0 victory over the Rams was especially pleasing to Landry because of the performance of strong safety Charlie Waters. Landry had defended and stood by Waters through some tough early years of his career in which Charlie had been asked to play cornerback when he really didn't have the speed and quickness to do so, had broken and

19

rebroken his arm and gone through a divorce which caused him to report to camp one year only a shell of himself. But Landry had moved
Waters to strong safety in 1974 and he became an All-Pro. Today he is
happily remarried, has a baby, and is one of the finer gentlemen and
leaders on the team. Charlie easily was the star of the NFC title victory
over the Rams, recovering a fumble to set up one touchdown and making pass interceptions to set up two others.

The final Dallas touchdown was a *coup de grace* by linebacker
Thomas (Hollywood) Henderson, who the week before the game had
publicly said the Rams "don't have enough class to make the Super
Bowl." Landry had cringed when he heard this but never said a word
to Henderson about it. Henderson picked off a Ram pass and returned
it sixty-eight yards for the final touchdown and Dallas was on its way to
Miami, to Super Bowl XIII.

Before the team left for Florida Landry said, "We have a chance this
time to make history, which is something we'll all be very proud of later.
I definitely think the NFL's best two teams are in the Super Bowl, which
probably isn't always the case, and that the Steelers should be favored."

"Pittsburgh," said Cowboy publicity director Doug Todd, "might
have a little better team but we've got two weeks to get ready. Give
Landry two weeks and he'd have beaten Nazi Germany."

There is nothing quite like the Super Bowl and, unless you have been
a part of the madness surrounding the athletic contest, then you will not
appreciate it fully. Certainly, the Super Bowl is game—sport—and yet
because of the unbelievable hype, the public relations by the NFL, it
becomes in our minds much more. Much more.

The Super Bowl is worshiped; we go to its altar to make sacrifices in
papier-mâché. Indeed, we make it bigger than life not only because of
the effect of the hype but also because, perhaps, we need to do so, need
to have the greatest of distractions from everyday life and what comes
with it.

Outside of the political conventions there is more media attention
given to the Super Bowl than any single event. It is on television and
radio. It is in screaming headlines, and pictures and store windows constantly remind us of the game as do our children, wearing No. 12,
tossing a football around the yard. No matter what you wish, what you
think or want, most of the kids would rather be Roger Staubach than
John Updike. They would rather play for Tom Landry than work for
Jimmy Carter. And our children grow up with the face of a man like
Tom Landry embedded in their minds, as was Tom Mix or Gene Autry
when Landry was a boy.

The NFL would have us hold the game in such reverence, and we do, that Roman numerals are used to designate its particular year, such as in 1979 when the game became XIII. Almost 2,000 credentials were issued to media covering the game and at least 500 more were turned down because there simply was not enough room for them.

Super Bowl XIII was viewed in 35,090,000 homes, more than any sporting event in history and, perhaps 150,000,000 people watched the game on television. It was carried by 218 stations in the United States and 378 in Canada (308 in English and 70 in French). It was televised in Puerto Rico, Mexico, Australia, Japan, New Zealand, Greenland, the Azores, Crete, Diego Garcia, England and the Philippines.

Over one million people have attended the annual game in person. The players' shares in SB XIII were $18,000 each for the Steelers and $9,000 each for the Cowboys, certainly more money than most people can make in such a short span of time.

During the week the players, from top to bottom of the roster, become celebrities, folk heroes, philosophers. We listen, hang onto their every word, the irony being that at ordinary times we might not walk around the corner to meet some of them. We would find what some say trite, hollow and not particularly interesting.

But everybody likes to be there, to be a part of the game, the hype, the overkill build-up, the atmosphere and the escape, for a while anyway, from the reality of daily existence. And, perhaps, it is good for a while to be in Camelot.

"The game has become so big that sometimes everything surrounding it takes away from the contest itself," said Landry. "But I understand why they have all the build-up, all the interviews. Everybody has a job to do and this is what people want to read about.

"Certainly, it can be distracting if you let it. But I just accept it, set aside time for the different things we have to do, try to enjoy the situation we're in. I imagine a lot of teams, a lot of coaches would like to go through the so-called distractions that we're going through. We're very happy to be here.

"The biggest problem for the players is that they have to get up so early—of course, you can't sleep much anyway—and you burn up a lot of energy before the game. There is just a lot of tension before the game and so much of the energy goes while waiting for the kickoff.

"Personally, I'm sure my [cool] appearance is misleading. Sure, I'm nervous. But in this situation we know what to expect because we've been here before and have had the Super Bowl experience. I've been here before. That helps you to relax.

"I'm not sure, however, that the play-offs are a true indication of the best team. You win a play-off game and it means you're the best team on that given day."

Because of the publicity demands the teams had to come to Florida on Monday before the game. Players had to meet with the press on Tuesday and Wednesday and the coaches had press conferences Tuesday, Wednesday and Friday.

George Allen, when he brought the Washington Redskins to the Super Bowl in Houston, did a lot of griping about the press taking up his time. Bud Grant voiced strong opinions about the distractions the first couple of times the Minnesota Vikings were in the Super Bowl, but mellowed the last two appearances. A number of players, such as the Vikings' Jim Marshall, griped a lot about having to undergo the interviews. Sometimes distractions are what you make of them.

The two teams who seemed most to enjoy the atmosphere have been the Steelers and the Cowboys. They have been to eight Super Bowls and won five between them. Once as a press conference was ending after the Steelers had made the Super Bowl in 1973, center Ray Mansfield noted the reporters were leaving and yelled, "Hey, you guys, don't go. Let's talk some more."

"What good," Landry once said, "would it do to gripe?"

The image of a stoic Tom Landry is so implanted in the mind of the general public that it wouldn't change if, for the next ten years, he put a feather in his hat and danced along the sidelines, carrying a cane. Actually he is a good, honest interview, always cooperative, but during Super Bowl XIII he seemed much more relaxed than ever with the press.

But as the Super Bowl Week began, comedian Don Rickles noted, "Chuck Noll and Tom Landry got into a grinning contest and neither side won, so they brought in another play-off team, Mt. Rushmore, and it beat both of them."

Both Noll and Landry are intellectuals but Landry clearly was the more personable of the two, easily capturing the press. For the most part, Noll remained very serious. He would answer questions with such remarks as, "I'm not a wordsmith," or "I'm not a historian," and "We're ready to play."

Once on the bulletin board in the press conference headquarters at the Americana Hotel on Miami Beach someone wrote, "Interesting quotes from Chuck Noll's press conference." Below, nothing was written.

However, Noll did get in a zinger at Thomas Henderson, the guy who said the Rams had no class. Henderson, whose nickname is Hollywood, was reminded that Pittsburgh Steeler defensive end L. C. Greenwood also had the nickname of Hollywood. Thomas responded, "L. C. Greenwood thinks he's Hollywood? How does this sound? L. C. (Hollywood) Greenwood. Or Greenwood (Hollywood) L. C. Or Hollywood Three Rivers L. C. Greenwood. That's the most ridiculous thing I ever heard. If he's the original Hollywood I'm gonna give it up. There's only one Hollywood. First I had Harold (Hollywood) Jackson of LA via New England. Now I got the guy who wears gold shoes for Pittsburgh who wants to be Hollywood.

"Maybe I should get some silver slippers and call myself Cinderella. If L. C. Greenwood can be Hollywood I'm gonna be Cinderella."

"I understand," said Noll, dryly, "empty barrels make the most noise."

Throughout much of the week those among the nation's press kept remarking and writing that Landry was showing a new side of his personality, but I wondered if many of them ever looked that closely anyway and heretofore had just accepted the general concept.

One morning Landry bumped into Doug Todd at ten o'clock. "What are you doing up so early?" Landry kidded him. "Oh, I've been up for hours," said Todd. Landry thought for a second and said, "Hmm. Nobody could be up that long and look as sleepy as you do."

Cowboy president Tex Schramm is part owner of a marina in Florida and one day when Landry asked where Schramm might be and was told that Tex was off on his boat, Landry sighed and said, "I'm going to come back in my other life as a president instead of a coach."

Landry's press conferences on Tuesday and Wednesday were held at the restaurant just to the side of the Bahia Mar. He would get up early, breakfast with the team, conduct team meetings and then hold a press conference-luncheon. When he had finished the writers went into a smaller, adjoining room to interview the players. Outside of Hollywood Henderson, Landry was the best interview, the best copy.

As Landry entered a typical press conference at midweek he walked slowly to the podium, then looked out across the room at the mass media. "I'm not sure," he deadpanned, "if this room's big enough to handle the Thomas Henderson interview but we'll try."

Before the press conference he had been asked what he would do concerning Thomas Henderson if he began talking about the Steelers as he did the Rams. Landry had grinned slightly and said, "Try to ignore it."

But then he seriously discussed the subject and his attitude toward those who were so outspoken. "I sort of mind the way he sometimes speaks out because that's not really my style," he said. "But I think we're in a different time now. I think a player should have great freedom of expression. My criterion is when it starts bothering the team and its effectiveness then I'll do something about it. But it hasn't.

"The main thing is that Henderson psyches himself up with what he says. When he does this, he has to back himself up. He's done it so far. It'll be interesting to see him when he doesn't. The only time I'd say anything is if he doesn't do well. Then I might suggest he change his tactics a little.

"It's just out of character for me as a professional player and coach to sound off that way. Except, once again, today we find in the NFL and almost any type of work there's a lot of expression by individuals. Whether they spike the ball or do this or that. It's something that's part of our times now. We deal with it as best we can.

"I don't resent it as a person. I don't resent people very easily. I can tolerate people and what they do pretty well. I don't feel any resentment at all about Henderson. He's underlined things that are positive, too."

When Landry had answered all the questions, members of the press left the dining room and went into the adjoining room to talk to the players, seated at individual tables. Landry came down off the podium and I stopped him. We stood there, talking about the Thomas Hendersons, the individuality which more and more had come into football and of another very different player he had coached, Duane Thomas, who had become as caustic as Henderson was good-natured, as withdrawn as Henderson was outgoing. Landry reflected back on the 1960s as the cause and effect of many things that had happened and were happening.

"I think, in many respects, the '60s was the worst era in American history for so many young people because of the pressures they had on them, regarding such things as the freedom issues, the drug culture," he said. "It was, perhaps, an era that was needed but one which was awfully difficult and, hopefully, one we'll never see again.

"There were so many negative aspects to the '60s but I think the kids taught us one very important thing; they taught us to look at ourselves and recognize each person as an individual.

"It wasn't easy for those of us who came up in a different era, a different atmosphere. I know it wasn't easy for me. But we had to learn the humanistic approach, for instance, to football. When I became aware of this, it helped me in my basic approach to life.

"Duane was a reflection of the social revolution of the '60s. What happened during that time brought him to where he was, the point to which he had come. I think it was very sad, what happened to him. I felt we were handling the situation until after his rookie year; he spent that summer in California and became involved in the culture out there.

"But . . . those times have changed. The players today, the ones coming out of college, are different from those in college in the mid and late 1960s. They're concerned more about their careers and what their success pattern will be. Yet, they still have the carry-overs from the '60s, which are freedom and individualism. That's good. I think those are very good qualities to retain."

Two other writers stopped to talk to Landry, who was through with the press conference and was in no way required to stick around. But he had. Samantha Stephenson, a free-lance writer who had worked out of Dallas for a few years in the early 1970s, had been at the press conference and motioned me over. She was doing a Super Bowl story on Landry for a publication in Philadelphia, where she lived.

"He's not going to remember me," she said. "Why don't you introduce me?"

"He might remember you."

"Gosh, it'll be embarrassing if he doesn't."

She walked over with me to Landry, who looked at her for a few seconds and said, "Hello, I haven't seen you in a long time. It's nice seeing you again." Then, he looked back at me and told her, "But you're keeping bad company."

Everyone laughed, including me. I don't know, truly, whether Landry remembered her or not but, just as important, he made her think he had.

Landry always is extra polite to women reporters but is very aware that some have gone to great lengths and even taken legal action to try to get equal treatment with newspapermen to the point of being allowed into locker rooms. "If it ever comes to the point in our society where it doesn't make any difference whether women go into the locker rooms, then football no longer will make any difference nor will newspapers because everything will have gone down the drain," he said. "There are some things you don't do and this happens to be one of them."

A man had been watching us. He looked to be in his '60s and came over and talked to Landry. "Tom, I saw you play when you were with the Giants," he said. "You seem so calm now. But you used to get pretty mad in those days—had a temper, all right. I remember you letting your temper go a few times. You were awful fiery."

"Now the truth comes out," I said. "You were a mean, dirty player."

Landry seemed briefly embarrassed and said, "I guess we all grow a little, mature a little."

When Landry left, the guy repeated, "Yessir, he sure had a bad temper then. But you wouldn't know it now, huh?"

No, you wouldn't know it now.

Players sat behind tables in the adjoining room enjoying the attention, hating the attention, and expounding on The Game, their philosophy on life, marriage, the pursuit of happiness and the funny things that happened to them on the way to the Super Bowl. What they were saying, the way they felt was devoured by the listening media, like food at a short order place. The biggest crowd was around Thomas (Hollywood) Henderson.

Larry Cole, the eleventh-year defensive lineman from Hawaii via the Air Force Academy, is one of the more thoughtful, reflective players. He has been shuffled around, from end to tackle to end, depending on the needs of the game, the season, and has never been one of the team's stars but remains a steady force.

"Times have changed on this team," said Cole. "It used to be, you know, 'This is the game plan. Do what I tell you because I'm the coach.' Now if you don't agree you can discuss it with the coaches. Yes, I think you can go all the way to Landry if you wanted."

"I think Coach Landry gives us [the players] more of the benefit of the doubt than he used to do," said linebacker D. D. Lewis. "It used to be awfully tough in meetings when he'd critique the films. Boy, he could mow you down, whether you were a fourteen-year veteran or not. Sometimes, at meetings, he'd ask you a question. It wasn't so much that you were afraid of him as a man but just the fact of the great knowledge he had. You might know the answer but you'd be so nervous you couldn't get it out. It's not so bad now.

"The man's knowledge is amazing. He coaches every position, knows everything. He doesn't panic when things go wrong and that's something that helps us all. He stays cool. If we're going bad he might throw some things out of the playbook but basically we'll do the same things but just keep trying to do them better.

"But I guess the thing that impresses me most about him is that he can put so very much into the game and not be consumed by it. He puts everything into it but can walk away and leave it there on the field. Not many coaches, if any, can do that."

Preston Pearson, the veteran halfback, had played for Don Shula in Baltimore and Chuck Noll in Pittsburgh, and had come to Dallas in 1975 on waivers. He was asked about Landry's impersonal relationship with his players. "The dealings I've had with the three coaches I've played for aren't that much different. You hear this coach or that coach gets close to his players. Well, those three can stand on their records. I don't think a player should have a personal relationship with a coach, going out for a drink or to dinner. That might tend to lead to favoritism."

Sometimes players have not agreed with Landry but I cannot remember any of them accusing him of favoritism, not even Craig Morton after Landry twice had picked Staubach over him as the No. 1 quarterback. Some fans have said that Landry chose Staubach because they were both very religious and strong in the Fellowship of Christian Athletes, but those who believed this do not know Landry. Staubach was in the FCA before he ever met Landry.

"I think," said Don Meredith, Landry's first project at quarterback, "if Tom Landry was going to create a perfect quarterback for his system it would be Roger. He has great character, which Tom likes, and the intensity and dedication to give that 110 percent, go that extra hundred yards. Roger's adapted well and, consequently, Dallas has won more games."

In the two Super Bowls Dallas has won, Roger Staubach was the quarterback.

Tom Landry, Jr., stood on the balcony of the hospitality room of the Bahia Mar Hotel. It overlooked a marina below. The fishing boats, docked, slowly swayed with the rhythm of the water. He is a little shorter than his father but has the same athletic build and had played football on scholarship at Duke before prematurely having to retire because of knee problems.

"He deserves this," he said. "Dad really deserves this. The Steelers are a great team and I'm sure Chuck Noll is a fine man but I just believe, with the things he's gone through, that Dad deserves to be the first to win three Super Bowls.

"But I guess about everybody figures the Steelers will win, don't they?"

"I think, man for man, the Steelers are better," I said. "Overall, their offensive line is a little better and the cornerbacks certainly are—but you never know. Your dad is smart enough that he just might pull it off if the Cowboys get the breaks, the close calls.

"But, sure, if you were a betting man, you'd have to take the Steelers, giving the oddsmakers three points."

"Dad's so dern smart, though," he added, staring blankly at the boats in the marina below but not really seeing them.

In a poll among the media covering the Super Bowl, 70 percent picked Pittsburgh. When the NFL head coaches were asked, only Dick Nolan and Bud Grant picked Dallas to win. President Carter bet his mother, Lillian Carter, the Cowboys would win. The general public seemed divided, which certainly was a change. For years the Cowboys had been, more than any other club, the nation's team, the one which most captured the imagination of the country.

"I wouldn't know which team most people wanted to win in this game," said Landry. "But in recent years when we'd go into the play-offs I believe there were more people in our business who wanted to see us lose. The more success you have, the more people would like to see you fall. I think it's normal to favor the underdog. We were underdogs for years and that's when we picked up a lot of fans.

"As far as this game, Pittsburgh should be favored, based on the schedule the Steelers played and what they accomplished. I do believe the two best teams in the NFL are here at the Super Bowl. I'm not sure that's always the case.

"At the championship level, the play-off level, there is a very narrow line between winning and losing. You don't have to take much away from a team to keep it from winning. The play-off system we have isn't necessarily a measure of the strength of two teams. You come out on a certain Sunday and for some reason your metabolism or whatever isn't right and you're out of it. Play-offs are just a measurement of the strength of a team on a particular day.

"I am not confident at all in this game. That doesn't mean I don't think we can win. But when you have two teams that are so evenly matched, something could happen that could throw the whole thing off for us. Just one little thing."

His final statement was a foreboding.

The limousine joined the early Friday morning traffic moving from Fort Lauderdale to Miami. Nobody pays that much attention to a limousine in the Miami area. Tom Landry sat in the back and read a newspaper. He was being driven to the Americana Hotel on Miami Beach for a final press conference. He was silent, concentrating, then put down the paper and said, "I don't know what anybody possibly can ask that hasn't already been covered." The traffic wasn't as bad as expected and so the limousine arrived almost three-quarters of an hour early, time Landry certainly could have used preparing himself for the game. But the wasted time, the inconvenience didn't seem to bother him.

Landry went into the coffee shop, sat down with a couple of writers and ordered hot tea. A columnist from San Antonio told Landry, "My daughter has informed me several times that her favorite teacher at school is your brother. She says he's excellent, a nice and understanding man."

Landry smiled politely and said, "I'm afraid it must be another

Landry. I don't have a brother who teaches school. The only brother I have lives in Houston."

"Oh," said the columnist, "I'm glad then I didn't write anything about it. I started to."

Landry chatted informally with the writers, sipping his tea. Then he went to a large ballroom for his final pregame press conference. No new questions were asked. There just were some different people there asking them.

That night Tom and Alicia attended the Super Bowl Party in the National Airlines International Terminal at the Miami airport. There were 3,000 people in attendance and most believe it is more difficult to get a ticket to the annual party than the annual game.

Previous NFL Super Bowl parties had been held in such places as aboard the Queen Mary, docked at Long Beach when the Super Bowl game was in Los Angeles, and at Hialeah Race Track in Miami in 1976. It was said the NFL spent about $1 million for shows surrounding Super Bowl XIII. At various places in the terminal different kinds of food were served and the entertainment ranged from bongo drummers to limbo dancers.

The Landrys sat at a table with Mr. and Mrs. Pete Rozelle. I walked around with Dick Nolan, who went by Landry's table and said, "Boy, I tell you, I ought to be sitting there instead of you."

"You can't win the Big One," said Landry, referring to what people used to say about Dallas before it finally won a Super Bowl in January 1972.

On Super Bowl Sunday buses stopped near the team entrance to the Orange Bowl and a path was made for Landry and his players to make a short walk through the crowd. There were no problems as people only yelled and waved Cowboy banners in the air. But not far away the pickpockets were at work. There must have been a pickpocket convention during the Super Bowl. Venders outside the stadium were robbed and by halftime over thirty fans had reported billfolds stolen inside the stadium. There would be hundreds taken before the afternoon was over.

Before the game I moved in the crowd, which edged along inch by inch. I saw a guy grab a man's billfold and yelled at a nearby officer. He looked and shrugged. There was nothing he could do. Officers did catch one thief but by the time they ran him down he had passed the billfold to friends.

Somehow, when a Super Bowl game finally begins it always seems a slight letdown after all of the build-up. But then you quickly get caught up in the time, the moment and significance and feel a great excitement. Most experts said the previous Dallas–Pittsburgh game had been the most exciting Super Bowl. This one would top that.

As the game began Dallas surprised everybody by moving the ball against Pittsburgh on the ground. With Tony Dorsett running wide, Dallas moved to a first and ten at the Steeler 34. Landry decided to pull a surprise early and called for a double-reverse pass. The Cowboys had worked on the play over and over in practice and removed all the kinks. Roger Staubach took the snap and handed to Dorsett who was to give the ball to flanker Drew Pearson on a reverse. Pearson, who once had been a quarterback, was supposed to stop and throw the ball to tight end Billy Joe DuPree. The Steelers fell for the trickery and DuPree was wide open for a touchdown. But Pearson fumbled the exchange and Pittsburgh recovered.

"That was the only thing which had never happened when we practiced that play," said offensive coordinator Danny Reeves. "Drew never fumbled it."

Critics later would strongly criticize Landry for calling such a play after the way his club had marched downfield. In fact, after the game Dorsett also was critical, saying Dallas should have continued to run. But against the Steelers' great defense it isn't likely the Cowboys would have continued to run the ball that well, which Landry suspected. I also believe Landry felt if he could shock the Steelers early he might be able to gain an advantage and keep it throughout the game. His team had run the ball and then, as Pittsburgh closed ranks to stop this, Dallas might have completed the trick pass for a touchdown. The Steelers would not have known from which direction the Cowboys were coming. But the pass had not worked.

It became obvious early that Terry Bradshaw would have a tremendous day, a continuation of the great season he had seen. Not only was he throwing well but the Cowboy defenders, especially the secondary, were having problems tackling the receivers once they caught the ball. Staubach threw a touchdown pass and linebacker Mike Hegman stole the ball from Bradshaw on a blitz, running 37 yards for a score. However, Bradshaw threw three touchdown passes the first half and Pittsburgh led, 21–14.

The Cowboy defense finally appeared to find itself in the third period and the offense also drove into position to score the tying touchdown. The defense held Pittsburgh to a net twelve yards on three third-period possessions, whereas the Cowboy offense drove from the Steeler 42 to a third and three at the ten. Staubach faked play-action and then tossed a pass to tight end Jackie Smith, all alone in the end zone, and what happened was one of those awful pictures of agony that you see in sports. Smith had the ball, then let it fall away as he dropped to his knees. He had waited a career for such a chance and, when it had come, he let it get away. Dallas had to settle for a field goal and Landry later would defend Smith, saying the play wasn't that big an issue. But it could have been. Landry felt great empathy for Smith's situation and was afraid, after Jackie's career, that the dropped pass would be what he and the fans would remember.

Dallas had regained the momentum. However, the Steelers faced a second and five in the fourth period at their own 44 and Bradshaw sent Swann down the right sidelines toward cornerback Benny Barnes, who back-pedaled. Barnes then became tangled up with Swann as the Steeler receiver turned back toward the middle of the field to go after Bradshaw's pass. They both fell. Actually, Swann appeared to cause the contact, stumbling into Barnes, but field judge Fred Swearingen called interference on Benny, a 33-yard penalty. Landry said later he was more upset with official Pat Knight, who had a clearer view of the play and should have told Swearingen.

Landry was yelling at both officials from the sidelines but it would not matter. The call would stand. It was all the Steelers needed to start rolling again, if indeed they needed even that. Pittsburgh moved to a third and nine at the Dallas 22 and Franco Harris scored almost untouched as Charlie Waters, moving in for the tackle, was screened off by an official, who was trying to get out of the way.

The ensuing kickoff went short to Randy White, who was playing with a broken thumb. He fumbled and Pittsburgh recovered at the Dallas 18 and Bradshaw threw another touchdown pass. Suddenly, a 21-17 game became a 35-17 Pittsburgh rout with 6:51 left to play. But Dallas didn't quit. Staubach, who had not played particularly well, got hot and Dallas moved 89 yards to score in eight plays with 2:27 left, cutting the margin to 35-24.

When Dallas recovered an onside kick Cowboy fans began to think of the great comeback against San Francisco in the 1972 play-off game and people in the Orange Bowl, ready to leave, started back to their seats. Staubach took Dallas 52 yards for another touchdown and the Cowboys trailed, 35-31, with just 22 seconds left. This time an onside kick failed and the Steelers ran out the clock and Landry's chance to make history.

In the Cowboy dressing room Landry had patiently waited for the television people to go live on the air and was very composed as he an-

31

swered questions. But when the interview was over he said, "It was such a shame. They just played their hearts out . . . just played their hearts out."

And when the press conference had ended that Monday morning after the Super Bowl, I still thought about how he had missed history again and the effect it had on so many. Landry, honestly, was more concerned about the great disappointment his players were feeling. But more people than he could imagine felt for him personally. They were people in Dallas with whom he had come in contact because of his profession and because of the kind of Christian man he is. They were people who had known and respected him so much while he was a player and assistant coach in New York. And there were those in the far corner of South Texas, the ones who had known him when he was a boy growing up in the little town of Mission.

2

MISSION IS A QUIET, somewhat unassuming Texas town of about 16,000 people which lies deep in the Rio Grande Valley, short miles from the Mexican border. Over the years its proximity to Mexico has caused a large migration and so the vast majority of citizens in the area have Latin ancestry. In fact, Hidalgo County, in which the city is located, is named for Miquel Hidalgo y Costillo, the Spaniard who first came to the area. Today the impact is still felt because many streets have Latin names and some residential homes are painted aqua, a much-used color in Mexico.

The city lies in a citrus fruit, farming area with rich, sandy loams and is known as the "Home of the Grapefruit." Tall palm trees line residential streets and the major highway, U.S. 83, which connects the city with the adjoining towns of McAllen and Pharr. Unlike most small Texas towns, Mission is not built around a square but rather the area has grown up on both sides of a main street, called Conway.

In the last decade or so Mission has changed its shape. A new stretch of stores and short order food places have appeared along Highway 83, as if drawn there magnetically. And the city also is now catering more to winter vacationers and, more and more, getting them to stop over en route to the Gulf Coast, less than 100 miles to the east.

But as one resident put it, "We don't get the kind who spend money, like the ones who go to the coast or stay in the big hotels. We get the ones in campers, coming for the warmer weather. But that is progress."

A number of distinguished people have come from Mission. Senator Lloyd Bentsen has his roots there and so do Congressmen Joe Kilgore and Eligio (Kiki) de la Garza. William Jennings Bryan once had a home in Mission and cowboy film star Ken Maynard was born there. Yet, the name for which the town is best known—the one which everybody knows about and will tell you about without any provocation—is Tom Landry.

"Yessir," said Sam Nixon, looking out across Conway Street from the window of his barber shop, "the Landrys were mighty fine people. They named a park here for Ray Landry, Tommy's daddy, you know. And of course we're all mighty proud of Tommy."

A group of kids, moving toward the Border Theater, a relic, passed the window. One boy had on a maroon and white Mission High School letter jacket. Another had hair down to his shoulders, a carry-over from the '60s. They passed a woman walking down the street who had to get out of their way.

"The kids in Tommy's day," said Andy Anderson, who has retired but works at times in the hardware store on Conway, "were a lot different. You get me talking about those days and it doesn't seem so long ago, really. Not so long ago."

When Thomas Wade Landry was in his teens there was an atmosphere in small-town America which never will be repeated, one of slow-moving dreams, of lazy days with fishing poles, of heroes on cereal boxes whose countenances were bigger than life, not so much because we were told this as much as we willed it so. It was a time that now has become as Americana as cars with big curving fenders and five-cent soda pops. The Depression had come, faded, and gone, and the survivors were into a new and exciting high. Dreams were in color.

And it seemed so far away, so very far away where the small, very animated man with the funny mustache was running amok in Europe and those bitten by the power struggle of madness were gaining so much influence in Japan. Soon it would not be so far away.

Soon it would bring an end to the final spring of our innocence . . . .

Tommy Landry was born September 11, 1924, in Mission at a time when all the businesses in the city were on Conway Street—the grocery, the drug store and the movie theaters—and when cities such as Dallas and Houston seemed so far away that you didn't even think about them. There were some 5,000 people living in Mission at the time but the Latin and Anglo population mixed very little, staying mostly to themselves.

Ray Landry had brought his family through the Depression better than most. There were no frills but his wife, Ruth, a daughter by the same name and sons Robert, Tommy and Jack did not lack for necessities. They lived in a comfortable though small frame house a block off Conway on Dougherty Street with a small yard in front and back and a vacant lot on the side.

Ray Landry's father, Alfred, was born in Bourbonnais, Illinois, one of six children of Canadians Stanislas and Marceline (Trembley) Landrie (the name was later changed to Landry). The family apparently originated in France and migrated to Canada where Stanislas, called Stani, was born in San Leon, one of six children. Stani crossed into the United States and, at the age of 19, joined and served in Company B of the 46th Wisconsin regiment in the Civil War. He was a lumberman and farmer by trade.

Alfred, or Fred, married Lillian Celena Anderson, whose father was Scotch-Irish and whose mother was French, in 1893. At that time he spoke mostly French and was taught English by his wife. The family settled in Illinois and the difficult winters took their toll as two of their six children died.

A family doctor advised Fred to leave Bradley, Illinois, and move his family to a warmer climate. His son, Ray, born November 17, 1898, was having awful bouts with muscular rheumatism and, fearing for the child's health, the Landrys signed on with the McColl Land and Development Company and moved to Mission in February, 1912. Fred purchased a small piece of land near Mission but later moved into town and became a bricklayer.

During the train trip south, the family kept singing, "It never rains in Texas" but they arrived at Mission during a downpour, somewhat shocked. However, the weather soon cleared, stayed warm, and Ray's sister, Mrs. Viola Bourgeois, who still lives in Mission, recalled, "Oddly enough, Ray never had any problem I can remember with the rheumatism after we came to Texas. The warm, healthy climate was just what we needed."

Ray was a good, natural athlete who distinguished himself as a fine pitcher and football player and also an outstanding debater. He was an easy-going young man whom classmates called "Happy." He also managed to distinguish himself with a young girl named Ruth Coffman, who had long braids of auburn hair, ending in curls. Ruth had been born January 5, 1899, in Haymakertown, Virginia, to Benjamin and

Banona Spencer Vandergrift. Her father, a farmer, moved his family from Tennessee to Oklahoma and, finally, to Mission in 1915.

Ruth was a much more serious and reserved person than Ray. She was a top student, sang in the glee club and, upon graduation, was valedictorian of her class. "Once they started dating in high school, neither of them ever dated anybody else," recalled Viola Bourgeois.

Ray graduated from Mission High in 1918 and went to Texas A&M. Ruth graduated a year later and her family moved to Los Angeles, California. Ray followed her to California, took a mechanic's course, worked for a while, and on May 8, 1920, they were married and moved back to Mission, where they would spend the remainder of their lives.

Ray's father, Fred, had been a very devout Christian. Once he caught Ray, then in his teens, smoking with a friend behind the barn. Ray felt the wrath of God was about to descend on him but his father, speaking quietly, said, "If a man's going to smoke he shouldn't sneak around to do it. Come on in the house and smoke with me."

They went into the house and Fred pulled out a box of his favorite cigars. He lit up, took a big puff and urged his son to do the same. Ray obliged. "Take a deep puff," said his father, "another deep puff." Ray did. "That's good," said his father. "Now once again." Ray turned gray and ran for the bathroom. He was very sick. But he never smoked again and the example he set carried over to his son, Tommy.

Ray worked as a mechanic, operating a small automobile shop, and he also served as chief of the town's volunteer fire department, a post he held for forty years until his retirement in 1973. He liked to hunt and fish and often took his boys with him. He wasn't known as a talker but as a doer. If there was a drowning, Ray was the first man in the boat. If there was a fire, he was the first to climb up to the attic. Ray Landry was just that way.

The Landrys regularly attended the First United Methodist Church, where Ray served as superintendent of the Sunday school for twenty-seven years, and Ruth constantly was doing church work. There is a Ray Landry Fireman's Park in Mission, and June Brann, editor of the weekly "Progress," wrote a few years ago, "Tom's a fine man but he has a lot of way to go to fill his daddy's shoes."

"My father was a fine man, a great man," Tom Landry recalled. "I can remember him feeding his family on $1.50 a day during the Depression. But we always had enough to eat. And I can't ever remember when we didn't go to church. It was something we always did, something I grew up doing. But I don't think I really became a true Christian until much later in my life, after I had joined the New York Giants. I just went to church because my parents always did and took us with them."

"When Tommy was growing up he wouldn't let his father out of his sight," said Viola Bourgeois. "I can remember when Tommy was about three. He was waiting, so anxious for his father and Uncle Arthur to come home from a hunting trip. When the men parked across the street Tommy just flew out of the house to see what they'd brought back. He ran right in front of a car, was hit and thrown down.

"Fortunately, the car that hit him was going slow or he'd have been killed. He did break his leg. I was outside in another car and Ray ran, picked up Tommy and got into the car and we rushed to the doctor.

"Ray and a friend had to pull Tommy's leg taut while the doctor set it, without using anesthetic. Tommy would scream and Ray would just about pass out. He'd have to turn the leg over to me to pull while he went and laid down. But when Tommy saw that his father was gone he'd start having a fit and his father would have to come back and hold the leg. I've never known Ray to be squeamish before or after that time, but he just couldn't stand to see his boy suffering so much."

When Tommy first began to talk he had a lisp, and the Murdock brothers, who ran the corner service station, loved to hear him talk. They had a lemon tree in back of the station and often would invite Tommy there to have lemonade. One day when they were making lemonade they gave Tommy a dime and told him to go buy some sugar. Soon, he came back crying and said the man at the store wouldn't give him any "tuga." So they wrote the word *sugar* on a piece of paper and sent him back to the store.

"Ray," continued Mrs. Bourgeois, "was such an outgoing person. Ruth was more quiet and reserved and I guess Tommy got a lot of his ways from her. But they were both such tremendous people, such fine Christian people."

"Ruth," recalled Wade Spillman, an Austin lawyer who is a lifelong friend of Tom and once dated his sister, "was a beautiful woman, with striking eyes. But she was the strong, silent type. She expected things to be done and done properly. I guess when Tom and I were growing up I was over at their house every day at one time or another. The impression I had was that Ruth was the disciplinarian and that Ray was the looser, more outgoing type . . . just a real friendly, lovable guy.

"There wasn't a great outward show of affection in the family but they felt it. You could tell they loved one another."

But Ruth did let her guard down at times. "I remember after Tommy was coaching with the Cowboys," said Mrs. Bourgeois, "that this television fellow came and interviewed Ruth. He asked her if she ever got excited watching the games. She said, no, that she stayed calm.

"Well, after the feller left, I looked at Ruth and laughed. Why didn't you tell him how you yell and jump up and down watching the Cowboys on television? I asked her. She just kinda grinned and blushed. She was such a lovely person, such a lovely person."

Robert, three years older than Tom, was also a good athlete, as was his younger brother James, now a computer expert in Houston.

"Our playground was the entire town," recalled Tom. "We'd get together on a vacant lot and play all the games without any organization, except what we did ourselves. We took a lot of bumps but we learned, and there was no pressure. I think kids these days miss that type of thing. It's all so organized now and so many of the parents or coaches of the kids put pressure on them. I was never pressured to play ball. It was just something I grew up doing."

"Tommy and some of the rest of us would meet and play football on a vacant lot somewhere," said Don Albrecht, an all-regional guard who played with Landry on both the junior and varsity teams at Mission High. "I mean, there was no touch football. We didn't have any pads but we'd play tackle. You always got scratched up a little but it made you tougher."

"I can remember when we all were ten or eleven years old," said Joe Summers, who now has a machine shop in Mission. "We'd play football in the park a lot.

"There was always somebody around who couldn't play much. Maybe they'd be too small or just not coordinated enough. A lot of the guys would tell them to go on, leave us alone. Not Tommy. He'd say, 'Let him play on my side.' Then he'd take the kid aside and say, 'You can play. You can do it. Don't let them tell you any different. You can play on my team.' "

But games were just rough. One was called "Saddle the Donkey." A boy would reach out, putting his hands on a tree or pole. Another would get behind and grab his waist. Then the others would back off twenty-five feet and take a running, flying leap on top of the pair, trying to force them to break apart.

"You know I used to get into some mischief, nothing serious like you hear of nowadays, but I never can remember Tommy even getting into a fight," said Albrecht. "I know he was an awful good swimmer and we used to go over to the Crystal Waters Pool and swim a lot."

"Tommy never really had to fight," recalled Summers. "He never really rubbed anybody wrong. Even the bullies didn't pick on him. He was a pretty good sized kid and very firm."

"Tommy and I were alike in those days," remembered Spillman. "We just didn't take to escapades much at all. I was there and, I give you my word, Tommy just wasn't the type to get into trouble.

"Nobody had much money but we made a little here and there, doing odd jobs. We used to pick up some money caddying. I guess that's where we learned how to play golf, caddying for those guys on the weekends."

Mostly the local newspaper was full of news about the exploits of the Mission Eagles but some small mention also was given to the big college stars such as Tom Harmon or Bronko Nagurski or Sammy Baugh, ol' Slingin' Sammy. Sid Luckman was a quarterback for the Chicago Bears and that big guy from Texas, Clyde (Bulldog) Turner, was the center.

"I know," said Landry, "we dreamed a lot. When I was real young I think our heroes were the movie idols, the cowboy stars and Tarzan. We lived in a fantasy world. These days kids grow up more with athletes as heroes."

They listened to the afternoon radio serials, following the exploits of Tom Mix and his horse, Tony, of Captain Midnight, the Green Hornet and Superman. You didn't want to listen to the radio too early in the day because of those silly soap operas, like Stella Dallas, stuff like that.

There were always the movie treats on Saturdays for ten cents. You could see the serials all morning and the main features, such as Tom Mix in *The Miracle Rider* or Gene Autry in *The Singing Vagabond,* or watch Ken Maynard or Tim McCoy get the best of the bad guys, who always wore the black hats. And there was a pretty good show called *Stagecoach* with John Wayne, who everybody said used to be a football player himself. A lot of Indians got killed in that show. A lot.

When you left the movies you went home and became the cowboys, the ones in the white hats, and all you needed to act out the dream was a vivid imagination and two sticks, the long one becoming your horse and the short one your gun.

Orson Welles scared a lot of people with his very realistic broadcast of H. G. Wells's *War of the Worlds,* making folks actually think the Martians were coming in 1938. That was the same year a young man named Bob Martin came to town. Martin had just graduated from South Texas State Teachers College in San Marcos, where he'd captained the football team. The school, which became known as Southwest Texas State, also had among its graduates a man named Lyndon Baines Johnson. After Johnson became President, Martin liked to remark, "I'm the only guy who went to the school in San Marcos who wasn't President Johnson's roommate."

Martin was hired to coach the junior team, composed of freshmen and sophomores at Mission High. The first time he called a meeting of his squad a group of twenty-four boys showed up.

"Boys," he said, holding up a football, "the first thing I need is somebody to take this and initiate every play we make. We need a tough, smart kid."

A tall, lean freshman with clear gray-green eyes stood up and said, "Coach, I'll do it." The kid was Tommy Landry but Martin said he started calling him "Tom" because it sounded tougher. The team did well and continued to do so when its nucleus became sophomores. As juniors, they would go to the varsity and all the town was talking about those prospects.

Most of the talk took place downtown on Conway at the vacant lot where everybody parked their cars. You had to get there early on Saturday to have a parking place, which also allowed you to sit on the fender of your car and hold court with your neighbors. They'd talk about the citrus crop, rain, politics, the war in Europe and football.

"Yep," said Andy Anderson, "people'd come into town, sit around, whittle and spit . . . spit and whittle."

Among the many stars of that junior team, moving to the varsity in 1940, were Tom Landry, Don Albrecht, A. B. Ward, Jimmy Mehis, Darroll and Carroll Martin, Audencio Mungia, Arnaldo Vera and Zelmo Hinojosa.

The varsity coach had been fired and the school board filled the vacancy by moving Bob Martin up from the junior team. Martin lived in a garage apartment next door to the Landrys and the summer of 1940 he started taking notice that his center, Tom Landry, also could throw the football. Ray had tied a rope through a tire and hung it from a tree. Tom spent hours tossing a football through the tire and also throwing to his younger brother, Jack.

"The kid had a good arm," recalled Martin. "He was growing tall, had some meat on him. I figured I needed me a quarterback and decided he'd be the one. So I moved him to quarterback and tailback before his junior year in high school. We'd shift out of the T-formation to the box, making the quarterback the tailback."

In those days Texas high schools were classified either A, for the small schools, or AA, for the larger schools, and no overall state champion was determined in either classification. Regional was as far as a team could advance.

When Tom Landry's class was in its junior year the Mission Eagles were 6–4, playing both A and AA teams. But the team won all its district games and went into bi-district to play Alice. That year Landry scored 46 points, threw for a number of other touchdowns, and his 34-yard run set up the only TD in the 7–0 victory over Pharr which gave

Mission the district title. But, although Mission gained more yardage, it lost to Alice, 7–6. Landry, then six feet, 150 pounds, made the All-South Texas team.

Bob Martin wasn't at all satisfied. He kept urging his players to try harder, to give more. He gave them a motto, "Eleven brothers are hard to beat." At that time players went both ways and so Landry, the quarterback-tailback, also played safety on defense. And he called his own plays on offense.

That Christmas of 1940 Martin sent each team member a card which read:

> You are the fellow who has to decide,
> Whether you'll do it or toss it aside;
> You are the fellow who makes up your mind,
> Whether you'll lead or linger behind;
>
> Whether you'll strive for the goal that's far,
> Or just be content to stay where you are.
> Take it or leave it! There's something to do!
> Just think it over [player's name written in],
> It's all up to you.

Franklin Delano Roosevelt had been elected President for an unprecedented third term, beating Wendell Willkie of New York. The German blitzkrieg had invaded Denmark, Norway, the Netherlands, Luxembourg, Belgium, and Czechoslovakia, and been joined by Japan and Italy in the Rome–Berlin Axis. A scientist named Albert Einstein had written President Roosevelt a letter about the feasibility of something called the "atomic bomb." People read John Steinbeck's *The Grapes of Wrath* and Ernest Hemingway's *For Whom the Bell Tolls* and Joe Louis was the heavyweight champion and, as the baseball season ended and football began, all over South Texas it was noted that Boston Red Sox slugger Ted Williams had won the batting title with a .405 average and that Joe DiMaggio had a 56-game hitting streak. And Hoagy Carmichael was still singing "Stardust."

Sometimes adults talked in low voices about the Germans and Japs and those wars going on overseas. They talked about another "New Deal" by Roosevelt and Bob Martin was saying that, although Mission High never had gone past the bi-district before, the season of 1941 was going to be a "New Deal."

"Coach cracked down and wouldn't even let us drink cokes," recalled Albrecht.

"Coach Martin was very strong," said Dr. J. M. Baker, now a veteri-

40

narian in Edinburg. "I was a couple of years behind Tommy in school but we worked out with the team. Coach Martin was the kind of guy who'd give you three licks if you lost a sprint and two if you won."

"I told them flatly," said Bob Martin, "that if any girls wore their letter sweaters, I wanted it to be their mothers or sisters. I wanted their complete concentration. That wasn't any problem with Tom. He wasn't going to break any of the rules but we used to joke about it.

"From where I lived I could look out the window and see him coming home. His dad had built him a bedroom up in the attic and the only way he could get in was to climb the stairs outside the house."

"Coach Martin," Landry would say, "I haven't got a chance. You can't check on the other guys but you can see for yourself if I'm breaking curfew."

Landry used to drop by Martin's apartment and talk football. He began to notice a picture of a girl there, which was inscribed, "Love, Dorothy."

"Hey, Coach Martin, who's that?" asked Tom. "We're not supposed to have girls during the season."

"Why, Tom, that's just my sister."

"Now, Coach Martin, that's not true. It says 'love' on it."

"Why, Tom, my sister loves me, too."

"I never did tell him any different," recalled Martin. "Then after the season he made the High School All-Star game in Abilene and I went up there with him." Dorothy came there, too. Tom kept staring at her and finally said, "Hey, Coach Martin, that's the girl in the picture." It was not his sister. Bob Martin and Dorothy soon were married.

Mission was a unanimous choice by Valley sportswriters to win the district because it had five returning players who had made All-Valley, including Tom Landry, Ward, Mehis, Albrecht and Carroll Martin.

Tom Landry's main interest was football but he also excelled in other things. He made the National Honor Society, was president of his class, and the local schoolgirls, noting his six-foot, 165-pound frame, his wavy brown hair and deepset gray-green eyes, voted him the "Cutest Boy" in Mission High. He had just as soon they hadn't.

Even after football season he didn't date that much. "In the first place it was kind of difficult," recalled Spillman. "None of the kids had their own cars then and, if your parents had a car, it was awfully hard to borrow. Tom was a big, good-looking guy and so naturally all the girls were after him. When he'd go out it usually would be with the best-looking girl. But, generally, he wasn't setting the world on fire as far as girls were concerned."

Schoolmates recalled Landry would go to dances but, mostly, stand

41

on the side and talk. He also did some singing in school but Albrecht, who had his own group called "Don Albrecht's Swingsters," noted, "Tommy had the worst singing voice of anybody in school. Just awful. I think that's about the only thing he couldn't do well."

One day Ruth Landry received some news about her son. He had made the National Honor Society and not so much as mentioned the fact to his parents.

"Son," she said, "I think everybody has heard about it but your father and I."

"Well," said Tom, "you always taught me to do my best and not brag about it. All I was doing was my best."

His parents never really heard him talk about his exploits on the football field. They either saw them firsthand, heard about them from friends, or read about them in Valley newspapers.

"Even after Tommy and I had gone to the University of Texas, I'd be the one to keep them up on what he was doing," said Spillman. "I'd get clips and tell them what was happening. Tommy was something . . . the perfect football hero at both the University and in high school."

The '41 season opened with Mission beating Edinburg, 12–0, as Landry threw two touchdown passes of 19 and 55 yards. The Eagles then ripped San Benito, 25–0. Landry broke loose for touchdown runs of 66 and 20 yards and threw 18 and 10–yard touchdown passes in a 28–0 win over Raymondville.

"Tommy wasn't fast," explained Martin, "but he was smart. He knew how to run, giving them the limp leg, picking his way. He also started on our basketball team, played tennis and ran track. He was on our relay team but not because he was so fast. We just didn't have anybody else."

Mission beat Mercedes, 40–0, as Landry scored on runs of 55 and 59 yards and he tallied four of seven touchdowns, including runs of 35, 36 and 64 yards, as the Eagles overwhelmed Weslaco, 47–0. The area press was full of news of his exploits, calling him "Terrific Tommy Landry, a six-foot, 170-pound back who can run, pass, punt with the best of them."

"The thing I always remember was his punting," said Sam Nixon, the barber. "We'd go to Burnett Field and he'd soar those punts into the sky, I mean. My son used to go down to the field and make bets with people that Tommy could stand on the 40 and punt it through the opposite goalpost. My son said he won as many bets as he lost."

Sportswriter George Wright, in his column called "In This Corner," noted one day that some people around town were saying that Tommy Landry got *all* the praise. "There's been too much praise for Tommy Landry and not enough for the other lads on the club, say they," wrote Wright. "Well, we'll agree with them that enough has not been said for the other boys. But we'll hold out for the belief that Tommy has deserved everything said about him. We're going on the results obtained and from remarks passed by observers who know their stuff, including other coaches.

"We've heard some complimentary stuff about the boy from nearly every coach whose team has played the Eagles. Only reason we haven't heard from all of them is because we haven't talked with all of them about this particular matter ... And we repeat that we still think Tommy Landry, whose head hasn't swelled a bit despite the adulation, deserves every kind word written about him."

People in Mission to this day are still talking about the sixth game that season in Donna. Word was that there were more people from Mission at the game than from Donna. People were calling the Eagles the "Totem Pole Eagles" and their fans the "Missionaries."

Landry threw a pass for one touchdown and his 40-yard run set up another TD as Mission led, 12–0. Landry also had a 60-yard touchdown run called back for clipping. But Donna moved the ball deep into Eagle territory and on third down a pass was thrown into the end zone. Interference was called and an official awarded Donna a touchdown, instead of putting the ball on the one-yard line.

Martin charged onto the field. "Get out of here!" said the official who made the call.

"You can't award a touchdown on a penalty!" yelled Martin. "They get the ball on our one-yard line!"

"I'm calling the game. Get off the field or I'll give you a 15-yard penalty."

"You can't give much more. You already gave them a touchdown."

"Get off."

"All right. But you'll be apologizing to me after the meeting on Monday."

Mission went on to win, 12–7. After the area officials had their weekly meeting on Monday, Martin received a call. "You were right, Bob. I apologize. It was no touchdown."

The boy who tackled the receiver in the end zone and was called for the interference penalty was Tommy Landry, the Mission safety. "After Tom went on to become an All-Pro defensive back with the New York Giants," chuckled Martin, "some of his teammates on that Mission squad couldn't believe it. He was a fine offensive player but some of them said all he did on defense was stand back there at safety with his hands on his hips. They said the opposition never got that far; the only tackle he ever made that year was on the interference call."

Before Mission played McAllen, a Class AA school, the fans there were saying that the Eagles were just a mediocre team without Tom Landry. This was hardly true, but Landry ran for touchdowns of 34, 19 and 48 yards and his 37-yard pass set up still another score in a 46–0 victory.

"The mornings after the games were great times," recalled Don Albrecht. "We'd meet there at the corner drugstore and let people lay the glory on us. Tommy would be there, too, talking about the game. We might have a soda. Everybody else was having cherry cokes."

Many felt the Eagles' winning streak would end in the game against Class AA Harlingen. Landry took a hard blow just below his right eye in the first period. He launched a 46-yard punt that went out of bounds at the Harlingen four, which led to a safety and, on the exchange, set up an Eagle touchdown.

But the side of his face was swelling so badly that he had to leave the game after the first period. His father came down to the bench and asked, "Can I help?"

"Yessir," said Bob Martin, "you can put ice on the boy's face. It looks pretty bad."

Martin later recalled, "That was the only time I ever remember Ray saying or doing anything to interfere with our team. And when he did, I needed the help. As a fireman, he knew first aid."

Landry's cheek bone was fractured and there was a question as to whether he'd be able to play the following week against LaFeria. Martin designed a special headgear, using two face masks, one upside down. Teammates were kidding Tom that he looked like the Masked Marvel. Landry played only the first period against LaFeria but by the time he left the game Mission had scored both touchdowns in a 14–0 victory.

He also saw only limited action the following week against Pharr, a 34–0 victory, but he was stunned, shocked, as was everybody else, at what happened. A substitute running back for Mission named Billy Brown broke loose from his own 12 and was on his way to a touchdown when Harvey Risinger, who played for Pharr, came off the bench and floored him with a body block. Risinger then crawled back off the field but an official had seen him. Pharr was given a 15-yard penalty.

Mission had won its fourth district title and would go to Aransas Pass for the bi-district game. Everybody in Mission was talking about the Eagles, saying how they had a chance for the first time in history to win bi-district, and make the regional championship game.

Students began passing around petitions, staging impromptu pep rallies, to try to get school officials to turn out classes early on Friday so they could go to the game. They also wanted the businesses to close down early. They succeeded and a special train, called the "Eagle Special," was chartered to take some 300 fans to the game. It was filled. The week of the game the Lions Club also had its banquet. Martin and some of his players made speeches. Landry, who had scored 111 points, stood up and talked about the team's strategy. He also was named co-captain of the team and picked by his teammates as the "Best Sport" and "Most Valuable Player." Fans gave Martin a new Chevrolet, which he recalled had a sticker price of $906.00.

Mission beat Aransas Pass, 19–0, and a newspaper account of the game noted, "The Eagles were sparked by 170-pound tailback Tommy Landry, who ran and, when slowed down passed, and whose toe kept the Eagles in good field position." Landry scored three times, going over from the 4, 38, and, late in the game, ran through what was said to be the entire Aransas Pass team for a 76-yard touchdown.

Two days after Mission had won its first bi-district game, on the morning of December 7, 1941, the Japanese launched an air attack off a task force on the U. S. Naval Base at Pearl Harbor, killing 2,403. It was a day President Roosevelt said would "live in infamy." War was declared on Japan the following day. On December 11, Italy and Germany declared war on the United States. World War II had begun.

"Honestly, until Pearl Harbor I don't think we were all that aware about the war, what was happening overseas," recalled Landry. "I know, personally, I wasn't. We were trying to win a championship in football and into school activities and just not conscious of what was happening.

"Then Pearl Harbor was attacked, people were talking about going to war and we became very aware then of what had happened."

Suddenly, everybody was talking about the war, the enemy, about what must be done to stop the Axis. But they also were talking about Mission playing Hondo for the regional championship. It was the time they had hoped would come, something they had planned for and some 3,000 fans jammed Burnett Field, purchasing reserved seats for $1.10 and $1.55 and general admission for 75 and 30 cents.

It had rained that week, the field was soggy, but nothing could stop the Eagles. Mission destroyed Hondo, 33–0, as Landry capped the first drive by scoring from the three, ran 45 yards to set up a score, passed 25 yards for another and then raced 65 yards for a touchdown. Mission, 12–0, had gone as far as it could. It had scored 322 points and was unscored upon, if you didn't count the touchdown (erroneously) awarded on the interference call against Donna. Landry was All-Valley, all-everything and there was a great deal of interest shown in him by Texas, SMU, Rice and Mississippi State.

"In those days," recalled Bully Gilstrap, then an assistant under D. X.

Bible at Texas, "we had two assistant coaches scouting. I had the south and east and Blair Cherry the north and west. We kept hearing good things about Tommy Landry, what a fine player and outstanding person he was.

"He was the top player in the Valley. Maybe not what you'd consider a great blue chipper but a fine player. I remember being a little afraid we might lose him to SMU because he was a Methodist. But in Mission we got a lot of help from an ex-Longhorn named Doc Newhouse. Doc kept talking up the Longhorns and telling us about Tommy."

Gilstrap recalled he told Landry, "Tommy, I want you to look around you in this town, this area, this state. You note the real important people and you'll find that the majority of those come from the University of Texas. You look at the leaders in the churches, the farming industry, the citrus industry, the lawyers, the politicians . . . the majority are from Texas.

"You go to another school, say SMU, and it'll be awful far for your parents to travel to see you play. But Austin's not that far. They'll be able to come see the games."

"I was pretty much sold on Texas," Landry once recalled. "In those days you just about had to have a Texas alumnus to recommend you to the school. Doc Newhouse was a big help getting me into school. It also helped that Jackie Fields, who was from Mission, was playing for Coach Bible at that time. I don't think the Valley was as much respected for football at that time as some of the other parts of the state, but Jackie had made a good impression.

"I'd never been anywhere to speak of and Austin was the closest place for Southwest Conference schools. That city was plenty big for me."

Although nobody knew it at the time, Mission High would not play football the following year due to the war. And when Tom Landry left town for Austin to attend the University of Texas, the war would be much closer than he thought. Much closer.

3

FLAK WAS THICK, heavy, hitting all around the B-17 squadron, exploding, then swelling, blossoming out like some ominous devil's flower and darkening the sky as if it were covered by a massive thundercloud. Sometimes the flak was so thick that it seemed to form a solid, black floor and looked as if one could step out of the plane and walk on it. One couldn't hear the shells or the flak exploding, really, because of the loud roar of the engines. You couldn't hear it unless it actually hit your plane and then it would be the last sound you ever heard.

The squadron of B-17s, the famed Flying Fortresses with guns in the nose, tail, on top and bottom and each side, were a segment of the Eighth Air Force stationed at bases in England under the command of Lt. Gen. James H. Doolittle. By that time, late 1944, the Allies had staggered the German *Luftwaffe* and thus the dreaded Messerschmitt and Focke-Wolf fighters no longer swooped down on the bombers like locusts before and after the target had been reached, although they were still around in isolated numbers. So those in the B-17s that day counted themselves lucky because their counterparts earlier in the war, in spite of fighter escorts, had been forced not only to run the gamut of concentrated *Luftwaffe* attack but also avoid ground fire from the antiaircraft guns.

On the other hand, the ground gunners had become much smarter, more accurate. Earlier in the war you could take a bombing run at a certain altitude and the flak would be closer and closer as the gunners zeroed in. But then you could take another run at a higher altitude and the gunners would still be shooting below you, at the former altitude.

Tom Landry, who had just turned twenty, was a copilot of one of those Flying Fortresses which were to bomb a German target in occupied Czechoslovakia. The flak shook his plane violently, as though it were in the middle of a storm, being yanked and shaken by a giant unseen force. Sometimes it felt as if the plane would be jerked apart even if a shell didn't hit it. During bombing missions you'd see another plane hit. Fire would spurt from its engines, belly, and tail, and it would disappear in a death dive or even explode in midair. This never seemed quite real, but you never saw the people in those planes again and so you knew it was. You always thought this happened to someone else, that it never would happen to you. But sometimes you were wrong.

Nineteen, twenty . . . it seemed so young, a time when you nudge against adulthood, worrying about your grade in freshman English, a date for Saturday night, and beginning to climb to your dreams, to what you'd be. But if you were nineteen and in the war you aged fast.

"Sure, you'd be a little scared," said Landry. "You were flying into the black cloud of flak and never really sure what might happen. You made your run, tried to concentrate on what you had to do, and then you got out of there as fast as you could, any way you could."

47

Bombs away! They dropped their payload of bombs, banked slightly, climbed and headed back to England, "The Flying Fortress was a great plane," Landry remembered. "Just a great plane. We'd get a few holes in us but it could take so much punishment. You could get an engine, even two engines knocked out and still fly on the other two."

The Flying Fortress, however, could not fly without gas. The mission from England to Czechoslovakia stretched the fuel supply to the limit and so the men were told if they couldn't get back to try to find an alternate field in France on which to land. Soon, it became evident Landry's plane would not make it. If they tried to cross the English Channel there was an excellent chance they'd have to ditch in the water, severely limiting any chance of survival. A fog had set in, the ceiling was very low, and their chances of finding the field in France also didn't look good. But it was their only hope. They had to try it.

"There must have been 2,500 planes, all looking for a place to land," Landry recalled. "Ceiling was under 300 feet, almost zero at times and you couldn't see anything below you. We also couldn't make radar contact."

The plane literally skimmed over the tops of trees, trying to find a field, an opening, anything. The gas was gone, the engines sputtered, silenced and they moved along in a glide to the ground, onto the trees. Suddenly, there was an opening in the trees and they set down, hitting the ground in a violent, jerking motion, then bellying along and plowing up the ground as they plunged forward, toward another group of trees. They slid through a small opening between two trees, shearing off each wing but slowing down the plane enough to reduce its impact when it smashed, nose first into another tree, buried all the way to the cockpit. It was still. Nobody breathed. Then everybody began to shout. Tom Landry and the entire crew walked away from the crash landing.

"We were awfully lucky," said Landry. "So many were looking for a place to land and didn't make it. No, as we were going down I don't remember being scared. I'm not sure why I wasn't. I guess I just hadn't had that experience before and so wasn't afraid."

Landry had left Mission, Texas, and gone to the University of Texas on a football scholarship in the fall of 1942. He joined the reserve because he wanted to, because it was the thing to do. World War II wasn't a war to protest against, to debate. Japan had attacked Pearl Harbor, and Germany, too, had declared war on the United States. You fought for your country, your way of life, democracy, and it was very clear that the aggressors, the enemies were Adolph Hitler's Nazism, Mussolini's

Fascism and the militarism in Japan, a country in which the Samurai, the warrior of war, was idolized to fanatical degrees.

"There was no question, really," said Landry. "If you didn't fight, there was a chance the country would be taken over by the Germans or the Japanese. We were fighting a war for our own country. We were united behind the war effort and everybody wanted to get into the service and help. Then, we were a country of patriots.

"If we hadn't been, we might have been saying *Sieg heil* or whatever the Japanese were saying."

While Landry was at Texas his freshman year the news came that his brother, Robert, three years older, was missing. Robert had joined the Air Force shortly after Pearl Harbor, completed his flight training, and was ferrying a plane to England when he disappeared. Finally, the news came that he had been killed. He had flown a route over Iceland and the plane had exploded in midair.

The news left a gnawing, hollow feeling inside Landry. He remembered so many things: growing up, playing catch with Robert, laughing, going through the silly games. He remembered as a kid, following his older brother around and wanting to be like him. He remembered the fun, the talks . . . and, perhaps, things left unsaid . . . some feelings left unexpressed. But Robert was gone, dead. He would not be around any more and the solace came when he thought of his brother now being in a better place, where there were no wars, no fighting. Just peace.

"It's something you never expect," recalled Landry. "It shocks you, shakes you up. But he had been missing for a long time and, although you always hope, you also prepare yourself for the worst. Certainly, it was most difficult to accept and live with, but you did so better in those times because people were getting killed in the war so frequently. In normal times, it would have been more of a shock."

Landry knew it wouldn't be long before his unit was called up and the war diminished everything—his education, football, everything.

"But even then, his freshman year," recalled teammate Frank Jeffers, "Tommy had a tremendous influence on other members of the frosh team. I don't believe I ever played with or against a greater competitor than Tommy Landry."

Landry was called to active duty in the spring of 1943. He was classified, sent to the college training program in Ada, Oklahoma, took preflight in San Antonio, graduated as a pilot in Lubbock and trained in multiple engine aircraft in Iowa. He was sent from there to Lincoln, Nebraska, where the crews were formed and they flew overseas to Epwich, England, not far from London, in the fall of 1944. There they would be based.

He was to fly thirty missions over Germany or occupied territory. "Tommy never said much about it but he volunteered for extra missions and said this was for his brother, Robert," recalled his aunt Viola Bourgeois.

And Tom Landry flew his first mission, in one of some 2,000 planes sent to destroy the oil fields at Mersburg, Germany. "We went in there and it was really something the first time to see and feel the flak. They tell you about it, warn you about it, but it's like nothing you've ever experienced. It was really a scary feeling."

The city was so dark on that first mission, Landry once said, that they'd gotten in and out so fast he wasn't sure if they had come close to the target or missed it by miles. But they returned safely and there would be many other missions.

"They kept us awfully busy," said Landry. "We were fogged in a lot and had to be ready to go when we could. We didn't have that much time off.

"When we were off, we'd go into London, sightsee, look around. But it was a very drab city then. Very dark and gray. When they'd have the blackouts you couldn't see your hand in front of your face, it was so dark. You just can't imagine how dark it was.

"But, mostly, there wasn't time for much of anything, just getting ready for our missions, taking them."

One mission was almost his last. They had made a bombing run over Germany and on the return flight to England the engines coughed, sputtered, and they thought they were out of gas. All the signs were there, and they were losing altitude. Soon all four engines conked out over Belgium and they dropped to 1,000 feet as the antiaircraft guns kept getting closer and closer with their fire.

"Let's get out of here!" said the pilot.

Everyone prepared to bail out. As Landry got out of his seat, he paused briefly and looked back at the instrument panel. He turned, reached over and adjusted the fuel mixture for the engines. They fired up again. The crew scrambled back to their places, the plane gained altitude and made it back to England. They had been over enemy territory. Had they bailed out, they would probably have become prisoners of war.

Once when he was asked about this story, Landry said, matter-of-factly, "I just realized something might be wrong with the fuel mixture. I wasn't sure. It just came to me that the fuel mixture might be off. It was just one of those things."

Defeat for Germany seemed inevitable. President Roosevelt and Prime Minister Churchill had decided to try to break Germany first, before Japan, because they feared the Germans were a more imminent threat.

In desperation the Nazis launched the V–I rocket, the *Vergeltungswaffe* or Vengeance Weapon, on England and later the V–II, the first guided missile. They also put into the air the first jet-propelled fighter plane, but it was too late.

"The Germans were the greatest of military minds," said Landry, who includes the history of WW II among his reading. "They had so many of the geniuses during the war—but the Allies, the people in the United States were just supremely determined."

President Roosevelt, the fine orator who had done so much to rally the country and to inspire the people during war, died in April, 1945, failing to realize victory. And Vice-President Harry Truman of Missouri, the man who didn't mince words or beat around the bush, became President of the United States.

On May 1, 1945, German radio announced Hitler had died while defending Berlin against the Russian onslaught. But investigations later determined that he had committed suicide with his wife, Eva Braun. On May 7, Germany surrendered.

In August President Truman gave his okay to use the atom bomb on Japan and when the bomber, the *Enola Gay,* dropped the A-bomb August 6 on Hiroshima, it killed some 92,000 people and launched the world into the Atomic Age. Three days later the A-bomb killed some 40,000 in Nagasaki, and Japan surrendered on September 2, 1945.

That November of 1945, First Lieutenant Tom Landry received his discharge and returned to Mission before trying to tie his life, his education, and his football career back together.

"Tommy and I got back to Mission, back from the war, about the same time," recalled Wade Spillman. "We'd been to war, aged, and returned as men of the world. We weren't kids anymore, and so we decided to cut loose. We planned to go across into Mexico, to Reynosa, and cut, shall we say, a wide path. So we took off one afternoon, figuring we'd stay a few days and really have a good time.

"Well, we got back home about 10:30 P.M. that same day."

In recent years I heard a writer ask Landry about his war experiences. "Oh, we got a few holes in our bomber every once in a while but nothing much happened, really," said Landry.

Nothing much. Perhaps the war matured Tom Landry but it didn't change him.

4

To MOST WHO have lived there, Austin is the best of places. The capital city of Texas has a great deal of atmosphere—and atmosphere is something which can't be manufactured or prefabricated. It is something that comes with time—and it is there, just there, or it isn't. Austin is a city whose streets climb and drop, some almost roller coaster-like. Ageless trees line its streets and their roots sometimes crack the sidewalks, as they should.

There are parks with rock paths, winding under giant oaks and elms, and the Colorado River runs through the city. At night, lights from both shores dance magically across its dark velvet waters. You find places such as Scholz Beer Garten where on lazy summer nights, a hodge-podge of students, writers, would-be writers, politicians (coming up and going down), professors and athletes crowd around tables in the back under trees lit by strings of bare light bulbs.

It is a city where, near the outskirts (or at least what once were the outskirts) you can climb Mt. Bonnell and look down on the river on one side and, on the other, watch the morning sun bank off the capitol building, giving it a pinkish tint. And it is a place where William Sydney Porter, better known as O. Henry, once worked for the local newspaper, and J. Frank Dobie taught. Short miles to the southwest you enter the Hill Country with its wild flowers of blue and red and yellow and its soft rolling hills. Austin always has been a good place to be when you are young.

In the past decade or so new buildings have grown taller than the capitol and Texas Tower. Expanded freeways have changed the look of Austin and the suburbs continually creep out in all directions. But when Tom Landry at twenty-three returned to Austin and the University of Texas in the fall of 1946, the capitol and Texas Tower were the most prominent architectural features of the city, standing above all else.

The city and the school were as he had remembered them—but the readjustment would take a while. He had been in a real war, where real people had died or were horribly maimed. Now he was back in an atmosphere of learning and athletics and living, where now he could really appreciate the things that, before the war, he had taken for granted. The sky was blue, peaceful without war planes, flak and death. Each day could be lived without wondering if there would be another.

His appearance had not changed that much. His weight, which had dropped during the war, was around 190 pounds again and he remained very clean-cut, his wavy, brown hair receding a little more around the part on the left side. And there were a few more wrinkles, caused more by the war than by the years.

At first he seemed a little quieter, a little more reflective, but those coming back from the war were either that way or loud and boisterous—letting go as if they'd held back for a long time. Landry talked very little to anyone about his war experiences. He turned his thoughts and attention to school and football, trying to recapture the competitive edge which had made him one of the brightest stars in Valley history and had earned him an athletic scholarship to the University of Texas.

When he had first received his discharge and gone home to Mission to await the fall semester, he'd started tossing the football around again. Discovering that his old high school coach, Bob Martin, was coaching high school football in Brownsville, just this side of the Mexican border across from Matamoros, he had gone to see him.

"I was surprised, but very glad to see him," recalled Martin. "We were in spring training and Tom just showed up one day and watched us practice. I told him he ought to put on a suit and scrimmage with us and he did. He played at quarterback and the kids really got after him. Here he was a big time college player and they wanted a chance to bust him. But he took it, never said a word, and I think during that time it helped him get back into the swing of football—a little, anyway."

When Landry reported to the Longhorns that fall, D. X. Bible was coaching his final season. Bible was a thorough, somewhat low-key man, who demanded excellence through repetition and hard work. But he seldom yelled at his players or raised his voice in an attempt to berate or shame them into trying harder.

"He was very efficient and a fine orator," Landry once told me. "I think he became more low-key after the war because I guess the older players were coming back and he felt that approach would be better than any of the Knute Rockne type talks he'd used before the war."

"Tom was a fine player," recalled Bible. "He was a leader, modest and quiet. He had a lot of influence without being loud or blustery. I used to tell the fellows if they would pay the premiums they would get the dividends. Tom paid them and still is."

Those were the Bobby Layne years. Bible used the Blond Bomber at both fullback and tailback in his single-wing formation. Landry played fullback and was used as a defensive halfback specialist in those days when colleges played platoon football with limited substitutions. Many of the players had been in the Armed Forces, such as center Dick Harris,

53

a friend of Landry's. He would go on to make All-American, and had returned to school the previous fall, blending back into the program effortlessly.

Landry had been away from football for so long it was difficult for him, but he was determined to succeed. Perhaps, many years later, this experience helped him to believe, when many didn't, that a guy named Roger Staubach, who had been serving a naval obligation for four years, could regain his competitive edge and make a career for himself in the National Football League.

Landry pledged Delta Kappa Epsilon and fraternity brother Bill Wiggins, now in the oil business in Dallas, remembered, "Tom was a serious young man then but not what you would call overly serious. He was a good sport. You could joke with him but he wasn't the type guy to go around making a fool out of himself. He stayed in control."

Landry ran around a lot with Lewis Holder and George McCall, who were ends on the football team and fellow fraternity brothers. Bobby Coy Lee sometimes joined them. Their activities outside of football were on the opposite end of the scale from those of Bobby Layne and Billy M. Andrews, known as Rooster. Andrews, who was slightly less than five feet tall and weighed some 120 pounds, had come to know Tom when he'd enrolled in Texas prior to the war. Andrews had tried to join the Armed Forces, too, but was turned down because of his size. He received the name Rooster one night during his freshman year when a group of seniors got him out of bed and demanded that he climb a tree and bring down their fighting rooster. They'd planned to take the bird to Elgin to enter in cockfights.

They failed, however, to tell Andrews that the bird was a fighting rooster. He gamely climbed the tree and reached for the rooster, who was standing on a limb. There followed one of the better fights at UT that year, which ended with both Andrews and the fighting bird tumbling to the ground. The rooster was fine. Andrews was scratched up and had broken his arm. Thereafter, he was called Rooster. He served as manager for the Longhorns but also was so adept at drop-kicking that sometimes he was used for extra points.

"With Layne in there you never knew when we'd score so sometimes I'd carry water on the field, wearing my helmet," Andrews said. "And Tommy Landry . . . everybody liked him. He really was a nice guy and, to tell you the truth, I don't think he's changed a bit since he was in school in Texas. He was a gentleman, was very much respected and, well, just didn't go around making an ass out of himself like Bobby and I did."

"Tommy," said Layne, "was awfully tame by our standards, but he wasn't the type of guy to put you down for what you did. Some people are one way, some people are another, and he understood that then."

"Tommy," added Andrews, "wouldn't let you upset him and he wouldn't upset you."

"Yeah," added Layne, "we all liked him but he wasn't the type of guy you'd go out with, have some beers and make a fool of yourself."

"They were," laughed Landry, "capable of doing a lot of things."

"You have to remember," said Dick Harris, "that we weren't kids any more when we got back from the war. We'd been through a lot."

"There were some fairly rowdy boys in school back then, but Tom was just very mature," said Ed Price, who was an assistant then and later became head coach at Texas. "He was no kid coming to the big city. He'd been to war. He was older than many and acted his age. I guess, really, it's surprising to a lot of people to find a man of such character and religious intent in a rough, tough game of pro football— but that's the way he was. I remember him as being quiet, poised, reliable, and having just all those good American traits."

Texas opened the season by beating Missouri, 42–0, and newspapers reported that among the many plays that thrilled the crowd was a 30-yard gain on a bootleg by Tom Landry. However, Landry still wasn't back in the groove and his duties mostly involved filling in at defensive halfback. The team finished 8–2 with most of the accolades falling on the shoulders of Layne and Bible, who was ending his career at UT with a 63–31–3 record and three SWC titles.

One of the two losses was 18–13 at the hands of Jess Neely's Rice Owls in Houston. "After the game," said McCall, now an Austin insurance man, "Tommy, Lew Holder and I took off for Galveston. There was this place at the time where they had gambling, which was illegal. We were a little curious what it was like at the place so we went inside.

"Well, we were looking around and I spotted this sportswriter from the Austin *American-Statesman*. It scared us to death. We weren't doing anything. We weren't gambling, drinking, or anything, but if he wrote in the paper that he had seen us at the place it would have been our tails. Coach Bible was so upset about losing to Rice and here were three of his players in a drinking, gambling place.

"I went over to the sportswriter and asked him not to write anything and he didn't, thank goodness. If he had, it wouldn't have mattered, I'm afraid, that we were just standing around."

By the fall of 1947, returning servicemen had swelled the enrollment at Texas to over 17,000. Styles were changing. Coeds, who had worn dresses up to their knees, were now wearing them down to mid-calf. Sweaters were in and so were sweater girls—the Lana Turners and

Rita Hayworths. Women also wore bobbysocks and white and brown saddle oxfords and penny loafers. The guys sported baggy slacks with cuffs, loose fitting sweaters and short, well-trimmed hair with sideburns no lower than mid-ear.

Blair Cherry, who had been the offensive assistant under Bible, took over the head coaching duties while his predecessor became athletic director. The previous season, Cherry had experimented with the T-formation with Bible's blessing. In 1946 he'd used a special team of players who ran the T in scrimmages in order to get the Longhorns ready for opponents who used the formation. But when Cherry got the head coaching job he decided to go all-out and make the T the major alignment for the Longhorns.

Layne, a tremendous passer, appeared the most likely candidate to become the quarterback, although Cherry also moved Tom Landry and Paul Campbell to the position. In high school, Landry's team had shifted out of the T into the box formation, but this was his first actual experience as the man under in the formation.

Layne wasn't overly sold on the idea so Cherry took him and his wife, the former Carol Kruger, to the College All-Star game to see how the pros used the formation. They also visited the Chicago Cardinals and the Chicago Bears, where Sid Luckman was one of the best at operating the formation for George Halas. Layne was sold. He adapted well, became the starting quarterback, and Landry would be his backup and come in for Bobby on defense, again playing halfback.

Cherry was a tough, more emotional coach than Bible. It was the practice of many during those days not to allow the players to drink water during practice, although of course now water breaks are common and necessary. But Cherry adhered to the practice of the times and, when a player fell out and became sick, trainer Frank Medina administered cold towels to revive him. Cherry worked his team so hard that observers were calling it the best conditioned team in Texas history. And some felt it also might be the best team in the Southwest Conference, although some sportswriters in Dallas were predicting big things for the SMU Mustangs of Rusty Russell, a team featuring Layne's old teammate at Dallas Highland Park, Doak Walker.

The Longhorns opened the season by bowling over Texas Tech. Then they crushed Oregon and its sophomore quarterback, Norm Van Brocklin, 34–13, with Landry playing mostly on defense. "He could have played any position except guard or tackle," recalled Bully Gilstrap, an assistant first to Bible and then to Cherry. "He studied, he listened and he knew all the assignments."

Ray Jones was the starting fullback, but a lot of talk centered around the prospects of a 200-pounder from Houston named Ray Borneman. One day Borneman was having problems on his timing and Cherry shouted to Landry, who was on defense:

"Tommy, get over here and show him how to run this play."

Landry responded, ran the play corrrectly. "Even in those days," said Layne, "Tommy was as smart as they come."

The third week of the season national attention focused on the game between the Longhorns and the powerful North Carolina Tarheels, featuring All-American halfback Choo-Choo Charlie Justice. Also, injury had forced a position change. Landry had suffered a broken thumb and, of course, couldn't pass or take snaps from under center. So he was moved to fullback for the Tarheel game.

"I remember being very apprehensive," said Landry. "But the way it turned out, maybe that was good."

Justice was held to only 18 yards rushing. The running star of the game was Tom Landry, who netted 91 yards on 12 carries as the Longhorn juggernaut crushed North Carolina, 34–0.

"Well," said Landry, "you do have to remember that Bobby was such a tremendous passer that it opened up things for me. I think I must have gained a lot of those yards on draws."

That year a striking young lady enrolled at the University of Texas. She had been raised in Dallas and, for a brief time, had lived in Houston when her family moved there. She was trim, had beautiful eyes and reddish blond hair and was to become a campus beauty, a Bluebonnet Belle. Her name was Alicia Wiggs and her father, Herbert Wiggs, was chairman of the board of an insurance company. Alicia was majoring in child psychology. As had Tom Landry, she had been raised in the church. Alicia had attended Highland Park High School during the time Layne and Walker played there and so she was a football fan, although she soon would become even more of one.

At that time George McCall was dating a girl named Ann Tynan, Sweetheart of UT, and through Ann introduced both Lew Holder and Bobby Coy Lee to girls they later married. Holder began dating Gloria Newhaws, who was a friend of Alicia. Gloria wanted Alicia to double date with them and suggested she take a blind date with one of the football players named Tommy Landry. Alicia declined.

"I didn't particularly like the idea of a blind date," said Alicia. "But Gloria kept after me and I finally went just because I thought so much of her and didn't want to disappoint her.

"You might say the first time I saw Tommy I was a little surprised."

Landry had played a game the day before and was very battered. He was bruised around the face, had a black eye, and was very sore.

"I suppose he was a little shy, as everybody says, but I was so shy then myself that I wouldn't have noticed," said Alicia. "But he was so polite and very handsome and we continued going out and, after I got to know him, I knew that he was exactly what I was looking for in a man. He had manners and we'd go to church on Sundays—and he seemed just perfect for me." Landry felt the same way.

"Alicia and I'd go to the movies, or down to New Braunfels where they had the rapids, or San Marcos," said Landry. "For a long time there it was a little difficult to get around. There weren't many of us who had cars. But I finally did buy a car, a convertible, from Frank Guest (a halfback on the team) and that made it easier.

"I don't know . . . we just did the usual crazy things."

"Sometimes I remember that Tommy came back from the war when I started to Texas," said Alicia. "Otherwise, had things gone normally in those times, I suppose we'd never have met because he'd have been graduated and gone by the time I got to Texas."

And there was always football. Football does not just happen or just come to Austin. The city literally vibrates with the sport all the way from some snack shop on campus, to the Texas Tower to the capitol. In a bigger city, Dallas or Houston, so many other things detract from the game, but Austin is just the right size to become completely caught up in the Texas Longhorns.

Texas followed the thumping of North Carolina with a 34–14 victory over Oklahoma in Dallas. In those days the Sooners had a fine halfback-punter by the name of Darrell Royal. By that time Landry was starting at fullback, dividing time with Ray Jones, and also playing full time on defense.

"I had thought I was a big football fan but after I started going with Tommy I *really* became an avid one," said Alicia.

"As a player," recalled Coach Price, "Tommy didn't have the break-away speed. He wasn't flashy but he was strong and tough—he could get the tough yardage for you."

"Tommy was a tremendous punter," said Layne. "We had two fine punters in those days, Tommy and Frank Guest."

The Longhorns beat Rice, and Arkansas, and then headed to the Cotton Bowl in Dallas for the showdown with Southern Methodist and its epitome of Saturday's hero, Doak Walker, who made the covers of *Time, Life, Look* and *Sport* magazines. A crowd of 45,000 came to the Cotton Bowl that Saturday afternoon to watch the No. 3 ranked Longhorns face the No. 8 ranked Mustangs in a game which would decide the Southwest Conference title. Others tuned to the game over the Humble Network to hear the very colorful Kern Tipps describe the action: "And the Blond Bomber Bobby Layne puts the ball into the belly of Tommy Landry who bucks into the Mustang line for a few hard-fought yards and tries to bull his way for more when Dick McKissack comes up and says, no you don't, that's the end of the line . . . ."

SMU, known for its trickery, ran a reverse on the opening kickoff when Walker took Harris's kick, then handed off to Paul Page who sped to the Texas 19, setting up an SMU touchdown which was scored when Walker handed to Page on the old Statue of Liberty play. Walker kicked the extra point, but Texas came back to tie the score after Byron Gillory's 40-yard punt return and Landry's plunge into the end zone followed by Guest's extra point.

The Ponies scored again as Walker slipped across the middle and took a pass from Gil Johnson which covered 54 yards and carried to the Texas one, from where McKissack scored. Landry was covering another receiver near the sidelines when he saw Walker break free and Johnson loft the ball toward him.

"Walker caught it right in front of me and took off," said Landry. "We chased him down and finally knocked him out of bounds at the one. He was just a tremendous player, could do it all."

Again, Walker kicked the extra point, giving the Mustangs a 14–7 lead, but his old Highland Park teammate Layne got hot and passed Texas on another touchdown drive with 12 minutes remaining. But this time Guest's extra point try was wide and SMU led by a single point.

Texas made one last drive, moving to what seemed a first down at the SMU 15, only to have the play wiped out with a penalty. When another play failed the Longhorns found themselves facing a fourth and one at the SMU 32. If they made it, they still had time to score, perhaps get close enough for a field goal. Needing the toughest of yards, they called on Landry, who says he'll never forget the play as long as he lives.

"We lined up and Bobby took the snap and turned to give me the ball," recalled Landry. "But I had slipped and fallen. I can still see the funny look on his face, standing there with nobody to give the ball to. I regained my balance but it was too late. There was no chance and SMU took over."

"It was such a freaky thing," said Price. "If Tommy had been anywhere else on the field he'd probably have made it. But there was a mud puddle near him and that's what made him slip."

Texas went through the remainder of its schedule undefeated but so did SMU, and the Mustangs became the SWC champions. "We really had a fine team that year," said Landry. "A fine team. We shouldn't have lost a game that year."

"'Football was such a big part of our lives," recalled Alicia. "Tommy talked a lot about it. Of course, we were getting pretty serious, although we had a little disagreement.

"I'd never smoked before in my life but it was something I'd thought about so I told Tommy I believed I'd give it a try."

Landry, who had never smoked, looked at her and said, "If you do, I won't kiss you anymore."

"So," said Alicia, laughing, "I never did smoke. But if I had . . . he'd still have kissed me."

SMU finished third, the Longhorns fourth in the final Associated Press poll. The Ponies were to beat Oregon in the Cotton Bowl and Texas was invited to tangle with Harry Gilmer and the Alabama Crimson Tide in the Sugar Bowl in New Orleans. Although Layne had the better statistics, most of the talk was about Gilmer, and Grantland Rice wrote, "Gilmer is the best college passer I ever saw, barring neither Sammy Baugh nor Sid Luckman." However, Texas was a 7-point favorite.

"Everybody was so proud of Tommy," said Bob Martin. "He'd gone through the war, was away from the game so long, and had become an outstanding player again through real dedication. I went to New Orleans to see the Sugar Bowl game that year. The Longhorns were staying at a dorm on the campus there and I went looking for Tommy.

"A bunch of the Texas players were sitting around on the grass outside the dorm, watching all the pretty coeds go past. You know, they'd whistle or holler at them. I asked one of the players if he'd seen Tommy Landry.

"'Oh, he's probably up in his room, concentrating on the game and studying the game plans,' said the player.

"Sure enough, that's where I found him," reported Martin. "I knocked, went in and he was sure surprised. He said, 'What are you doing here?' I told him I'd come all the way to see the game and that I expected him to be superb. We talked for a while and I let him get back . . . to studying."

Texas easily beat Alabama, 27–7, before 73,000 fans on a bright, chilly day in the Sugar Bowl. The Longhorns limited Gilmer, the best college passer Grantland Rice ever saw, to 41 yards on four completions while Layne hit 10 of 24 passes for 183 yards and was named the game's Most Valuable Player. It had been a banner year for the Longhorns, who finished 10–1, with Layne, Harris (who had been moved from center to tackle that year), and end Max Bumgardner making All-SWC and Harris and Layne being named All-American. Landry was the All-SWC second-string fullback. It still was one-platoon football with a few defensive specialists being used and so no mythical defensive team was named.

The Longhorns also had a banner celebration in the French Quarter after the Sugar Bowl victory. "A bunch of us went dining at Antoine's Restaurant," said Rooster Andrews. "I remember Dr. Kruger, Bobby's father-in-law, was with us. Whenever they'd make a crêpe suzette, you know, they'd turn down the lights and strike a match to it. It kept happening and Dr. Kruger said, 'This might be a great restaurant but the electricity sure is bad.'"

"One thing led to another," said Layne. "You know, everybody kept talking about our two million dollar band. Well, we decided we'd form our own million dollar band. So we got some brooms, mops, plungers and took off, marching up and down the streets of the French Quarter. I don't know. I think Tommy might have been with us."

"I doubt it but, heck, he might have," said Andrews.

"No," said Landry, "I wasn't. Ray Jones had gotten hurt and so I had to play full time on offense and defense. I played 58 minutes of that game and I was just dead when it was over. I went back to my room and rested."

"Tommy was a fine student, of course, but we all were having trouble with this course in letter writing," said Harris, who today is a banker in Amarillo. "This prof who taught the course was busting all of us. Tommy went home with me that summer to Wichita Falls and we took the course at Midwestern."

The teacher who taught the course at Midwestern was a big football fan and wanted badly to see the UT–Texas A&M game the following year. Harris confided that he would be able to secure her tickets to the game. Both Harris and Landry passed the letter writing course.

"You might say," reflected Harris, "that Tommy helped me pass statistics and I helped him pass letter writing."

When he wasn't in football, Landry participated in intramural sports and won the UT light heavyweight boxing championship. "He was so strong," recalled fraternity brother McCall, "and certainly had courage. He was weighing about 190 but got his weight down to about 180 in order to box light heavyweight."

As school began the fall of 1948 Landry was having problems with impacted wisdom teeth. They were bothering him a great deal and hindered him in football, although he tried to ignore the problem. Layne had graduated and gone into pro football but the Longhorns still were strong. Harris returned to center and was named with Landry as co-captains of the Longhorns. There also was a newcomer named Bud Mc-Fadin, who would make his mark.

The big problem was replacing Layne, and that duty went to Paul Campbell, a slim 174-pounder who was a fine ball-handler but at times became an indecisive passer.

"Paul was a fine person and turned out to be a good quarterback for us," said Harris. "However, I still think Tommy would have been a better quarterback. But that year he still couldn't take snaps or throw the ball as he once had because of the thumb he'd broken. So he stayed at fullback and defensive right halfback."

With the problems of the wisdom teeth and, even after he had them taken out, Landry felt weak, his playing weight staying almost ten pounds below normal.

"I still had the poison in my body from the wisdom teeth problem and I didn't regain my strength and stamina until the last couple of games of the season," said Landry. "So I didn't play as much my senior year as I had as a junior."

Campbell had begun to click after a slow start that season, but his early problems contributed to Texas losses to North Carolina, Oklahoma, and SMU, which again claimed the SWC title. Furthermore, the Longhorns were tied by Texas A&M, 14-14, which was considered a major disaster among the Orange and White supporters. Naturally, the 6-3-1 record was very disappointing after being picked as a contender for the SWC title and Cherry became the center of a great deal of criticism. So it was a great surprise when the Orange Bowl committee picked the Longhorns to play highly ranked Georgia in the Miami game. The Bulldogs of Wally Butts had lost only one game, 21-14, to a North Carolina team which had shattered Texas, 34-7. The natives were restless in Miami; there were threats of forming another bowl game. Critic writers called Texas a third-rate team, said the Orange Bowl had scraped the bottom of the barrel to come up with the Longhorns.

"Everybody was talking and writing about what a poor opponent we were for Georgia," said Landry. "But we noted all this and really geared up for the game."

Perhaps it was just a year of upsets. The polls had predicted Thomas Dewey of New York would easily win the presidential election over Harry Truman, and columnists noted that the only way Truman would have become president in the first place was through the death of Roosevelt, that the voters never would have elected him. On election night the Chicago *Tribune* printed screaming headlines which said, "Dewey Beats Truman." The next morning when the votes were counted, Truman had won the election. To this day, the stigma remains with the *Tribune*.

"Coach Cherry really impressed me before we played Georgia," said Harris. "He told us flatly that the Bulldogs would use a 4-4 defense and we prepared thusly, adjusting our plans. It never was clear whether he picked up the fact they might use it against us in the films or what. There were some rumors that somebody had tipped him off. But, sure enough, that's the defense Georgia used."

After a slow start, Campbell had a good day and Landry, as he had had to do the year before, ended up playing the entire game at fullback and defensive halfback because, this time, Ray Borneman, the other fullback, injured a knee. The game was evenly matched for three periods and Georgia led 28–27 with 11:15 to play. But Landry, running hard and tough like his old self, led Texas on an 11-play, 70-yard touchdown drive and then, breaking tackles and running over other tacklers, crashed 21 yards to set up still another touchdown as Texas won, 41–28. Landry had perhaps his best day in his final game as a Longhorn, finishing as the game's top rusher with 117 yards on 17 carries and playing a fine, rugged defensive game.

In the jubilant Longhorn dressing room, players were yelling, "Who's third-rate?" And Butts told a group of writers, "Next time you writers call a team third-rate, you're going to have to play them yourselves . . . the bottom of that barrel was full of snakes."

Landry had been drafted as a sophomore (had it not been for his years in the war his class could have graduated) by both the New York Giants of the National Football League and the New York Yankees of the All-American Football Conference, which was dominated by Paul Brown's Cleveland Browns.

As Landry walked off the field at the Orange Bowl in Miami after the Longhorn victory that day, he was met by Jack White, an assistant coach for the Yankees. "I had the contract in my pocket and he signed it," said White. "He wasn't hard to deal with. He was very fair and we just made him a better offer than the Giants. I believe we gave him a bonus of $1,500 or $2,000 and a salary of $7,500, but that was good money in those days.

"We knew he was a class guy. He was a big raw-boned kid and a tremendous punter, too. He could turn and back-pedal and seemed a natural on defense. He had a lot of courage and would really come up and bust the ball-carrier.

"I remember when we first began checking on him. I talked to Dutch Meyer at TCU and Dutch said, 'He's a hoss. Landry's a hoss.'"

White, who after 38 years of coaching and holding down other jobs in pro football, retired to a ranch in Oregon, recalled that Landry's play in the Orange Bowl also caught the eye of some other teams.

"Paul Brown came over to me at the winter meetings and asked if I'd trade him Landry," said White. "I told him there was no way!"

That January of 1948 Tom Landry and Alicia Wiggs were married in Houston and then returned to Austin, where Landry received his B.A. degree. He had decided by then to become an industrial engineer and would continue his schooling at the University of Houston.

"Pro football was such an unknown thing then," said Alicia, who left school as a sophomore to go with her husband. "Tommy was going to go ahead and get his degree in engineering. But neither of us had been up East and it was kind of like an adventure for us. So we talked about the future and decided that he'd play in New York for a couple of years, get his degree during the off-season, and then go into engineering. It was just to be an adventure for us."

But pro football would become an adventure that would last them a lifetime.

5

THE GAME between the Los Angeles Rams and New York Giants was in the rickety old Polo Grounds in Coogan's Bluff during the final stages of the 1954 season. The NFL conference winners would be Cleveland and Detroit and the opponents in question that afternoon would go nowhere. There occurred a play which, even to this day, causes Tom Landry to literally crack up, to shed what many who do not look deeply enough believe to be a granite face.

Now in those days the Rams were still the glamor team with such players as Norm Van Brocklin, the Dutchman who had an affinity for giving nicknames to his teammates, receivers such as Tom Fears, Elroy ("Crazylegs") Hirsch, and a pair of bull-like running backs nicknamed by Van Brocklin "Deacon" Dan Towler and "Tank" Paul Younger.

Deac and Tank had rattled the rib cages of more than one defender, especially a defensive back who might have the ill fortune to be in their path once they cleared the line of scrimmage and got up a head of steam. That was the first year Landry had become a player-coach for the New York Giants and the team had added another defensive halfback from Maryland named Dick Nolan, who later would become an assistant for Landry with the Dallas Cowboys and head coach of the San Francisco 49ers and New Orleans Saints.

In those days Nolan weighed in at about 175–180 pounds, giving up some 30 to 40 pounds to backs such as Deac and Tank. Dick had a great deal of nerve and was aggressive, although he did not particularly enjoy seeing the likes of the Ram runners break into the secondary and thus have to face them head-on.

At that time there were no bars across helmets and many players had the faces of boxers. Goal posts also were set on the actual goal line then, not at the back of the end zone, and they were unpadded. In fact, it often was good strategy for runners to use the steel poles of the uprights to shield off would-be tacklers as they plunged for the end zone.

During the course of the game, which the Rams would win 17–16, Los Angeles drove inside the Giants' five-yard line. The Giants tightened, preparing to meet another bullish charge from Towler or Younger. Deacon's number was called and as he lined up his face became stern, grim, but inside he was smiling because he liked the contact, to feel defenders crumble against his awesome power. He set and on the snap lunged forth to take the hand-off from Van Brocklin. It was the right play at the right time and a huge hole opened over guard and Deacon was unchallenged at the line of scrimmage as he charged forward in all his fury, his head lowered and his helmet set to butt anything in his way. So he gained speed, picked up steam and drove with all his might to the end zone without the expected opposition. Only thing, he ran smack into the goal post with his head.

There was a bone-rattling collision, muscle and power, albeit human flesh, against steel set solidly into the ground with concrete. Nolan later recalled looking at films, and said you actually could see the goal post give, bend a little, and then catapult Deacon backward some four or five yards, sending the ball flying out of his hand as though it had been dynamited loose.

"The goal post," said Nolan, "went shoooooshhhhh."

Deacon, thrown on his back, sat up, stunned, his eyes blank, looking like Orphan Annie's, his helmet askew, slightly cracked, and the man having no idea what great force had hit him. He tried to shake loose the cobwebs in his head and the stars dancing madly in front of his eyes.

"I just stood there for a while," said Landry, "looking at him to see if he'd ever move again."

Emlen Tunnell, the Giants' safety, was concerned and said, "Deac! Deac! You all right? You okay?"

Nolan, not about to miss a chance, moseyed over to Deacon, bent over him and stuck a finger right in the Ram running back's face. "Yeah, Deac," Nolan barked, "you come through there again, you sonuvagun, and next time I'll *really* hit you!" Deacon stared at Nolan in disbelief.

65

Landry, laughing aloud as he recalled the story, said, "I couldn't look at either of them. I ran off the field and got to the sidelines before I broke up.

"Those were great years and that Nolan could be crazy at times."

New York has always been alive with itself. At the time Tom Landry was in New York there was much less decay in the city and it buzzed with the great musicals on Broadway—*South Pacific* and *Peter Pan*. There were all-time sports heroes like Joltin' Joe DiMaggio, and fine places to hang out such as Toots Shor's. There you might bump into a movie star or even Rocky Marciano, who had knocked out the great Joe Louis in his comeback try in 1951. Rocky had become the world heavyweight champion in 1952. And also there was El Morocco and the Stork Club. You could send your kids to play in Central Park and go there yourself without fear of being mugged or worse. It has always been a key place where successful people migrate, a place that author Willie Morris, a Southerner, once called "The City of Finalists." But when Landry was there it was also a city that didn't have such a dirty face.

This was the 1950s, when a war in Korea would begin and end and a power-hungry egotist named Joseph McCarthy would ruin scores of lives by simply hinting that a person might be a communist. And it was a time for Eisenhower ("We like Ike") to become President and young Richard Nixon, the lawyer from California, to be Vice-President and the rising star of the Republican Party. Johnny Ray would sing a song called "Cry" and sound very much as though he actually were doing so. And Elvis Presley would twist his torso in such a shameful way that some were saying the devil himself must be inside him. Herman Wouk would emerge with *The Caine Mutiny* and James Jones would come out with *From Here to Eternity*. Thomas B. Costain would have a best seller called *The Silver Chalice* and Lloyd Douglas had *The Robe*.

Fine Western movies such as *High Noon* with Gary Cooper and *Shane* with Alan Ladd would draw the attention of movie-goers throughout the nation, and Steve Allen would keep television viewers up on the "Tonight Show." People had begun to talk about too many cars but, certainly, not too little gas.

The '50s, to say the least, were exciting times and, as Tom and Alicia Landry had said when they left Texas for New York, "It would be a time of adventure for us."

Baseball was the biggest of games and its players the greatest of heroes as the '50s began, but in the final part of the decade there would be the perfect marriage of television and professional football. A nation of sportsmen would come to totally embrace the National Football League.

66

"It was just a great experience, being in New York in those days," recalled Landry. "The game of professional football really caught on. It grew up during those days and, I suppose, those of us who were there felt a part of this process.

"During the 1950s the thing I remember was that television wasn't a dominant force at all and the newspapers didn't carry that much about pro football around the country. Playing pro football when I started was less than a six-month-a-year job and, when I'd go back to Texas during the off-season, nobody would come up and ask me about pro football.

"Things were a lot more low-keyed then. Pro football people were a pretty closely knit group. The game didn't have the sophistication, the big salaries and the media exposure. Really, none of us knew anything about big business. We were Depression babies, just happy to be playing football and getting paid for it. There just wasn't much money talk and nobody knew what the other guy was making."

Tom Landry had begun his career with the New York Yankees, who merged with the Brooklyn team in the All-American Football Conference in 1949 and became the Brooklyn-New York Yankees. The AAFC was in its fourth and final year before being absorbed by the National Football League. So, including the Giants and Bulldogs of the NFL, New York City had three professional football teams that year.

"The All-American Football Conference wasn't stable," said Landry, "but actually we [the Yankees] were owned by the baseball Yankees and were probably more stable than the Giants and even might have outdrawn them."

As one day others would observe about the American Football League, the purists, The Establishment chuckled about the AAFC, saying its teams were inferior, a point that the Cleveland Browns and the very innovative and intelligent Paul Brown would soon prove ridiculous.

Landry, the rookie from the University of Texas, was the Yankees' punter, averaging 44.1 for the season, second only to Frankie Albert of San Francisco. He returned three punts for a 17.3 average and intercepted a single pass, which he ran back 44 yards. And on October 31 of that year he had become a father. In Houston, the Landrys' off-season hometown and where he was working on an industrial engineering degree at the University of Houston, Alicia gave birth to Thomas Wade Landry, Jr. Tom phoned a number of times but didn't get to see the baby for over six weeks, until the season had ended. They were learning early you could not live what was considered a normal life when you were in professional football.

Cleveland won that final AAFC championship, as it had each of the previous four years, with San Francisco finishing second and Brooklyn–New York third. In the play-offs Cleveland beat Buffalo and San Francisco toppled Brooklyn–New York in the semifinals and the Browns whipped San Francisco, 21–7, in the title game. In the NFL, the Philadelphia Eagles beat the Los Angeles Rams, 14–10, for the championship.

"To begin with I played offensive halfback behind Buddy Young but I didn't do a very good job," said Landry. "Then we lost our cornerback Harmon Rowe and they sent me in to play. Man, Otto Graham went crazy when he saw me. That game I'll never forget. I've never seen so many passes caught in my life. They killed me, but I learned how I'd have to play the game, that I'd have to use my head, rather than any great physical talents which I just didn't have."

The game in question was on November 20, 1949, and Graham, picking on the inexperienced Landry, mostly threw to Mac Speedie, who set an AAFC record with 11 receptions for 228 yards as Cleveland won, 31–0.

The experience would have destroyed many players before they ever really began. But, of course, it did not Landry, for he would go on to become the biggest obstacle Paul Brown and his team would face in the ensuing years.

After a great deal of hassling, prophetic of things to come in later years between the AFL and the NFL, the National Football League finally agreed to take three AAFC franchises in their entirety, including the champion Browns, the San Francisco 49ers, and the Baltimore Colts. Players from the other teams would be drafted, with regional preference observed. The Giants, as an example, chose five players from the Yankees.

Steve Owen, who had played for the Giants in the formative years and then become head coach in 1931, conferred with those in the organization and picked from the Yankees Landry, mostly because of his punting ability, and defensive backs Rowe and Otto Schnellbacher, tackle Arnie Weinmeister and guard John Mastrangelo. Unlimited substitution had been installed in the NFL in 1950 and Landry, Rowe and Schnellbacher were to become mainstays of a tremendous New York secondary and Weinmeister a fine tackle.

"I suppose the fastest I'd ever run the 100 was about 10.3," said Landry. "I'm sure the only reason the Giants picked me was for my punting ability. Steve Owen told me I might play some on defense, too.

"I was just too slow to play cornerback in the league, so in order to keep my job I had to study a lot. I had to try to figure out what the other team was going to do. I watched films, picked up tendencies."

And Landry was extremely competitive; he would find a way. So he would analyze the opponent to such an extent that he would be there waiting long before the receiver concluded his route. Landry, even then, was picking up the keys that would unlock the secrets of the offensive huddle.

Commissioner Bert Bell wasted no time in getting the immediate and undivided attention of those who followed pro football the first year of the merger. On Saturday, before the regular season began on Sunday, he scheduled a contest between the AAFC champion Cleveland Browns and the defending NFL champion Philadelphia Eagles, featuring Steve Van Buren. Fans of the AAFC rubbed their hands together in anticipation and NFL fans wondered just who were those guys named Graham, Marion Motley, Speedie, Dante Lavelli, Lou Groza and a so-called innovative coach, Paul Brown. The question was explicitly answered. Cleveland crushed Philadelphia, 35–10, before 71,237 fans in the City of Brotherly Love.

In attendance that day was Steve Owen. That day Brown had made a popular NFL defense, the Eagle Defense (created by Philadelphia coach Earle Greasy Neale), look obsolete. The predominant defense before and during the war years was the 5–3–3 (five linemen, three linebackers, three defensive backs). Neale tired of seeing fast backs outrun the linebacker on passing plays, so he conceived the Eagle Defense, a 5–2–4 alignment, putting in another defensive back for the linebacker.

However, the Eagle Defense was quite vulnerable up the middle when an offensive team sent its backs into the flat, occupying the linebackers, and then moved the ends back across the uncovered middle. Brown had done this and had also introduced the Eagles that day, and the NFL, to the comeback patterns in which Speedie and Lavelli would run downfield toward the backs, then turn and come back a couple of yards to take the ball from Graham on timing.

Owen, a defensive innovator in his own right, was very much aware of what he had seen. Many NFL observers watching the Browns and Eagles that day would talk about how their players must try harder, hustle more against the Browns' receivers, but Owen saw that help had to come from another direction, a new defense.

The Giants were to play the Browns the following game, so as the week's preparations began, Owen walked into the team meeting and went to the blackboard. "Gentlemen," he said, "this week we will make changes. This week we will use the 6–1 [six linemen, one linebacker, four defensive backs] against the Cleveland Browns." He then diagramed the alignment and added, "Sometimes we'll be dropping off the ends into the hook zones, the flare zones and at other times, we'll let them rush Graham. Gentlemen, this is how we'll beat the Cleveland Browns this week."

With that statement, Owen walked out of the room. The players and coaches looked at one another. "Steve Owen was not a great detail man," said Landry. "He'd just do things like that and figure you would work out the details for yourself on the field. I learned much of my coaching by playing under him because I had to work out the details of what he meant.

"The day he drew the 6-1 on the blackboard and walked out of the room, there was some confusion. We had never played that defense before and I knew somebody had to get up and explain it. Somebody had to exert leadership. I'd never done anything like that before but I just got up, went to the blackboard, and began to explain in detail what he meant."

Landry explained that the defense would fan out in a semicircle downfield with the middle linebacker as a kind of stem. Sometimes, he told them, the ends would be standing up and dropping off (into pass coverage) and sometimes they would get down in a lineman's stance and rush. The idea was to keep the Browns off balance, never letting them know what was coming. What Owen had devised and Landry helped explain was what came to be known as the Umbrella Defense, which would replace the Eagle Defense as the most used alignment in the NFL.

When Tom Landry got up that day and explained to the team what Owen meant, he was 25 years old. One day he would take the Eagle Defense, the Umbrella Defense, and go a step further.

"We had a great game against the Browns that day," said Landry. "Graham didn't complete a pass in the first half against us. Certainly, that's one of the games I'll always remember."

When Graham got under center for the first time he thought he was looking at a straight 6-1 defense. But as he faded to pass, ends Jim Duncan and Ray Poole dropped off with the receivers. Speedie and Lavelli were, in effect, double covered. Graham not only didn't complete a pass but had three intercepted.

At halftime Paul Brown made adjustments, telling Graham to throw short passes or run wide, toward the retreating New York ends. But Owen countered, having Poole and Duncan charge the passer most of the time and sending Landry and Em Tunnel, both large for defensive backs, up to make the tackles. The Giants won, 6-0, in the beginning of what was to become a fabled rivalry. No matter when or where the Giants and Browns played, it always was like a championship game.

The Giants also won the second meeting between the two teams, 17–13, and finished with a 10–2 record, tying the Browns for what then was called the American Conference of the National Football League. However, the Browns won the play-off game, 8–3, over the Giants and then edged the Los Angeles Rams, winners of the National Conference of the NFL, 30–28, for the championship on Groza's field goal with 28 seconds left to play.

"I still think," Tunnell once said, "that the 1950 team was the best the Giants ever had. Imagine, holding a team like Cleveland with a single touchdown in three games."

Some experts, even today, agree that this was indeed one of the great accomplishments in NFL defensive history.

In 1951 the Giants finished second to Cleveland in the conference, although this time the Browns lost the NFL championship to the Rams. Cleveland beat the Giants twice, 14–13 and 10–0, but Landry intercepted a pass in the first week and returned it for a touchdown. He duplicated that feat the following week against the Eagles. Landry also served as the Giants' punter from 1950–55. This ranked him second only to Don Chandler, one of the all-time great punters, in Giant annals in total punts and total yardage punting.

"In those early years we lived in a resort hotel on Long Island," recalled Alicia Landry. "It was almost vacant during the season, the winter months, and so it was a nice thing for us. Tommy would commute to work at the Polo Grounds. I loved it there, then. We'd have some nice snows and it was so much cleaner than now."

After Tom went to training camp in 1952, Kitty was born on August 25 in Houston. Again, he phoned but was unable to see Alicia or his daughter until the Giants played an exhibition game in Dallas.

The 1952 season was one in which Tom Landry would begin to assert himself as one of the NFL's top defensive backs. It also was a year in which Dallas, ever so briefly, would have a professional football team. The chain of events had begun in 1949, the final year of the AAFC–NFL war. The Boston Yanks left that city and moved to New York, becoming the Bulldogs. When the leagues merged the Bulldogs became the Yankees of the NFL, being given the same name as the AAFC team upon which Landry had begun his career.

But in 1952 Yankees' owner Ted Collins sold his team back to the NFL, which, in turn, allowed it to be bought by a group of Texas businessmen headed by Giles Miller. The team played in the Cotton Bowl but the talent was inferior, the losses almost sure and nobody came to the Cotton Bowl to watch. So at mid-season the franchise was given back to the league and became a "traveling" team, playing the

71

remainder of its games on the road. The Dallas Texans were the last NFL team to fail. The following year the team was purchased by Carroll Rosenbloom and moved to Baltimore, becoming the Colts and soon an NFL power. It would be eight years before another NFL team, the Cowboys, appeared in Dallas.

Landry was superb that season, leading his team with eight interceptions, punting well, and becoming a coach on the field. He was also getting a reputation for being able to back up his brain with brawn.

"Tom," recalled Pat Summerall, a kicker for the Giants who later became a national television commentator, "was big [198 pounds] for a defensive back and just a great hitter, even a late hitter at times in his enthusiasm. He wasn't mean, like some who played then. He was just aggressive and I also remember what a tremendous punter he was."

Nolan, who came to the Giants in 1954, said, "Tom was such a tough competitor. I guarantee you he'd knock your block off. He was so smart, just amazing. The Rams used to have a sprinter named Bobby Boyd (not to be confused with the defensive back who later played for Baltimore). The guy could fly and would just take off and run past the defensive backs. But not Tom. Tom gave him fits because Tom *knew* when Boyd was going deep and would be there, waiting."

Years ago when I was at the Dallas Cowboy training camp in Thousand Oaks, California, a group of writers often used to go into Encino and eat at the Rams' Horn, a fine restaurant at the time operated by former LA linebacker, Don Paul. One night Paul got to talking about Landry and told us about a time when Tom chased Mr. Outside of West Point fame, Glenn Davis, all the way back to the bench. Davis, a fine halfback-receiver for the Rams, had beaten Landry for a touchdown.

Davis agreed the incident as told by Paul was fairly accurate. "I caught a pass about ten yards behind Tom and scored," Davis recalled. "But I could still hear Tom coming after me. I knew he was going to punish me for what I'd done and, sure enough, he really crashed into me in the end zone. I got up and said, 'If you want the ball that bad, here!' I threw it at his head and then I took off for the bench. He came after me. Fortunately, I had friends over there."

Landry just grins at such stories, the grin meaning they might be true or might be an exaggeration. Sometimes his grins are like that, very noncommittal.

Again, as in the two previous seasons, the Giants were battling the Browns for the conference title. New York, certainly, was improving and had added SMU All-American Kyle Rote in 1951 and Southern

72

California glamor boy, halfback Frank Gifford, in 1952. The conference title came down to the last three games, the first of which for the Giants was against the Pittsburgh Steelers, featuring one of the best, toughest and meanest men ever to play the game, Ernie Stautner. Stautner, a Hall-of-Famer who is now defensive coordinator for the Dallas Cowboys, had wanted to play for the Giants, although the Steelers had drafted him. It appeared something might be worked out, if the Giants were interested.

"I was a defensive tackle and weighed only about 213 pounds when I got out of college," said Stautner. "I went to talk to Steve Owen and he took one look at me and said I was too small to play in the line for his Umbrella Defense."

Stautner's famous temper boiled. "I tell you something, Mr. Owen," said Ernie, "I'll play in this league and you'll rue the day you refused me."

Obviously, he did. Stautner carried on a personal vendetta against the Giants and, although the Steelers had poor records during the '50s, they held their own with the Giants, becoming a strong reason New York kept finishing behind Cleveland, such as in 1952.

"When we played the Giants near the end of that season we could do nothing wrong," said Stautner. "First we knocked out Charlie Conerly, then got their second-string quarterback [Fred Benners, of SMU] and they had nobody to play quarterback. Tom had had a little experience at the position at Texas and so they put him in there."

"We were lucky to be playing in Pittsburgh," said Landry. "The ground was soft there . . . I could draw plays in the dirt."

"I was rushing Tom when he went back to pass," said Stautner. "You know, like always, foaming at the mouth, hell-bent-for-leather. I broke through, doubled up my fist and smashed him in the face, right through his face mask. The blow broke his nose, bloodied him up, knocked him over.

"I just casually started walking back to the defensive side when Tom jumped up and pounded me on the back. I kept going. I knew I'd done a bad thing but I hated the Giants so bad because they'd told me I was too little to play."

That day Pittsburgh beat the Giants, 63-7. It was the last time Landry ever played quarterback and, after the game Owen, originator of the Umbrella Defense, remarked, "It's a good thing I'm known as a defensive genius or the score would have been 100-7."

The Giants then lost to Washington, but beat Cleveland in the final game, 37-34. They'd also beaten the Browns, 17-9, in an initial meeting that season but, because of the loss to Pittsburgh as much as

73

anything else, finished a game behind Cleveland for the conference title.

"Tom never forgot that game and that I'd broken his nose," said Stautner. "After I went to work for him in 1966 he just looked at me one day and said, 'Ernie, I remember you breaking my nose that day in Pittsburgh.'"

It came as a shock for almost everybody concerned, but the Giants fell apart in 1953, finishing with a 3–9 record, and twice losing to Cleveland, including once by the humiliating score of 62–14. There were key injuries to Rote and Ed Price, the fine running backs, and so Owen asked Frank Gifford to move to offense. He went on to become one of the all-time stars at halfback, a man who could not only run but also catch and throw passes, adding a new dimension. In 1976 Gifford visited Dallas to honor Tom Landry and I stopped him in the hallway of the Fairmont Hotel. He was rushed but said he always had time to talk about Tom.

"Most of us in those days just played the game," said Gifford. "Not Tom. He studied it, studied everything. When I was playing on the defensive unit with Tom in 1952, defense was just hit or miss with most everybody in those days. Not with Tom. He put the same kind of discipline in the defense that the offense had. He had begun to create pro defense as we play it today.

"He had begun to give us keys, although we didn't call them that in those days. But you had to be disciplined. One time I remember I intercepted a pass. I'd just gone for the ball but I was out of position. Tom didn't say, nice play. He just said, 'Frank, you know you were out of position on that play.'"

When the season ended the rumors that had been circulating in football circles around New York became fact; Timothy Mara fired Steve Owen. Owen had been a loyal Giant all his pro career, playing for the team for ten years and then coaching for twenty-three seasons in which he won NFL titles in 1934 and 1938, took nine conference or divisional championships and tied for still another. His critics said the game had passed him by and that he was a stubborn man who resisted change. Certainly, the NFL offenses had begun to exploit his Umbrella Defense. But Owen was hurt deeply when the ax fell and refused a job in the organization. Jim Lee Howell, a soft-spoken 6 foot 4 inch, 250-pound man from Arkansas who once had played end for the Giants, was given the job as head coach.

Two major steps were taken. First Mara told Howell he wanted him to talk to a young assistant at West Point under Earl (Red) Blaik.

If the young man met Howell's requirements, he should hire him. So Howell hired Vince Lombardi to handle his offense. The next step he took was to ask Tom Landry to become a player-coach, to assume responsibility for the defense, something that he already, to a degree, had taken upon himself. Landry, at 29, became the youngest assistant in the NFL.

"I hadn't planned on a coaching career at all," said Landry. "It just happened. I had my work during the off-season and planned to pursue another career when I retired as a player. I had been working in real estate and insurance. Then, of course, I retired as a player [in 1956] and became a full-time assistant. But, even then, football only lasted half the year and I could pursue other interests."

"And it also was during those days that Tommy and I established a tradition we still carry on, that of going out to dinner at least once a week, no matter what is happening," recalled Alicia.

The season of 1954 would be Tom Landry's best as a player and a suggestion he made one day in practice would not only prolong but add even more stardom to the career of Kyle Rote. As a halfback Rote was continually having knee problems. His knee simply could not stand the pounding from the position.

"Oh, I'd run patterns against Tom in practice from my position, which, basically, was a halfback split out wide," said Rote. "I suppose I'd run pretty good patterns and catch the ball fairly well so one day in practice Tom stopped me."

"Hey," said Landry to Rote, "why don't you try it at end? I think you'd do a good job there."

Rote took the suggestion and became one of the great ends of his time in the NFL. "Tom knew I couldn't run out of the backfield any more because of my knees," said Rote. "I just couldn't do it. When I moved to end it was the biggest break of my football career." Rote played end for the Giants until his retirement in 1961.

The Giants finished third in what then was called the Eastern Conference. Landry not only coached the defense but also intercepted eight passes, tying Tunnell for the team lead. He finished fourth in the NFL in punting with a 42.5 average and had a long kick of 61 yards. His hairline was receding on both sides, just as his father's had done, but some of the Giants joked that he lost hair because he was hitting opponents so hard. Years later others would say the same thing about Cowboy free safety Cliff Harris.

"We'd get into the defensive huddle," said Nolan, a rookie then, "and Tom would call the defense. He'd look over at me and say, 'Dick, if they put the flanker out in front of you, then you key the fullback and, if the fullback swings out, the flanker will run a down-and-in, so be ready.' He was usually right."

Landry was always at his best against the Browns, perhaps because deeply embedded in his mind was the time as a rookie in 1949 when Otto Graham had picked him apart. One day he caught Graham in the open field, running with the ball, and crashed into the Browns quarterback with a shot that could be heard around the stadium. It was the final play of a particular series and as Landry started off the field, the usually calm Paul Brown charged a few steps on the field and yelled, "Cheap shot, Landry! Cheap shot!"

Calmly, Landry turned toward Brown and replied, "You know better than that, Paul."

Tunnell, the first black man to play for the Giants, an NFL Hall-of-Famer and a man many believe to be the greatest safety to play the game, once said, "Landry was real smart. He never said much, really. But he always knew what was going on. We didn't have words like they do now, keying or something like that. Tom would make up his own keys and teach them to us.

"But socially . . . he seemed kind of weird to me sometimes. We played alongside each other and played great for all those years but outside of football we didn't communicate much at all. Tom was his own person, going his own way, and I was mine. Some of us would go out for a beer but Tom, mostly, would just disappear, go off with his family. But I say this, I had a lot of respect for him."

"Tom was so strong-minded and such a stickler for the way things should be done," recalled Nolan, a grin creeping across his face. "One time we were playing—Detroit, I believe. Anyway, I was at right corner and Tom played the left corner. John Henry Johnson, a big, mean, sonuvagun of a fullback, headed in my direction. He had all three guys leading interference for him and it seemed like they all were coming at me. Anyway, I do know they all hit me, leaving me all in pieces on the ground. My shoulder was separated and I just laid there, trying to see whether or not I was dead. The first thing I saw when I opened my eyes was Tom, standing over me.

" 'I know,' I told him, 'you want me to stay in the game.'

" 'No,' he said. 'You had bad technique on that play.' "

Landry made All-Pro at cornerback in 1954, along with such people as Otto Graham, Doak Walker, Ollie Matson, Lou Groza, Leo Nomellini, Les Bingaman, Chuck Bednarik and Bucko Kilroy, who later became a scout for the Cowboys and then player personnel director of the New England Patriots, and later general manager.

Again in 1955 the Giants finished third in the NFL Eastern Conference with a 6–5–1 record, but they did so in a different place—Yankee Stadium. They had moved there from the old Polo Grounds. It was a much better field, with improved dressing facilities, but Yankee Stadium still was "The House that Ruth Built" and baseball was still king. It also marked the year that Landry retired as an active player, becoming a full-time assistant or defensive coach for Howell (he had become a player-coach in 1954).

Longtime Giant publicity director Don Smith recalled the year and the transition once by saying, "When Tom became a full-time coach it was as if he had been doing it for twenty years. There was no sense of time passing. Even today when you see him, you get the feeling no time has passed. It's just like you wake up, pull a shade and all the wisdom of a lifetime is under the pillow."

Although the record didn't reveal what was happening, the Giants were getting awfully close to becoming a power in 1954 and 1955, with the credit going not only to the fine array of talent being assembled, but also to Howell's young assistants, Landry and Lombardi.

"In the early years Vince was a fine coach but not the great coach he later became," Landry said. "When he came into pro football with us it was his first time in the game (he hadn't played professional football), so he was not only doing the job but also learning.

"But it was pretty obvious to all of us that Vince one day would be a really great coach. He was very basic in his approach and was a master of knowing how to utilize, to get the most out of personnel.

"Vince was a very emotional man. If the offense didn't look good sometimes it'd be two, three days before you could talk to him. He really hated to look bad. He was that sensitive. But that was just Vince and we understood him. We got along very well—we were friends. It was just that if the offense played well and won, he was very outgoing, emotional and, if not, the opposite."

Wellington Mara once said of the pair, "Lombardi was on the surface a much warmer person than Landry. He went from warm to red hot. You could hear Vince laughing or shouting for five blocks. You couldn't hear Landry from the next chair. Lombardi was more of a teacher. It was as though Landry lectured the top 40 percent of the class and Lombardi taught the lower 10 percent."

"There's no doubt," said Nolan, "that Landry and Lombardi were the main guys. Vince was gregarious and, you know, he was the type guy who could get a guy to jump through a hoop for him. He would get a guy to play above his capabilities. Tom would tell you exactly what to do and if you did it you were successful. It was that simple."

77

Jim Lee Howell gave Landry and Lombardi the reins and let them go. "I just pump up the footballs and keep curfew," he once said. "With those two around I had very little to do.

"Vince was very aggressive, sometimes to the point of being abrasive, but that was just his personality. On the field he would walk guys through plays before there was contact. He wanted every player to understand his assignment before the play was carried out. And he was daring, which I liked.

"Tom was the best defensive coach in the business, a brilliant man, a great organizer. His manner was very different. Vince was a yelling and shouting type guy. Tom never raised his voice; he was very quiet and got his point across just as effectively as Vince. Tom was extremely talented at analyzing films. It would take him, maybe, twenty minutes to dissect a team's performance, whereas it might take somebody else hours. He also was outstanding at evaluating players, which later helped him so much at Dallas.

"It was a wonderful situation. They were friends, competitive, and each had a fire in him to win."

"They were good friends," said Nolan, "but Tom knew more football."

Rote once remembered walking down the hall at the Giants' training camp at St. Michael's, Vermont. "I looked on one side of the hall and there was Lombardi looking at films," said Rote. "I looked on the other side and there was Landry looking at films. I continued on down the hall and saw Jim Lee reading a newspaper."

"I doubt there will ever be a situation like that again," said Landry. "I mean one where you have three men like that working together and a head coach just turning things over to his assistants like Jim Lee did Vince and myself.

"Jim Lee was a very soft-spoken man. But I'm sure if we'd messed up he'd have said something to us. But as long as we were doing the job he just let us handle it. Vince and I ran our units during the week and during the games."

"It was extremely competitive," said Nolan. "You can't imagine how competitive it could be. But it just happened . . . the offense and defensive units separated. The toughest competition either ever faced was when it scrimmaged the other."

"The defensive unit in those years was very close," said Landry. "As I look back on those times in the mid and late 1950s, I think of them as some of the best experiences of my time in football. It was as close as any team with whom I've been associated. I didn't have any help coaching the defensive. I coached everybody . . . the line, the linebackers, the secondary [he also coached the kickers] and it was a great time.

"We all worked hard. It seemed like we worked until we were about ready to drop and then we'd work some more."

Of course, Lombardi would always want the offense on the field and Landry would want the defense out there. Nolan remembered seeing Howell run up and down the sidelines, yelling at Landry, "What should we do! What should we do!"

"Punt," said Landry. "Give them the ball."

Lombardi had installed the power sweep with the fullback blocking, the two guards pulling and the halfback following with the ball. It was perfect for Gifford, a fine runner who was also a threat as a passer. This was the same set-up Lombardi later exploited at Green Bay with Paul Hornung.

And Landry had taken the defense a step further. He began using a 4-3 alignment (four linemen, three linebackers, two cornerbacks, two safeties) when he was a player-coach. The unit was solid but something was lacking. In 1956 he found that ingredient in a man who was to become the epitome of middle linebackers of his era. This was the year the Giants took steps to establish a dynasty in the Eastern Conference and head on a collision course with the Baltimore Colts two years later. That game would change the nation's television viewing habits, making pro football the national sport, television's game.

WHEN THE New York Giants began training in 1956 at St. Michael's, Vermont, a baby-faced lineman from West Virginia was among the rookie crop. He had an innocent, easygoing air about him but at times when he was on the field, he could become overly aggressive or as some put it, "downright mean." But the kid was only 6 feet 1 inch, about 225 to 230 pounds, and he was a guard. The times had changed and so the pros wanted their blockers taller and bigger to withstand such huge rushers and the Colts' Big Daddy Lipscomb, who weighed 280. The kid also was too small to play in the defensive line. The only guy who could do that at about the same size was Ernie Stautner, and the Giants didn't even like to think about letting him get away to Pittsburgh.

The kid and his roommate, Don Chandler, a punter who the coaches hoped would take Tom Landry's place as the team's kicker, became very disenchanted in camp. The kid was hearing talk that he was a man without a position and so felt he'd be cut anyway, and there were just too many sacrifices to be made for nothing. So the pair packed their bags, sneaked out of camp and headed for home, where the kid planned to become a schoolteacher.

One story has it that Vince Lombardi stopped them before they left the dorm at training camp. Another says Lombardi came roaring up in a car before they boarded a train and stopped them, putting an end to their idea of going AWOL.

But, with the fury that he could show so well, Lombardi mesmerized them, saying, "Listen, you two might not make this club but nobody runs out on me! Nobody!"

So they came back, their heads lowered. And Tom Landry, then a full-time defensive coach, began to get some ideas about the baby-faced kid whose name, incidentally, was Robert E. Lee (Sam) Huff. He would become the epitome of a position called middle linebacker and his violent world would be talked about by pro football fans from New York to Texas as he became a part of the defensive renaissance.

Landry had already experimented with the 4-3 and by that year had begun, more and more, to explore all the aspects of the alignment. Other teams around the league also had begun to drop off their ends from a six-man line to defend against the end sweep, but Landry still was ahead of his time.

Wellington Mara, one of the sons of the Giants' founder, Timothy, and later president of the club, recalled, "What everybody was doing was forcing the play back inside. But Tom came up with the idea of defensing the end run inside-out, stopping opponents up the middle with the idea that pursuit would take care of the outside. Simply, Tom was talking about today's 4-3 defense, where the four defensive linemen are charged with the responsibility of keeping the five offensive linemen from getting a clear shot at the middle linebacker. Jim Lee Howell accepted this theory and the rest is history—the 4-3 defense."

"Even during the days I was playing offense I felt defense was the most challenging part of the game," said Landry. "The offense has its plays diagramed for it and knows ahead of time what to do. The defense must constantly anticipate and react. On defense you have to accept the fact that you're going to give the other guy the first shot.

The initial advantage is his. I just always have had an analytical mind and this was most intriguing for me.

"Again, the 4-3 was a combination of the Eagle Defense and the Umbrella. The Eagle Defense had begun taking on a 4-3 look because they'd put an extra back in for the linebacker to help on passing downs. He'd be standing up. It was just becoming obvious to me that the thing to do was to keep the ends dropped off, covering the flare areas, making them linebackers.

"But what I needed was a guy in the middle who was pretty quick, pretty active and could key. Sam seemed like he might be that guy. We tried him and it worked out well for all concerned."

"Ray Beck got hurt in an exhibition game," said Huff. "And they stuck me in there. By early season I was the starting middle linebacker."

"Well, it was obvious he ought to be tried at middle linebacker," continued Landry. "In those days, we kept things very simple, easy to make the adjustments. I gave him a couple of keys and that's what he looked for.

"Actually, when we got Randy White with the Cowboys, I felt the same way about him, that he should be tried at middle linebacker and could be tremendous due to his size and ability. But the game had become so much more complicated. It would have taken a much, much longer time for Randy. Had Randy been around during the days when Sam came up, he'd have moved in and done extremely well at middle linebacker, too.

"But Sam . . . he just was excellent at following instructions. He was very disciplined and would listen. He also had a mean streak, which you need as a linebacker.

"Our defense was coordinated and you had to have discipline to play it, sometimes sacrificing individual plays for the betterment of the overall defense. It's based on the ability of a unit to react together. Most defensive players get hit and fight through the block. We hold. We do not fight through a block. We control an area. That's based on my engineering background, coordinating people."

"I don't know who takes credit for the 4-3," said Frank Gifford, "but it was Tom . . . he exploited it, coordinated it, made it work. Few people outside of football realize what a great coach he is, what a great innovator he is. Most coaches should be worshiping at his feet."

Dick Nolan remembered the 4-3 and Huff. "Sam was perfect but Tom made him what he became with that defense. If the right defense hadn't been there for him, if Tom hadn't been there, I don't know what would have happened to him.

"But against some of those big fullbacks Tom would tell him exactly

81

what they'd do. If they line up like this, and he's here, then he'll do this. Tom could look at an opponent's films, even in those days, and know what they'd do. He was so far ahead of his time . . . you just can't imagine how far."

When the Giants broke training camp eighteen players and coaches moved to the Concourse Plaza, near Yankee Stadium, not far from Central Park. Kyle Rote, Jr., remembered that he used to go to Central Park and play games with Tom Landry, Jr., and Jeff Gifford. And when the team, before it played a home game, would go through a light workout on Saturday morning, the boys would go to Yankee Stadium and wear Giants' T-shirts or old jerseys and run around, throwing the football.

"We weren't far from the Planetarium and the Museum of Natural History," said Landry. "Alicia and I would go there with the kids and stay for hours."

"But all the children," said Alicia, "were born in Texas. We wanted them to be Texans, although the people we knew were so nice. Oh, sometimes people at stores would be a little rude but you'd play this game with them. You'd keep being nice to them and just see how long they could go before they started smiling and being nice back to you."

Huff, the rookie, also moved into the Concourse Plaza. "You might say I learned to play middle linebacker while sitting in the Landry suite at the hotel," Huff said. "I'd be there in my room, you know, after practice, relaxing, and the phone would ring. It would be Tom."

"Sam," Landry would say, "what are you doing?"

"Oh, hello, coach. Just resting, sitting here watching television."

"Good, I'm glad you aren't doing anything. Why don't you come on up to my room and look at some football films with me? There's some things I want to show you."

Huff recalled, "Tom had this projector in his apartment and we'd go over the team we'd be playing that week, over and over . . . . tendencies, what to look for, keys. I didn't get to finish watching a lot of interesting television programs that year but I learned more football in that one season in Tom's apartment than I'd learned throughout high school and college."

"It was good to get out of the Polo Grounds," admitted Landry. "Yankee Stadium had a great deal of tradition and it was an exciting place to play, to be. Of course, it seated a lot more people [62,000] too, and we were going to draw the crowds."

"One time in the Polo Grounds," said Nolan, "we played before 8,000 fans." He said he thought he'd never experience anything like that again and didn't, until he got to Dallas.

There was no doubt the Giants had something special going in 1956, especially on defense. The club had a fine new defensive lineman in Jim Katcavage, who soon would join Andy Robustelli, Rosey Grier and Dick Modzelewski in the front four; linebackers Huff, Harland Svare, Bill Svoboda and Cliff Livingston; and a secondary of guys such as Nolan, Tunnell, Jim Patton, Ed Hughes and Lindon Crow. Before the 1950s had ended they would have fans looking at the defense as much, if not more so, than the offense. They would become the heroes, and fans who before had only watched the ball, suddenly would chant throughout Yankee Stadium, "DEEFENSE! DEEFENSE!" and then, "Huff-Huff-Huff-Huff!" until it sounded almost like a locomotive gaining speed.

There had been great defensive players and coaches in the past, but because of the attention Landry and his unit were to receive in the nation's largest city, its largest media market, the defense in all sports would take on new proportions as far as the general public was concerned. The defenders would begin to reach the same stardom, the same status as those on offense.

New York would one day hold an opponent to zero yards passing and the confrontations with the explosive Cleveland Browns and Jimmy Brown would get the nation's attention.

"We really did have an exceptional football team," said Landry. "I think by 1958 and the great championship game with Baltimore that our defense was the catalyst in giving the defensive in professional football recognition as a unit. It was the beginning of the change which has carried through all these years."

But the Giants also had great offensive stars in Conerly, Gifford, Rote, Alex Webster, Roosevelt Brown, Bill Austin and young Don Heinrich, and outstanding kickers in first Ben Agajanian and later Pat Summerall, and a tremendous punter in Don Chandler.

In 1956 changes had come and were coming. The Western Conference Los Angeles Rams dropped from the top to the bottom, and the Baltimore Colts were on the rise when a free agent named Johnny Unitas, cut by Pittsburgh, took over for injured quarterback George Shaw. The always potent Cleveland Browns took a step backward when Otto Graham retired and Paul Brown tried to find an adequate replacement. The times were right for the New York Giants.

"Everybody worked so hard," recalled Howell. "Landry would be in my office one minute, asking for more time in practice for his defense, and Lombardi would walk in the next minute, wanting more time for the offense."

"It hadn't been that way before but it finally got to where the offensive and defensive units were separated, in meetings and otherwise," said Landry. But, of course, one depended on the other.

Conerly had been through some lean years in New York, and then Howell used the theory of starting Heinrich to probe the defense, see what was happening, discuss it with Conerly on the sidelines and then send him in, usually after about a period or less.

"A lot of the fans were on Charlie," recalled Landry. "They'd boo him pretty badly at times. They wanted the young guy in there, you know. But Vince was a strong supporter of Charlie, whom he called 'The Pro.' Everybody called him that."

When Landry took over the Cowboys he would experience the same situation with fans wanting Don Meredith to replace Eddie LeBaron at first, and later, Jerry Rhome or Craig Morton to replace Meredith. It just gave him another experience upon which to draw later.

But this was 1956. Ike was in office, Debbie Reynolds and Eddie Fisher were married, and the Yankees beat the Dodgers in the World Series.

And the New York Giants defense limited famed Chicago Bear fullback Rick Casares, who was to lead the NFL in rushing with 1,126 yards, to a mere 13 yards rushing when the teams played. The teams had tied 17–17 in late season and many felt it was a preview of the NFL title game. It was. With the fine defense and Gifford having an outstanding year offensively, rushing for 819 yards and catching 52 passes for 603, the Giants took the East with a 7–5 mark. The Bears won the West with a 9–2 mark, beating out Detroit by a single game.

On December 30, 1956, they met in Yankee Stadium before 56,000 fans for the NFL championship. Temperatures were near 18 degrees and dropping by midafternoon, ironically reminding some old-timers of the weather in 1934 when the Giants had beaten the Bears, 30–13, in the NFL title game. That day the Giants had played on the hard, frozen field with sneakers instead of cleated shoes and were able to maneuver much better than the Bears. Howell said they also would use sneakers in this one, in order to get better footing. The move paid off again.

Rookie Gene Filipski returned the opening kickoff from George Blanda 54 yards to the Bears' five and the rout was on. The Giants led 34–7 at halftime and won the championship, 47–7.

"The way our defense and offense played was a great tribute to two men," said Howell, "Landry and Lombardi."

Most felt the Giants would repeat in 1957, but something happened beyond their control. Paul Brown drafted the big running back from

Syracuse, Jim Brown. It wasn't that Cleveland could handle the Giants but, with Brown running wild and Tommy O'Connell having a good year at quarterback, Paul Brown's team beat practically everyone else.

The Browns won the first meeting of the two clubs, 6–3, on Lou Groza's two field goals but, obviously by the score, Landry's defense couldn't have played much better. Cleveland also won the second meeting between the two clubs, 34–28, as the defense didn't play so well but Landry still got in a word.

Brown was on his way to leading the league in rushing with 942 yards, a 4.7 average per carry, but before the final game with the Giants, Landry chided Giant running back Mel Triplett.

"Mel," said Landry, "how is it Brown makes more yards in one game than you do the entire season? Is he that much better than you are? Is that what it is?"

Jimmy Brown rushed for 114 yards that day. Mel Triplett rushed for 116.

Cleveland won the Eastern title with a 9–2–1 record, while the Giants finished second at 7–5. Detroit claimed the West and routed the Browns, 59–14, for the NFL title.

Studying and working during the off-season, Landry had earned his industrial engineering degree to go along with the B.A. he had taken at the University, and had moved his family in 1955 to Dallas, where he worked during the off-season in real estate and insurance. On March 14, 1958, a third child, Lisa, was born. This time Tom was there.

"He was working but took off and stayed at home and helped me with the baby and the other kids," said Alicia. "He really worked hard, taking care of the baby. But Tom always has been a good father and the fact that he was there with me just made up for the other two times when he was away and couldn't be with me."

Prior to the 1958 season everybody was talking about Jimmy Brown and just what he might accomplish, of ageless George Halas reinstating himself as coach of the Chicago Bears, of Texan Buddy Parker, abruptly walking out on the Detroit Lions and going to the Pittsburgh Steelers, where he quickly traded for Bobby Layne, and Norm Van Brocklin moving from the Rams to the Eagles.

But nobody had any idea of the great significance the 1958 season would have when it finally ended. There would be a title game that would become legendary, one that would turn the eyes of the nation to professional football and unite the game with television, once and for all. It would become *the* television sport, and the New York Giants and Tom Landry were very much a part of it all.

Most were picking the Giants behind Cleveland and, perhaps, the

Eagles because of the addition of Van Brocklin. The Landrys had moved away from the city to Stamford, Connecticut, where Tom would commute to Yankee Stadium with Ed Hughes, who had taken his place at right cornerback when Landry had retired as a player in 1956, Andy Robustelli, Cliff Livingston, and a lawyer turned sportscaster named Howard Cosell.

"Howard," remarked Landry, "wasn't as caustic in those days. He was doing mostly boxing."

When reminded that Cosell, a strong Lombardi and Don Shula disciple, had been critical of Landry over Monday night football in recent years, often saying his team was overrated, Landry just smiled and said nothing.

"Oh," said Alicia when it was pointed out that Cosell had knocked her husband, "we don't pay much attention to things such as that. When people get very critical or attack Tom we just consider the source."

She also has fond memories of the years in Connecticut. "The times I enjoyed most were when I'd go into the city and meet Tom for lunch," she said. "It was lovely there."

Hughes, now an assistant for Nolan, his brother-in-law, at New Orleans and formerly an assistant for the Cowboys, recalled, "In those days Tom used to have a saying. He had just about everything figured out but, of course, there's always a gray area. So if it came to that gray area Tom would say, 'Well, then you react like a football player.'

"It was funny but years later when I was into coaching I wrote Tom and asked him how to handle a certain situation. I got a thirteen-page reply back from him, explaining all aspects. 'But, of course,' he said, at the end of the letter, 'there's a gray area, not black or white, so in this case you must react like a football player.'"

Cleveland, with the great Jimmy Brown running rampant, got off to a 5-0 start. Brown was averaging 163 yards per game and 6.9 yards per carry and had scored 14 touchdowns. The Giants, losing Gifford temporarily to injury, were 3-2, but got back into the race by beating Cleveland, 21-17.

It was almost like a script had been written because it all came down to the final game with the Giants hanging on by their fingernails. They had to beat the Browns to tie Cleveland for the NFL Eastern Conference title and cause a play-off.

Snow had been falling in New York, making it look somewhat like a Christmas card, on that Sunday in mid-December. The game was a typically fierce battle between the two teams with the Giants trailing 10-3 at halftime but tying the game 10-10 when Gifford twice completed halfback passes. Jimmy Brown had opened the game by bursting through the Giants' defense on a 65-yard touchdown run but thereafter he was almost shut down completely by Huff and the defense. Many believed that Landry had Huff following Brown on each and every play, but this wasn't true. Landry had discovered a tendency used by Paul Brown, who called the Cleveland plays. Most of the time, if Brown lined up in such a way in a certain formation, he very likely would run a certain play. Landry simply had unlocked the Browns' offense by watching films.

All Cleveland needed was a 10–10 tie and it seemed they would get this when Summerall missed a 37-yard field goal with less than five minutes to play. Cleveland wanted to kill the clock but Landry's defense held and the Giants moved to the Browns' 42-yard line with 2:07 remaining. They faced a fourth and ten.

Howell had planned to pass on fourth down, but he suddenly turned to Summerall and told him to go in and try the impossible, a 49-yard field goal in the snow. "You always have hopes," said Landry, "but with the snow and all, Pat couldn't even see the goal post."

When the Giants lined up the yells and screams in Yankee Stadium became little more than muffled murmurs. Conerly cleared a spot in the snow and put down the snap from Ray Wietecha. Summerall, in picture form, moved forward, locked his ankle, kept his head down, and met the ball solidly, sending it soaring toward the goal post. It sliced the uprights and the Giants won, 13–10, forcing a rematch between the teams for the NFL Eastern Conference championship.

When the teams met again the Giants' defense, Landry's 4–3, his keys, his game plan, his analysis of what Cleveland would do, especially what Jimmy Brown would do, and a fine array of players completely dominated the Cleveland offense as Brown was held to eight yards rushing and the Giants won, 10–0.

After the game a stunned Lou Groza remarked, "There's only one man who could have done this to us . . . Tom Landry. Nobody else."

The game ball was handed to Andy Robustelli, who said, "This doesn't belong to me," and gave it to Landry. Jim Lee Howell said, "Tom Landry is the best coach in football."

The Giants had survived a season, won a title, by depending on a great defense and doing the things offensively that they had to do, a field goal here, a big play there. Meanwhile, Baltimore had swept the Western Conference behind Unitas and names such as Ray Berry, Lenny Moore, Jim Parker, Gene (Big Daddy) Lipscomb, and Gino Marchetti. These names were soon to become household words. The stage was set for the historical meeting, a classic match up of the best

87

offense (the Colts had scored 381 points in 12 games) against the best defense (the Giants had allowed but 183 points in 13 games). The Giants already had won a regular season meeting between the two teams, 24–21, but Unitas had missed the game with injured ribs and Johnny U., as fans were calling him, made a lot of difference, all the difference. So the oddsmakers made Baltimore a 3½ point favorite.

Seven days after the Giants had beaten Cleveland for the NFL Eastern title, they met the Colts in Yankee Stadium in a game many have called the greatest ever played. This, of course, is only opinion, but there is no doubt that it was a game replayed by fans many times. Those who participated became a part of pro football nostalgia. The game had the media's undivided attention because of the great success of the Giants in the nation's largest city. It also became a focal point of that particular Sunday's television viewing around the country. People watched the game, became intrigued with it, excited by what was happening, and were hooked on professional football.

Some 64,000 fans watched on a mild, wintry day as the Colts dominated the first half when Unitas led an offense which gained 200 yards and Landry struggled for the answers to stop the onslaught. Baltimore took advantage of Rote's fumble at his own 20 to score one touchdown, but then had driven 88 yards for another score to take a 14–3 halftime lead. Landry talked to the defensive players at halftime and told them what they must do or they'd be blown out of the stadium.

The Colts moved to the Giants' three-yard line as the second half started and Landry walked the sidelines and yelled at the defense to hold, that they must hold. Ameche got a yard to the two but was slammed back and Landry screamed, "That's the way! That's the way!" Unitas made another yard but on third down Ameche was stopped for no gain and the crowd began chanting, "DEEFENSE! DEEFENSE!"

Coach Weeb Ewbank and Unitas discussed the situation, fourth and one at the New York one, and decided to go for it. They felt the Giants had shut off the middle but they might get Ameche wide on a play in which he would first draw back his arm, as if to throw, and then run for the flag. But this time the 4–3 defense and the people who played it performed perfectly. Ameche was hit first by Katcavage, then Modzelewski and Huff came over to finish him off. He'd lost four yards, the crowd was wild with what their heroes had done, and the game had been turned back as the momentum switched.

After Baltimore had been stopped, Conerly launched a long pass from his own 19 to Rote, who gathered it in and took off. However, after covering 62 yards he fumbled. But Alex Webster, racing downfield to block, picked up the ball and raced to the Colt one, from where the

88

Giants scored to get back into the game. In the final period the New York team went ahead, 17–14, when Conerly found Gifford on a 15-yard touchdown pass. The Colts had been silenced, shut out in the third and most of the fourth periods and the game was in the grasp of the Giants, who were trying to run out the clock.

But then came one of those terrible breaks with which Landry was to become so familiar as the coach of the Cowboys. Needing four yards for a first down, which would perhaps give them time to run out the clock, Gifford got the ball and swept wide, cutting back inside. Marchetti hit him and then screamed as Lipscomb came over to finish him off. Gifford seemed to have made the four yards, a little more, but confusion erupted as Marchetti began to scream for people to get off him. His leg had been badly broken and when the bodies had been cleared, official Ronnie Gibbs marked the ball a few inches short of the first down.

Years later Gifford recalled, "I know I made the first down. You know things like that. I asked Gibbs about it later and he said, 'I blew it.' But there was so much confusion with Marchetti getting hurt, I can understand it happening."

However, Chandler got off a beautiful punt that went out of bounds at the Colt 12, the clock was running out, and the Giants' defense had dominated the second half. But then it began to happen and couldn't be stopped. The rest is pro football folklore, faded photos in our minds but pictures which will always be there.

Landry, desperate, had decided to double-team both Ray Berry and Lenny Moore. But when you are magic and have a date with destiny, it makes no difference. Unitas went to work, taking his team downfield against the clock in what would be a classic two-minute offense, one that would forever characterize the excitement that can be the NFL. He would throw to Berry, who would take the ball just as he stepped out of bounds, stopping the clock. He hit Berry, who was doubled, at the Giants' 35 with 43 seconds left and then found him again for 22 yards as the Colt split end made a diving catch, saving the ball just inches off the ground. The Colts were at the Giants' 23 with 25 seconds left. Steve Myhra came in and kicked a field goal to tie the game, 17–17, with nine seconds remaining and, as had been determined if such a thing occurred, professional football went into its first sudden death overtime.

"There was such a big psychological factor involved," said Landry. "We were just inches away from winning a championship and then they kicked that field goal to tie the game. There was a big letdown. All of a sudden, you've let go of what you seemed to have had, what seemed a victory and wasn't. From a psychological standpoint it ruins you. Now, Baltimore had its second chance.

"When Frank missed the first down by inches the momentum had completely changed. Defensively, when something like that happens to change momentum, something happens to you psychologically. You're going to get penetrated, no matter how good you are.

"And, remember, the Colts were the best offensive team in the league."

The Giants won the toss but again on a crucial play Conerly was inches short of a first down and Chandler had to punt. The crowd and some of the players, sensing the Colts had become unstoppable on offense, wanted to try to make the first down but Howell played the percentages and Chandler punted the Colts back to their 20. With the same faces, the same attack, Unitas moved his club 79 yards to the Giants' one, the big play being a 21-yard completion to Berry on third and 15.

For the Colts, there would be no easy field goal. What followed was a play that would remain indelibly etched in the minds of those who saw the game. In the gray darkness of late afternoon, which seemed hardly brightened by the lights being turned on, Ameche took a handoff from Unitas and bore up the middle into the end zone to give the Colts a 23–17 victory in 8:15 of sudden death overtime.

"I'm not sure whether it was the greatest game ever played," said Landry, "but there's no question in my mind that it marked the time, the game and the place where pro football really caught on, where the public attention was aroused and brought the game into the spotlight it enjoys today."

No. Perhaps it wasn't the best game, but it was the one which still holds the most solid place in NFL history because it was a game, a day, which those touched by it always would remember. People watching across the nation would remember the names, the place, where they were, what they ate, what they said and thought—and that is what legends are made of.

Although the same teams would meet again for the 1959 NFL championship, the cast was altered and never would be the same again. Prior to the opening of the season Timothy J. Mara, founder of the Giants, died at 71 years of age. Vince Lombardi took over the head coaching job at Green Bay, a team which had in 1958 lost ten games with players such as Paul Hornung, Jim Ringo and Jimmy Taylor. Allie Sherman took Lombardi's place with the Giants' offense and Em Tunnell retired.

Plans also were being made that would again change the face of professional football. Dallas millionaire Lamar Hunt, becoming extremely disenchanted and frustrated in his dealings with the NFL to bring a

90

franchise, especially the failing Chicago Cardinals, to Dallas, announced he would form another league. Hunt led a group which included Denver's Bob Howsam, Houston's Bud Adams, Los Angeles's Barron Hilton, New York's Harry Wismer, and Max Winter and William Boyer of Minneapolis–St. Paul and formed the American Football League. It would begin competition in 1960 and be headquartered in Dallas.

The NFL had planned expansion in 1961 with Dallas and Minnesota being mentioned as the likely candidates. NFL officials, behind closed doors, noted Hunt's intentions, his power and money, and decided to expand to Dallas in 1970 and Minnesota a year later. But Dallas definitely was the key, a city in which the NFL hoped to fight the AFL and perhaps bury it.

As the season began Texas E. Schramm, former public relations director and general manager of the Los Angeles Rams, who had spent the last three years as assistant director of sports for CBS, was put in touch with another Dallas millionaire, Clint Murchison, Jr., who was very much interested in the expansion team he might bring to his city. George Halas remembered Schramm's work with the Rams, where he was one of the innovators in a scouting system from which all others one day would be modeled. He told Murchison that Schramm would make a fine choice to lead a team in Dallas, if indeed, the city got enough votes at the NFL owners' meeting in January of 1960. He strongly hinted this would likely happen.

Landry's New York defense was better than ever in 1959, allowing opponents just 170 points, which truly is amazing considering that in the second game of the season Norm Van Brocklin led the Eagles to score 49 points in beating the Giants, 49–21, in Philadelphia's Franklin Field. Van Brocklin and his understudy, Sonny Jurgensen, had a field day throwing to former Oklahoma All-American Tommy McDonald.

Nolan, who had the ill luck to be swapped to the Cardinals in a deal for Summerall and Crow in 1958 after spending his first four seasons with the Giants, was brought back to New York in 1959 and remembered that Eagle game. "'Tom was livid," said Nolan. "If you knew him you could look at him and tell, but all he actually said was, 'That'll never happen again.'"

Ed Hughes, who commuted with Landry from Stamford, recalled, "You know, in those days, we were taking turns driving from Connecticut. Well, for the Eagle game we drove a car into New York, left it at Yankee Stadium and caught a subway to the train to take us to Philly.

"We got our butts kicked and, I think, Robustelli and Livingston

91

were with us coming back after the game. With the train ride, the subway ride, then the drive back home we were together maybe three and a half, four hours.

"Tom was really upset about the way the defense played. Lombardi had screamed and yelled and cut guys to pieces. Tom could do the same thing with just a look, making you feel about two inches tall.

"Anyway, he wouldn't talk to any of us all the way back home. We even stopped for coffee and I bet he didn't say two words."

When the teams met two weeks later in Yankee Stadium the Giants won, 24-7. Landry had devised a plan to double-team McDonald in which Crow picked him up short and Patton covered him deep. "We knew we had to stop McDonald to win and that's what we did," said Landry after the game.

Conerly had his best year, to the surprise of most, leading the league in passing but, although the offense had its moments, the main scoring punch was Summerall's kicking. He had come from the Cardinals as a mediocre kicker. He showed improvement in 1958, hitting 12 of 23 field goals, but in 1959 he led the league, connecting on 20 of 29.

"The big difference was Tom Landry," said Summerall. "He was the kicking coach, too, and would watch films of me kicking and pick up any flaws I had. He also studied Wietecha and Conerly, the center and holder, to see if they were doing anything wrong. He put it all together so we all had a really good year kicking."

The Giants twice beat the rival Cleveland Browns to finish with a 10-2 mark, the best in the entire NFL. Cleveland and Philadelphia tied for second. New York beat Cleveland, 10-6, in the first meeting and 48-7 the second time, ending all hopes for Paul Brown's club to catch it in the championship race.

"That Landry," said Nolan, "here we were 40 points ahead of the Browns and he'd be out there yelling, 'Don't let them score! Hold them! Hold them!'"

The Colts won the NFL Western Conference title with a 9-3 mark, a game ahead of the Bears and two in front of the vastly improved Packers under Lombardi. In the title game the Giants' defense dominated the game for three periods as New York held a 9-7 lead. But Conerly was off, losing three interceptions, one of which was returned for a touchdown, and Unitas rallied Baltimore for 24 final period points and a 31-17 victory in a game watched by, among others, Vice-President Richard Nixon, who soon would become the Republican Party's nominee to oppose John Kennedy for President.

A month prior to the NFL title game, in November, Murchison had hired Schramm to head what he hoped would be a pro football team in

Dallas. Schramm attempted to get the standard NFL contract from acting commissioner Austin Gunsel, who had taken office when Bert Bell died watching an Eagle game that October. Gunsel refused, so Schramm duplicated the standard NFL contract and hired Gil Brandt (a former baby-photographer and self-made football talent expert) and Hamp Pool, and sent them out to sign all the free agents they could to the counterfeit contracts. If Dallas didn't get a team, the contracts would be voided.

"I also worked out a deal with the Rams," admitted Schramm, "to use their scouting information on players who weren't drafted. It cost us $5,000." Brandt and Pool signed 28 free agents.

Landry wasn't sure what he'd do. He'd been approached by Bud Adams to coach the Houston Oilers of the AFL. Murchison also had done some checking around the league and Landry's name kept coming up as being one of the truly fine young coaches in football. He was only thirty-five but his reputation as a defensive coach was unmatched. Murchison talked to Schramm about trying to hire Landry. Schramm also expressed interest in Sid Gillman, who had coached the Rams when Tex was in Los Angeles. But in the end, they went for Landry.

"You just kept hearing so many good things about him," recalled Schramm. "When you hire an assistant, you might hit on one of four or five, but he was so highly regarded around the league that I just felt he'd be the one, the right one."

"Even when I was coaching the Giants I don't think I actually thought of myself as a coach," said Landry. "I still leaned a little toward a career in business. Constantly during the off-seasons I was getting ready for what would be a career in business when I finished what I thought would be only a temporary job as an assistant coach.

"I'd worked in Houston until I got my degree and we'd been living in Dallas for years during the off-seasons. I'd heard from Adams about the Houston job and Jim Lee Howell was considering stepping down as coach of the Giants and I might be strongly considered for that job.

"But when Tex approached me about the Dallas job, it just seemed ideal. It was where we were living, we liked the city and the area, and the idea of such a big challenge intrigued me."

After the Giants lost to Baltimore in the title game, Landry was announced as the coach of the proposed expansion team in Dallas, which would be called the Rangers. He was given a 5-year contract, calling for $34,500 annually. Everyone concerned breathed much easier when it became official. At the owners' meeting in Miami Beach on January 28, 1960, Clint Murchison, Jr., Bedford Wynne, and John Murchison were awarded an NFL franchise.

Howell said the Dallas team had hired the best coach in the business but was also quoted as saying, "Tom is a warm person but not so much with his players. Sometimes he gets impatient with them, doesn't pat them on the back. He expects them to go out there and do their jobs. One thing is that he's so much smarter than most of them. Maybe he should be more of a dope like me. He's like Paul Brown, a perfectionist. But he's smarter than anybody."

In an obvious attempt to hurt the AFL and Lamar Hunt's Dallas Texans, the club would begin playing that 1960 season, with its record counting in the Western Conference but having a schedule that included all NFL teams, giving the fans of Dallas a chance to see the league from top to bottom.

And, unlike teams before and after, Dallas didn't have the benefit of the draft because it already had been held. Fortunately, however, Murchison, with a big assist from Halas, was able to sign SMU All-American Don Meredith to a personal services contract. Halas had drafted Meredith, but sympathetic to the Dallas plight and angered by the AFL, asked only a future third-round draft pick from the team that Schramm finally talked Murchison into calling the Cowboys.

Dallas was allowed to stock its franchise by selecting 36 veterans from existing NFL teams. Each team was allowed to freeze 25 names on the roster of 36 and Dallas could pick no more than three from each existing club. The league gave the Cowboys only 24 hours to make those selections. However, Landry, getting an idea of what might happen, hadn't been caught with his eyes closed. Prior to the announcement of the process in which the Cowboys would get players, Landry had made a whistle stop tour of the NFL, looking at films of each team. He'd also made a deal with the Giants in which New York could freeze more players if Landry were able to sign Don Heinrich as a player-coach.

Schramm also was able to trade a future draft choice for Eddie LeBaron, the 5 foot 8 inch Washington Redskin quarterback who once had led the league in passing, but had retired. LeBaron said the only reason he came out of retirement was that he had such respect for Landry and wanted to be a part of what was happening in Dallas.

The days in New York were over for the Landrys. As Alicia had put it, they'd gone there on a kind of lark, and stayed ten years. "It was a period," said Landry, "that I'll never forget. It was a great time of fun and adventure for us."

The Cowboys and Dallas, however, would become a time of his greatest football frustrations and achievement. There would be trying times when a weaker man would have given up. But something happened to Landry during his off-season in Dallas in 1958, something which would change his life and, perhaps, help him cope with the great pitfalls and frustrations that were to follow.

7

Tom Landry was up very early that Wednesday morning in winter. On the surface he seemed to be a man in charge, his life in place, as he dressed and prepared to drive over to the Melrose Hotel, just out of the shadows of downtown Dallas. He showered, shaved, said good-by to Alicia, went to his car and joined the early morning traffic. It wasn't bad yet; it was too early to become crowded with those hurrying to their various job cubicles before the clock struck 9 A.M. Besides, people in Dallas just thought the traffic was bad. They should sample it in New York City!

As he drove, stopping and starting as the traffic lights changed, he wasn't sure he should be going in the first place. Certainly, he felt skeptical about the whole thing. But he had promised to be there, and so he would. But, perhaps, subconsciously, he was looking, hoping for some answers he didn't have, something to help rid him of a deep and well hidden emptiness he felt. Sure, the recent loss to Baltimore in the 1958 NFL championship game was disappointing. He thought the Giants could have, no, should have won, and his defense hadn't been able to stop the Colts at the end. But the season was over and he was back home in Dallas. Besides, there would be other seasons. And already he had played a big part when the Giants won the NFL title in 1956. Winning the NFL championship was the ultimate achievement in pro football for a player or coach or club official. But success was not new to him. His sole goal during his days at Mission High School had been to help the Eagles win the regional title while playing as well as he possibly could. Mission had won the title and he had been named to the All-Regional team. Landry later sought success at the University of Texas and found it. He had been a big part of the Longhorn teams which one year beat Alabama in the Sugar Bowl and another year Georgia in the Orange Bowl. He had achieved at Texas, being named co-captain. And he had been blessed with a fine, beautiful wife, three children—so what was it? What was the emptiness?

95

A friend, Frank Phillips, had asked him to come to the Melrose for a men's breakfast in which the participants probed the Scriptures.

"I think you'll enjoy it, Tom," Phillips had said. "There's a lot of good fellowship."

Landry agreed and his attendance that morning after the 1958 football season would be the beginning of the biggest change in his life.

"I had been in and about the church all my life," Landry recalled. "But, really it was only half-hearted. I considered myself a church-goer and a pretty good guy. Certainly, I thought of myself as a Christian but found out I really wasn't. I was just a church-goer, which is a lot different. If you just go to church, it's like going to the Lion's Club or something like that. Oh, man, there's no comparison.

"Anyway, I wasn't sure Bible discussion was for me, since my scientific approach made it difficult to accept certain parts of the Scriptures."

But nonetheless, he arrived at that first breakfast at 7:30 A.M. and found four tables of eight to ten men each. After eating, the men at each table chose a moderator to begin discussion of the Bible. Landry's analytical mind was properly challenged and so he returned, week after week, to the informal sessions in which those present searched for answers in the Bible. Finally, the mental anguish he suffered at the meetings caused him to ask himself a most critical question: "Isn't life more important than football?"

His football accomplishments stacked up high, yet the dissatisfaction remained. But perhaps what he had sought was tunnel vision. So what was lacking? He wasn't sure, but was now more than willing to search for the unknown factor that would complete the equation to happiness. This forced him to turn his thoughts more seriously to Christ. He had read about him throughout his life but who was he really? Did he really accept Christ? And if he did, then he must accept what Christ said. If he accepted what he said, then the way he was living his life was wrong.

"At that point, I nearly stopped going to those Bible sessions," Landry admitted. "My whole life had been carefully structured throughout the year and I was almost convinced that my future lay in being a coach. This was no time to become confused about my goals in life."

Yet, the challenge was there and he continued regular attendance at the Bible study breakfasts until he was convinced that Jesus Christ was the missing link in his life. "I find it difficult to pick out any one specific turning point for me," said Landry. "I can't pinpoint it by time or place. There was no emotional experience. As we talked about the Galilean during one of those Bible sessions, I found myself drawn to him."

Landry recalled that his earliest urge to accept Christ was drawn from two passages in the Bible, both in the Gospel of Matthew. He quotes them:

"Therefore I say unto you, Take no thought for your life, what ye shall eat, or what ye shall drink; nor yet for your body, what ye shall put on. Is not the life more than meat [food], and the body than raiment [clothing]?" (Matt. 6:25).

"Therefore whosoever heareth these sayings of mine, and doeth them, I will liken him unto a wise man, which built his house upon a rock. And the rain descended, and the floods came, and the winds blew, and beat upon that house; and it fell not: for it was founded upon a rock" (Matt. 7:24, 25).

He read the passages over and over and began to wonder if, indeed, his house was founded on rock. Certainly, he and Alicia and the children went to church, but what did it really mean to them? What kind of foundation was he building for his family? What kind of real foundation?

"For a self-centered person, those can be disconcerting questions," said Landry. "For the first time I began to feel a quickening desire to get to know this Man, Jesus Christ. At the next Bible meeting I asked, 'How can we be sure Jesus is who he says he is?' No one there could answer the question in a way that satisfied me."

So Landry spent a great deal of time analyzing what he had asked, researching the Man, Jesus Christ. Football had taught him to measure things in terms of results. Players are trained to accomplish certain objectives, such as a kicking specialist putting three points on the scoreboard when the ball is in his range, and a passer throwing the ball so a receiver can catch it a great percentage of the time. Landry began thinking about Jesus in terms of what he did and the results of his life. In doing this, he discovered Christ's compelling impact on the lives of countless millions of people down through the years.

"At some period during the spring of 1959, all my so-called intellectual questions no longer seemed important, and I had a joyous feeling inside," said Landry. "Internally, the decision had been made. Now, while the process had been slow and gradual, once made, the decision has been the most important one of my life. It was a commitment of my life to Jesus Christ and a willingness to do what he wanted me to do as best I could by seeking his will through prayer and reading his Word."

This in no way meant that he would have to give up football or stop trying to be the best at his profession. "I simply believed that Christ wanted me to bring him into my daily life, including football.

"I also began trying more and more to think a little less about football systems and a little more about the people involved, although the adjustment took time. I really had a lot of maturing to do as a Christian."

Because it is his nature, Landry continued to strive for perfection, but as the years passed with the Dallas Cowboys his somewhat dictatorial approach began to lessen. He became more capable of understanding the different, more individually oriented players and also those who, unlike Landry, would give less than 100 percent. And his faith certainly was a factor in helping him try to understand and cope with the much-troubled Duane Thomas and to give a fairer assessment of free spirits like Thomas (Hollywood) Henderson, or even to a degree, Tony Dorsett.

"I've become more tolerant," he said in recent years. "I give everybody a full opportunity to make a change."

Landry does not force his faith upon his players but he tells them how he feels and they know it is always there, within him. "I don't want them to feel pressured or obligated to be a part of it," he explained. "I don't want to come across as a pious type person.

"We have four, five players who are very strong Christians. Roger Staubach's a Christian, for instance, and he's our quarterback. But a lot of people think we have a Christian atmosphere on our team. That just isn't correct. The atmosphere we try to create is one in which we hope to develop good character, although everyone is not a Christian.

"I would hope our influence is such that whether we are out in public or on the field, we conduct ourselves so as to show Christian traits. If we have someone who has no values at all, then I won't tolerate this. When a guy has good character he's at least pointed in the right direction."

However, on some occasions Landry has been known to more directly share his faith with his players and at times reassure them with words from the Scriptures during low points and pressure times. He has told them, "God does not give us fear, but power and love and self-control. The thing that eats you up is fear and anxiety. Once you commit your life to Christ, it's in God's hands. He has a direction he wants to take you which isn't based on winning and losing. The more you dwell on your own power, the more anxious you become."

"I don't think anybody resents it when he tells us something from the Bible or about his faith," said Charlie Waters. "He doesn't try to force it on us. I appreciate hearing what has guided a man as wise as he is."

Danny Reeves, first a player and currently the offensive coordinator for the Cowboys, believes Landry gets his religious message across to the team without having to actually put it into words very often. "He shows you by example what a Christian life is all about," said Reeves. "That's more impressive than any words a person might say."

The Cowboys have a team prayer session before each game and an early morning nondenominational service before road games, but attendance is optional. Players are also encouraged to attend a service of their own faith but, of course, this is optional as well.

Over the years I have seen and actually been present when a coach would say a pregame prayer and ask God to give his team the strength to win. Once I got into a terrible argument with a well-known coach when I told him how I felt. "God," I said, "really doesn't care who wins a football game." Once Landry was asked about the subject and he said, "God doesn't interfere in games. We have great Christian friends all around the league. What God does is give you the courage to excel—the confidence to perform to the best of your ability. So many players don't do that, don't use the talent they have."

Landry does not think a man must be a Christian to become a great athlete, although he does feel it helps. "I put some emphasis on a religious commitment in relation to everything," he said. "I feel a man who is not committed to Christ is handicapped in almost anything he does. A person who is committed to Christ has more freedom and is, therefore, able to develop himself to the fullest. A Christian shouldn't have the fears and the anxieties to hold him back. I find that our Christian players seem to get more out of their jobs. I believe they enjoy them more and reach higher levels than they would if they were not committed.

"I'm not saying that you will become a great athlete by receiving Christ, but I do believe that if you have the natural ability, your commitment to him will enable you to achieve a greater degree of excellence. The most unfortunate thing in my life was that I did not discover Christ until I was coaching. I didn't have the pleasure and enjoyment of knowing him while I was a player. If you have a positive attitude, good things will happen. Why has positive thinking become a multi-million-dollar industry? They're just teaching what God gives us in the Bible.

"When I first started coaching I thought mostly of physical ability: quickness, agility, control, strength and explosiveness. Then, as we developed into a stronger team, character became more important. The character and competitiveness of a player became more the controlling factors. I just believe that when you reach a championship level what separates you is basically the character in your team. If your team has enough character they'll usually pull themselves out in tough situations.

"I think that's why Roger Staubach and Drew Pearson pulled out the Minnesota play-off game in 1975 with that long pass in the last seconds. It wasn't so much the play, it was the quality of the players involved and their attitude in this situation. The player without character usually finds excuses for why he shouldn't produce with everything he has. A player with character looks for the best in every situation. There's always hope for him even though the clock is running out. He's looking for a play to win the game. That's the difference and it has won a lot of big games for us.

"Roger Staubach, for example, has been that type player for us—and he was that way when he played for the Naval Academy."

On the surface, the only place so many look, there seems to be a conflict between the passive image of Christianity and the violence associated with professional football. One appears the antithesis of the other . . . on the surface.

"This is a misconception more than anything else," Landry once explained. "Religion is anything but passive. Every man must have his right relationship with God, and if he has certain talents, he must demonstrate them. Whatever field a man is in, God expects him to be at his best. Some of the greatest competitors I've seen in pro football are Christians. If there is any conflict from a religious point of view, it would be playing on Sunday. The occupation mandates this, so most Christian athletes feel all right about it."

One of the more admirable traits of Tom Landry, at least from the perspective of those who have been around him a great deal, is his ability to bounce back so quickly from painful setbacks and disappointments. He will feel the hurt but he's able to put it in perspective more quickly than other head coaches and, perhaps, this is why he has lasted so long in a profession that literally has made nervous wrecks out of so many fine coaches. The profession has taken tolls on such men as Allie Sherman, Don Coryell when he was at St. Louis, Tommy Prothro, and Woody Hayes. It has caused John Madden to prematurely retire with bleeding ulcers, and has had adverse mental and physical effects on the majority involved in it. But Landry does not drink, take pills to relax or to perk him up, nor does he have ulcers or trouble sleeping.

"As a Christian I know my life is in God's hands. He has a plan for me. Therefore I never worry about tomorrow and try to keep the winning and losing of football games in this perspective. The knowledge that my life is in his hands helps me keep my composure or regain it in tough situations."

Alicia Landry shares her husband's faith. One of the first things they did when they moved from Houston to make their home in Dallas during the off-season of 1956 was to become active members of Highland Park Methodist Church, housed in a large, impressive building on the southwest corner of the Southern Methodist University campus. It was

100

Alicia's childhood church, where she was baptized, and also has one of the largest memberships of any Methodist church in the country.

Landry organized a Bible study group several years ago at the church and also served as a member of the church's official board. But his religious activities are far from being confined to the church. In 1972 he served as general chairman for the Billy Graham Greater Southwestern Crusade, which ran for ten days in Texas Stadium, home of the Cowboys. He has also spoken at a number of crusades conducted by Graham, who is a personal friend.

Much of Landry's free time is devoted to the Fellowship of Christian Athletes. He's been a guiding force since the FCA's inception and it has always been one of his main interests outside of football. Basically, the organization is aimed at confronting coaches and athletes and, through them, the youth of America with the challenge and adventure of following Jesus Christ and fellowship in the church.

"It's the greatest organization for young people that I know of," Landry has said. "There's no question that it will have an effect on the life of a boy or girl. When one has Christian principles to live by, he's less likely to end up on drugs and in other types of trouble."

Considering his busy schedule, Landry's commitment to the FCA is astronomical, particularly in the off-season months of April and May. It's not unusual for him to travel across the country, speaking three or four nights a week to high school and college groups.

Bill Krisher, a 1957 All-American guard at the University of Oklahoma who now heads the National FCA from its Dallas headquarters, says he is much in awe of Landry. "He humbles you into making you want to do more," Krisher explained. "I've known him since 1958 and he's been giving himself for all that time. It's exciting to hear him give his witness. Let me tell you, Tom Landry walks the walk, meaning he backs up what he says with his life. He lives it. And he does such an eloquent job in doing so. He's such a tremendous father, churchman, speaker and gentleman."

Krisher, of course, is in a position to know, having watched Landry give his time and money unselfishly to the FCA for more than twenty-one years. "He's been chairman of the FCA's National Board of Trustees, he's currently back on the board and has been president of the Dallas FCA Chapter since 1968," said Krisher. "Tom and Grant Teaff [Baylor University head football coach] probably give more time than any of the other active coaches in the country. Coach Landry ranks among the top in all aspects of the FCA. Even during his busy season we have an FCA executive meeting in his office once a month."

Invitations for Landry to speak or attend various meetings and activities are far too numerous for any one man to handle, so he's forced to say no when he would like to say yes to many of them.

He also loves to play golf, has a ten-handicap or less and has scored a hole-in-one, but rarely gets a chance to enjoy the game due to his limited time. Each spring he does participate in several charitable fund-raising golf events, one of which bears his name for the benefit of the FCA. For the past two years more than 200 golfers have annually contributed $100 to the FCA for an opportunity to compete to have their name inscribed on the Tom Landry Trophy at the Dallas Athletic Club.

Whenever Landry speaks he commands attention and often lets loose with jokes, although he is no threat to Bob Hope. However, because Landry tells them, they become funnier due to the source. There is one particular story he likes to tell, using it on various people who might be in attendance. For instance, at a roast for Kyle Rote, Jr., in Dallas Landry said:

"I have this dream where I die and go to heaven. Sure enough, it's a beautiful place. When I arrive, St. Peter gives me a grand tour. He takes me to a gigantic room jammed with clocks. I ask him to explain why such a huge and magnificent place has nothing but clocks in it. 'Well, Tom,' St. Peter says, 'this is the room where we keep check on the daily sins of those people still on earth who have yet to join us here. We judge each person by the number of revolutions that person's clock makes. When there's only a small amount of sinning, the clock's hands move only slightly. The more one sins, the greater the revolutions of his clock.

"'Take that one over there,' St. Peter said, pointing to the clock of Danny Reeves. 'You notice the hands stand at three o'clock, which means Danny has been pretty good lately. Now, look over there at Gene Stallings's piece. Not bad, either, at five o'clock.'

"Then I noticed an empty space where a clock had been, and asked St. Peter why it was missing. St. Peter smiled at me and said, 'Tom, that one belongs to Kyle Rote, Jr. It's been broken down for some time now and the last time I checked with the people in the repair shop they were using it for a fan.'"

Landry's beliefs as a Christian aren't, obviously, reserved for Sundays and religious holidays. He begins each day with a prayer. During these times, he explained, he has asked many things such as, "Lord, I need your help today when we make our squad cuts, so please let me be fair," or "Please give me the right words to say to the coaches at our meeting," or "Help me to forget football today when I'm with Alicia and the children."

Landry's day ends similarly, when he privately takes inventory of himself with prayer. "Was my criticism of the quarterback handled right? Did I get across to the squad my moral convictions without preaching? Was I too stern with my daughter over her last report card?" Yet, the main evaluation he concerns himself with at the close of each day, he has said, is whether he brought the Lord into the situations he faced or whether he barged ahead on his own.

Few men, regardless of profession, can come to grips with themselves on such a daily basis. It can only come, Landry believes, through a strong faith in Jesus Christ. And he feels the church is not challenging the young people of America today to truly discover him.

"This is one of my greatest concerns," Landry has explained. "That's because I deal with young people all the time. And I tell you this, they want Christianity to help them solve their problems, but we're failing to show it to them."

Landry, especially through the FCA, has been able to get the message of the Lord to the younger generation. He greatly admires others who are trying to do the same things, people like weight lifting champion Paul Anderson. "You've got to show the kids, and that's what Paul Anderson does," said Landry. "He does it when he stands up in front of young people, takes a twenty-penny nail and drives it into two one-by-sixes with his bare hand, then brings up eight or so kids, puts them on a table, gets under it and lifts the table off the stage and then comes back to the microphone and tells them, 'It takes courage to be a Christian; it's no sissy game.'"

It also takes courage for a man in Landry's position to publicly declare that his greatest goal isn't winning a Super Bowl, but is in serving God as he feels he should. He can declare something like this while working and functioning so well in a game in which the great majority of people believe winning is everything, the only thing.

"I'm a Christian, that's where I live," he said. "It's a difficult thing to explain but it's what I am, where I am."

Landry had been in the church all his life, but after that 1958 season, at thirty-three, he became a true Christian. There would be shaky times, frustrating times, and times so disappointing that they would scar many others, but his faith would sustain him, and it is doubtful that without his faith he would have survived all the trying times with the Dallas Cowboys, especially the formative years which were much worse than he could have imagined.

FINALLY, TOM LANDRY thought, it was all there. The Dallas Cowboys were ready to break loose from their magnetic line of mediocrity and become a winner, once and for all. He had seen his predicted "Five Year Plan" to make the Cowboys a winner go down the drain in the fifth year, 1964, when the team had won five, lost eight and tied one. But in 1965 he had some good athletes, his defense was playing well and the Cowboys had won their first two games by impressive scores over New York and Washington. Then Dallas had gone into a tailspin, losing four in a row by ten points or less, including a very tough loss, 13–3 to Lombardi's Packers when the Cowboys had allowed the Packers only a minus ten yards net.

Don Meredith, the man upon whom the franchise had based its future, in 1964 and 1965 had suffered through more injuries than most sustained during a career. But he had courageously hung in there when others would not have attempted to play. In 1965 he had gone into a terrible slump and during the four straight losses Landry had benched him and gone with Craig Morton and Jerry Rhome, the much-heralded rookie quarterbacks. Sometimes Landry had used one of the rookies, sometimes the other and sometimes both, shuttling them on each down while he had called plays, a practice he had used with Eddie LeBaron and Meredith in the first years of the team.

But that year, 1965, Meredith had looked good in practice as the Cowboys prepared to travel to Pittsburgh to play the struggling Steelers and Landry felt certain his team would turn the season around. So Landry had said Meredith would again start against the Steelers, although most of the area's media didn't understand why he did so. Morton and Rhome figured to have good futures but Meredith had the most experience, had the best instinct, and the signs were there that his slump had ended.

Actually, Dallas was better than the Steelers, who had been shocked as the season opened when Coach Buddy Parker resigned. Landry knew the Steelers inside out and had laid his best plans for victory. Even with backfires, he felt Dallas would win and move toward its first successful season. If he knew anything at that time about football, he knew this would happen. But that Sunday afternoon the Steelers had won, 22–13, sending Dallas down to its fifth straight defeat in a game, appropriately perhaps, played in Pitt Stadium, adjacent to a graveyard which could be clearly seen from the press box. Meredith had been miserable, hitting just 12 of 34 passes for 187 yards. He had tried, Landry had tried, but it just hadn't worked and as Landry got up to talk to the team after the game his words seemed to come very slowly, his voice almost shaking. He said that was the first time he truly had been ashamed and that, perhaps, the fault did lie in his system, his approach. Then he coughed softly and tears came into his eyes. This man who they said had a stone face, the man with no emotion, was crying.

"It was so unexpected we didn't know what to think," said flanker Pete Gent. "It just wasn't something, well, you'd associate with him."

"I felt a little ashamed and then disappointed because I just didn't expect him to do something like that," said center Dave Manders.

Meredith said he felt awful, that he'd never tried so hard and done so badly. Landry didn't say anything else; he walked into the coach's locker room and closed the door. When he came out again, he hinted to the press that, certainly, he had to seriously consider going with Morton or Rhome. Those present agreed it was the only thing he could do. After that game in Pittsburgh, Meredith's Nielsen rating in the Dallas area would have been zero.

On Wednesday, December 3, 1965, Tom Landry's weekly press conference was filled with speculation as to exactly what he'd do: Would he go with Morton? Would he go with Rhome? Or would he shuttle Morton and Rhome on each play? Everyone had his opinion with, perhaps, Morton being the consensus favorite.

Landry had done a great deal of soul-searching before the press conference, weighing each player's performance. He had prayed that God would help him make the correct decision.

"Our offensive team is very young," he told the press, his voice strong, his looks again unruffled. "We have three rookies starting, Leon Donohue [a guard] is a veteran but has been with us only two months. The only veterans with experience on our offensive team are Jim Boeke, Don Perkins and Frank Clarke. We need a quarterback to lift us to our potential and that's why I have made the decision . . . Don Meredith will start the next seven games this season."

You could have heard a pin drop and Landry continued, "After five straight losses a decision of this nature is difficult, but I had to go with the man I felt everyone on the team had the most confidence in; the man I felt could make the team rise up and play well enough to make up the seven to ten points we've been losing by all season."

Radio men ran to the phones, reporters hurried downtown to tell of the decision and write their stories. Most everybody disagreed—but Landry was the man, he made the decision.

Recently reflecting on various decisions he's had to make over the years with the Cowboys, Landry said, "The Meredith decision I made that year was the most difficult I've ever had to make. Everything seemed to be going against Meredith. The press and the fans were down on him, and he was getting booed something awful. But I felt strongly he was the right choice. It was more difficult than when I was faced with the Morton, Staubach decisions. The team, the town was divided over Morton and Staubach and they both were doing well. But that time in 1965 Meredith wasn't doing so well."

Later Landry reflected, "A lot of people had just forgotten what Don had done for us in 1964. It's hard for me to forget. He quarterbacked for us when no other man could have stood on the field with the injuries he had. When he was healthy for one short span in 1964, he won three straight games for us. I'm not foolish enough to put a quarterback out there, from personal sentiment or otherwise, if I don't think he can win. I have no doubt Don can win."

It was the correct decision, one which launched the Cowboys into a winning era, a far cry from the beginning in 1960 when each day for Landry seemed more trying than the day before and players no one else wanted appeared and disappeared as if they were going through a swinging door.

The early 1960s were a time of the Freedom Riders, when an actor named Paul Newman emerged as one of the all-time box office favorites with his role in *The Hustler,* when Ernest Hemingway, a physical and mental shadow of what he had been, would kill himself with a shotgun, when a group from England called the Beatles would drive adults up the wall and send the young feminine generation into screaming, yelling frenzies. It was a time in Dallas, Texas, when water fountains in the downtown area were clearly marked "white" and "colored" and when John F. Kennedy's New Frontier would come to an end that awful day with an assassin's bullets.

Most of the original Dallas Cowboys who showed up at that first training camp in Forest Grove, Oregon, in July of 1960 were, frankly, the dregs of the league. Dallas did not draft and was able to fill its team only from a player pool made up of men whom other teams felt were expendable and free agents Gil Brandt and his helpers had found after searching under every rug from the Canadian to the Mexican borders. The team was made up mostly of nonentities, the malcontents, the injury prone, clubhouse lawyers and only a handful of good athletes such as Frank Clarke, Jerry Tubbs, Eddie LeBaron, Don Perkins and, of course, Don (Call Me Dandy) Meredith.

If it had been possible to design and then construct a working model of an NFL quarterback whose temperament and attitude were radically different than Landry's, one who was at the beginning absurdly ill-fitted for what Tom hoped to accomplish, off the drawing board would have popped a walking, talking Don Meredith.

Landry's first Cowboy lineups were written on Magic-Slates, but it was the irrepressible Dandy who left the lasting impression. More than anyone, he typified the splendor and more often the sorrow of the early Dallas teams. But even before the dramatic decision of 1965, Meredith was a man Landry stuck by, though at times he would get burned.

The pair were the Odd Couple. Whereas Landry was studious and pensive, Meredith was finger-snapping flip; while Tom looked at the game as an intensely serious business, Meredith came into pro football with the notion that the game was just another chance to go out and have a little fun. Landry had developed his skills through exhaustive repetition, painstaking analysis and an almost mystifying devotion to the game. Dandy had come by his skills naturally. It was as if one day they were just dumped into his lap and he accepted them with an easy grace. "Why do they call you Dandy?" he would be asked and would reply, "Because I am."

Yet Meredith came with strings attached. At times his talents would desert him as if yanked by some unseen hand or force which pulled the strings. For years he suffered from inadequate blocking and an inconsistency that Landry felt could be overcome with devotion and hard work. To Dandy, football was still a game. And in his early years he was known to have come into the huddle singing a few lines from some honky-tonk song.

Meredith had come to the Cowboys after a great deal of personal success at SMU. Twice he made All-American and established an NCAA passing accuracy record of 61 percent. But the best the Ponys ever did when he was there was post a 6-4 record in 1958.

Landry, with the help of Don Heinrich and, especially, Eddie LeBaron, nursed Meredith through some frustrating early times. Sometimes they would be almost at wits' end with each other, but the bond was there. In later years Landry, certainly, began to understand Meredith better, knowing that under the flippant exterior, Meredith hurt and felt as much as anyone, probably more. Flippancy was just his way of hiding his emotions.

Years later, Meredith was to say, "I've come to love the man, Tom Landry." And two summers ago when Meredith, a most successful television personality, visited training camp, Landry hurried acorss the field and greeted him warmly. It appeared for a second or so that they actually might embrace.

"Tom was closer to Don than he was to anybody else on the team in those early years," recalled defensive end Larry Stephens. "At least they seemed to be close most of the time. Don always seemed to have some idea how Landry felt about the team, what was happening. Tom never said much to the rest of us."

Many just didn't know what to think of Landry. He was thirty-five when he began coaching the Cowboys, not much, if any, older than some of the veteran players who had come in the expansion pool. He was detached, all business to most of them, and seldom even exchanged pleasantries.

"I felt if Tom had been more personable with his players in those early days he might have gotten more out of them," recalled Tom Franckhauser, a defensive back who now is a successful stockbroker. "A lot of us didn't particularly like his stand-offish attitude."

L. G. Dupree, who had played for Baltimore in the 1958 championship game against the Giants, also came in the expansion pool to Dallas during the twilight of his career, but said, "I could understand what Tom was doing. He was concentrating so hard on trying to build a winner that he had to be shifting people around all the time, constantly trying to find the players who could fill the gaps."

It just seemed to many that Landry was aloof, as though he were smarter than everybody else. "Well," said Jerry Tubbs, one of the few truly outstanding defensive players in the early days and now a Cowboy assistant coach, "the fact is that Tom *was* smarter than everybody else."

"Some of the other guys," said LeBaron, who first became a successful lawyer and now is general manager of the Atlanta Falcons, "didn't see eye-to-eye with Tom. They had been around the league and were pretty set in their ways. But I never bought the idea that he was cold and detached. To me he's always just been intense, yet where I've been concerned he's been a warm person. In practice situations or games he doesn't have a great sense of humor. It's serious business for him. But off the field, even in the early days, I saw the warm side of him."

During that first training camp the Cowboys set a room aside in the coachs' and club officials' dorm for social gathering, called the 5:30 Club. It was something the Giants had done when Landry was in New York and seemed like a good idea to carry on with the Cowboys. The room is furnished with easy chairs and couches and cold drinks and beer in the refrigerator. Coaches, writers, club officials and visitors usually gather in the 5:30 Club after practice to talk informally about the day's events.

The Cowboy organization knew it had little chance of winning, but was locked in a battle for the sports dollar with Hunt's Dallas Texans. It was hoped Landry could, at least, field an exciting team. Landry knew

108

immediately that, outside of Tubbs who was to become a Pro Bowl player, he had few defenders to stop the opposition. He would try to outscore his opponents . . . or at least score points and keep up the interest of the fans.

So Landry devised the multiple offensive concept with its phone book of plays, its motion, false direction and continual shifting. The Cowboys didn't just run the two basic formations of football, they ran practically all formations. What Landry did, in effect, was try to destroy the 4–3 defense he had nurtured while with the Giants.

"I felt the best way to attack the 4–3 we'd established in New York was the multiple offense," he said. "I knew that defense so well that I had a good idea of the best way to beat it. Remember the 4–3 was based on formation recognition with man-for-man basic pass coverage. To be effective, the defense had to have a jump by recognizing first the formation, then knowing what plays could be run from it. I felt if we used multiple sets, shifting from one to the other, we could confuse the defensive players. They had worked all week on perfecting certain keys and if we could destroy those keys we might be able to move the ball and have a chance even to win."

Today the multiple offense has evolved into a situation in which the Cowboys will run The Flip formation (wide receivers on the same side), Double and Triple Wings; the basic alignments such as Red (fullback and halfback setting up behind the tackles with the fullback to the strong or tight end side), Green (the halfback going to the strongside), Brown (fullback lines up behind quarterback and center with halfback on weakside), Blue (fullback behind quarterback with halfback on strongside), the I (fullback and halfback, in order, lined up in straight line behind quarterback), and the Spread (used in obvious passing situations and in two-minute offense). Dallas also lines up in a certain formation and shifts into another. There are some forty basic plays in the Cowboy offense but from the different sets the club has numerous variations.

LeBaron, who at first called his own plays and then became part of a quarterback shuttle in which he would alternate on each down with Meredith while Landry told each the next play he wanted run, recalled, "Tom and I often talked about the theory of what we were trying to accomplish. The shifting and moving was necessary because we just didn't have the personnel to blow anybody out. We had to do things differently so we basically relied on deception. I was never concerned about who called the plays really. What happens is that your thinking becomes so similar that it really doesn't matter. I understood pretty well what Tom was trying to do. He wasn't a yeller or a hard-sell guy but I don't think he ever lacked confidence. I mean you had the feeling he knew what he was doing. He had a terrific way of selling a game plan. You knew it would work because Tom said it would work. It was that simple. It was just that . . . well, our talent was so inferior. We didn't have much of a chance but we took what we had and went for it."

LeBaron, of course, was an NFL class quarterback. Tubbs was a fine linebacker who had planned an early retirement after a great deal of frustration in San Francisco. But Landry talked him into playing and he enjoyed many fine seasons as the club's first middle linebacker. And then there was Frank Clarke, who came from Cleveland in the expansion draft and was going nowhere until he reached Dallas. Before he was through, Clarke would become one of the NFL's premier receivers, twice ranking third in the NFL in receiving, once catching 65 passes in a single season and scoring 14 touchdowns.

"People would question what Tom did at first but, soon, they would learn he was right," recalled Clarke. "I was just fortunate to end up in Dallas." Originally, Clarke had been a high draft choice of Cleveland in 1957, but quickly found himself on Paul Brown's bad side. Frank recalled during one particular game he missed a block, taking a bad angle, and when he came off the field Brown told him he couldn't play for the Browns, that he couldn't play in the NFL.

"During 1963 with the Cowboys we were driving for a touchdown and Meredith threw a pass high for me in the end zone," said Clarke. "Sure, the pass was high, and I jumped but just didn't go after it with much intensity. When I went to the sidelines all Coach Landry said was, 'Frank, do you think you could have made a better effort on that pass?' I remembered how Paul Brown had treated me and then how Coach Landry treated me and I was determined I would make a better effort, for my own sake and for that of Coach Landry."

Dallas played its first game in history against San Francisco in preseason, losing 16–10. Overall, Dallas was 1–5 that first preseason, beating only Landry's old team, the Giants, 14–3, as Clarke caught a 73–yard TD pass from Meredith.

Meredith also had another game-stopper. Mostly operating in a state of confusion, Dandy had gone back to his natural instincts for the touchdown to Clarke. However, earlier in the day he was faced with the menacing figure of Sam Huff, looking him right in the eye as he set up to bark signals. Meredith would start his count and Huff would adjust the defense. Meredith then would remember an audible to call. Huff moved accordingly and seemed to know exactly where the play was going.

Meredith's signal calling went something like this, with appropriate stares into Huff's eyes. "Four-three Set! . . . uh, Red Right . . . uh, 22 . . . . Ah, * * * *! Time out!" Huff, the entire New York defense, plus the Cowboy offense broke into laughter. Landry only managed a smile.

But when the regular season opened, as expected, Dallas generally could put up points but couldn't stop any opponents as it lost ten straight games before going into Yankee Stadium to play the Giants on December 5 with 55,033 fans in attendance. The fans remembered what Landry had done in New York and gave him a tremendous ovation as he came on the field with his team.

Dallas was a two-touchdown underdog but LeBaron, the Little General, hit three touchdown passes and the game was tied 24–24. New York scored again and it looked like another day at the office for Dallas. Then Joe Morrison lost a fumble at the Giants' 40 with 2:27 to play. LeBaron guided Dallas to the New York 11, from which he found Billy Howton with a TD pass, tying the game 31–31. This marked the first game Dallas did not lose.

Jim Lee Howell, in his final year of coaching the Giants, was amazed at the performance of Landry's band of misfits. He had called Landry the best defensive coach in football when he was with the Giants, but after the tie he went a step further and said, "Tom Landry is the best coach in all of football."

Dallas, finally, was able to draft in 1961 and picked Bob Lilly, the giant defensive lineman from TCU. Lilly was to flounder at defensive end until 1963 when Landry would move him to tackle.

"Lilly," said Nolan, "just wasn't a very good defensive end. He didn't have the long range speed. He'd have ended up being just a mediocre defensive end, but Tom saw some traits in him that seemed to lend themselves to making a tackle. So Tom moved him to tackle, I guess, in 1963. And he was great, maybe the greatest to play the game at that position."

"It was just becoming pretty obvious as I watched him that Lilly had all the attributes of a tackle," said Landry. "He was so very quick, had strength and short range speed to make it at tackle. He was just tremendous. In Lilly, we had a guy around whom to start building our defense."

It also was during that 1961 season that Tom Landry would get his first victory as a head coach. This came in the league opener against the Pittsburgh Steelers before some 50,000 empty seats (23,500 fans) in the Cotton Bowl. Landry had said he planned to use both Meredith and LeBaron as starting quarterbacks, depending on his feeling the particular week and the circumstances. Meredith had started and did all right until throwing an interception to Johnny Sample, who ran it back 39 yards for a touchdown to give Pittsburgh a 24–17 lead. Landry then put in LeBaron for Meredith, who retired quietly to the bench, joked with those around him and then sat down by himself and cried.

LeBaron took the club 75 yards to tie the score, 24–24, and in the waning seconds Jerry Tubbs intercepted a Bobby Layne pass at the Dallas 38 with only seconds left. Meredith, although he didn't know it at the time, would have seen the irony in what happened next. LeBaron dispensed with the regular offense, turned to Billy Howton and told him, "Just take off deep. Everybody else block." LeBaron found Howton on a 40-yard completion, the Cowboy receiver stepping out of bounds at the Steeler 22 with one second left. Rookie Allen Green, who had missed two earlier field goals and had a punt blocked, then kicked a 27-yard field goal to give Dallas a 27-24 victory.

"I think," recalled Landry, "we all stood there stunned for a while, not believing. And then it was great, just great."

Dallas went on to win three other games, including a 28–0 victory over Minnesota when Landry began to employ his quarterback shuttle in which he could call the plays but give Meredith needed experience.

The Cowboys finished 4-9-1 and then 5-8-1 in 1962 under Landry's quarterback shuttle system. It was then Meredith casually pointed out that Landry had a mind like an IBM, which probably was the beginning of the metaphor generally used in referring to the Cowboy coach.

The year of 1962 was very trying. In the second regular season game Pittsburgh beat Dallas, 30–28, on a play that nobody would ever forget. It sent Landry onto the field to argue to no avail with officials. In the third period, LeBaron faded into his end zone to pass, with the line of scrimmage the Dallas one. He caught a glimpse of Clarke flying down the sidelines and threw the ball as far as he could. Frank caught the ball and apparently scored on a 99-yard play.

But back in the end zone there was a flag. Official Emil Heintz said Cowboy guard Andy Cvercko was holding in the end zone and cited long forgotten Rule 9, Section 5, Article 2. It stated that a safety would be awarded if an offensive team was guilty of a penalty in its own end zone. The TD was taken away from Dallas and Pittsburgh was awarded a safety, which turned out to be the winning margin. The rule was removed from the books the next year.

However, there were other trying periods, such as the life and times of one Sam Baker, occupation: place kicker-punter, man-about town. If, at times, Meredith was a minor annoyance, Baker wrote the book! He was one of the league's better kickers but just wasn't overly serious about rules and did like his beverage now and then. He once showed up for a Cowboy game in Pittsburgh carrying a potted orange plant and wearing a silly grin.

Another time the team flew to an exhibition game and then returned to training camp. But Baker was AWOL. Arriving on a commercial flight at 3:30 A.M. he phoned training camp, asking for Gil Brandt.

"I imagine the Man wants to talk to you, Sam," said Brandt.

"Now?" asked Baker, slurring his words. "Right this minute?"

When he arrived in camp he marched to Landry's door and knocked, as though he were trying to break down the door. When Landry finally woke up and opened the door, Baker swung to attention, clicking his heels and giving a *Sieg heil.*

"Sam Baker reporting for duty, sir," he said.

"Good," said Landry, blinking. "That'll cost you $1,000." He closed the door and went back to sleep.

Baker lasted two seasons and went to Philadelphia where he continued to be one of the league's better kickers.

"You can't imagine how frustrating those early years were," said Nolan. "Boy, we had some ragnots. We'd be working so hard, rooting so hard for something to work and it wouldn't. Sure, we had some real characters around then but, generally, we just took what we could get until we could bring in enough top players through the draft."

Nolan had played on the 1961 New York Giants team which lost to Lombardi's Green Bay Packers, 37–0, for the NFL title. He was having a lot of trouble with his shoulder and so figured he'd retire when Landry phoned him.

"He asked me if I'd like to coach in Dallas," said Nolan. "By February 15 [1962] I was in Dallas. He turned the defense over to me. I knew the system, what he was trying to do, because that was what he installed with the Giants. At one time I was the only defensive coach he had. Now they have three.

"My weight had gone up to about 195, maybe 20 pounds over my playing weight, but I had come to Dallas to coach, right? So before a game I'm out there on Saturday at practice. I'm just throwing the ball around and Tom walked over to me and said, 'Dick, how would you like to play again?' I said I didn't know, hadn't even thought about it but I didn't think I could. Tom said, 'Good, I've activated you and you're playing tomorrow.' So we kept playing catch and I threw the ball and dislocated my shoulder again. Tom rushed me to the team doctor to put it back in place so I could play. They wrapped it and I played . . . what? About all the games that season. My shoulder was knocked out four more times."

Nolan was the first and probably the last Cowboy assistant who, at times, sassed Landry. "I remember once after we'd lost a game to the Washington Redskins," said Nolan. "Tom called me up one night and

113

said that there had been an article in the Washington *Post* about us having a fight on the sidelines, that we were on the outs with each other.

" 'What are you talking about?' I asked Tom.

" 'Well,' said Landry, 'the Washington *Post* said you and I were arguing on the sidelines.'

" 'I don't know what they're talking about.'

" 'Well, Dick, I thought I'd call and let you know what the paper said.'

"So, the next week we played the Cardinals and Tom told me, 'We'll have to be careful what we do on the sidelines.' I told him, sure, okay. Anyway, Cornell Green got beat on a 30-yard pass and here comes Tom storming down the sidelines and he gets right in my ear and says, 'Did you see that? Did you see that?'

" 'Yeah, I saw it. I saw it. What the heck do you want me to do? I can't do anything about it now.' "

Landry kept on questioning him about the play and Nolan, remembering what Landry had cautioned him about, just kept walking on down the sidelines, trying to get away. "I'm looking up the field toward the open tunnel side of the Cotton Bowl, you know, where the playing is coming back. He keeps talking and I just keep staring at the tunnel. So, anyway, Tom had Alicia watching him on the sidelines and she told him that people had interpreted what was happening as a fight between us on the sidelines."

After the game Landry came over to Nolan at a party and said, "Dick, I'm sorry about what happened on the sidelines."

"What happened?" asked Nolan.

"Well," said Landry, "you know, I'm sorry about arguing with you out there."

"Heck, nothing to be sorry about. You've been doing the same thing ever since I met you in New York."

Nolan sat behind his head coach's desk in the New Orleans Saints' offices and continually chuckled about the beginning years with the Cowboys. But he also would get serious when he remembered some of the frustrations.

"Boy, those days were tough," he continued. "Very trying on everybody, especially Tom. I remember one time on a charter flight back to Dallas, I was near Tom and he motioned for me to come over and sit by him. He said he was really feeling down and didn't want to talk to anybody. So whenever somebody would come by I'd motion for them to go on, to leave him alone."

The Cowboys were 5–8–1 in 1962, but lost the rival Texans, moved by Lamar Hunt to Kansas City. It is said Murchison and Hunt flipped a coin, with the loser leaving town, but this never was verified.

Prior to the 1963 season coaches around the league had taken note of the progress of the Cowboys. Paul Brown chided local writers by telling them they didn't appreciate what a fine team Landry was building. Tex Maule flatly predicted the Cowboys would win the NFL Eastern title in a *Sports Illustrated* cover story before the season.

At times the Cowboys would almost put it together and then fall apart at inopportune moments, when unfortunate things would happen. Amos Marsh, another one of the club's phenoms, was big and had great speed but he also would often drop the ball on such things as pitchouts. Once during a game Marsh circled under a high, spiraling punt. The ball came down and hit him right on top of the head. However, Dallas did retain possession and Marsh wasn't seriously injured on the play. "That was nothing unusual," remarked a team cynic. "That was just Amos's way of doing things." But there were highlights and it was obvious Lilly was taking to his new position at tackle.

The team finished 4–10–0 in 1963, with one less victory than the previous year, and some element of fans began howling for Landry's job. Clint Murchison, Jr., responded by awarding Landry a ten-year contract, the longest in sports at that time, which would begin when Landry's contract expired in 1965.

"I had concluded in my mind that Tom was a damned smart coach and had all the ingredients to make a winner of the Cowboys," recalled Schramm. "I talked to Clint about this and we felt we should make a commitment that this was the direction we were going and let everybody, the players or fans or whomever, know how we felt. No, I felt no pressure from outside that Landry wasn't doing a good job but I suppose in some parts of the city that was the feeling. There always are people like that."

From the first Landry had felt he was fortunate in dealing with Murchison and Schramm. In his original contract it was agreed that he would be solely in control of the actual team he put on the field. And, when many would have been fired due to public opinion at the lack of instant success, Landry was rewarded. Looking back on the early years and some of the frustrations that were to follow Landry explained:

"I've been very fortunate in Dallas in that I've had an owner like Clint Murchison and a president like Tex Schramm. The whole organization stems from the outlook of Clint. He's always been one who will put somebody in charge and, basically, leave him alone. He did that with Tex when he first hired him.

"Consequently, when Tex hired me he gave me what I wanted from the beginning . . . complete control of the football end, anything relating to the players other than actually signing them. That includes drafting, trading, releasing players. We discuss these things but the final decision always has been mine. He's done the same thing for Gil Brandt in the scouting department. It's just been an excellent working arrangement for us over the years.

"And both Clint and Tex have stayed with me so I could contribute over the long haul. They're not susceptible to being influenced by fan reaction or by the pressures of winning or losing. When you have people like that you're able to go through situations where other coaches might have been fired by owners."

"We were getting a lot of criticism," said LeBaron, who retired and turned the reins over to Meredith after 1963. "If it had happened somewhere else, they might have fired the coach and later regretted it. We'd had some lean years, and there would be others, but Tom kept the faith in his system, went down the road with it and the club kept faith in him. Tom had his mind set on things he wanted and, as time went by, the players improved and the system became more believable to them."

After Dallas had gone into a tailspin again in 1964, Murchison noted, "I was having lunch with this friend of mine and he noted the team had been losing and said, 'Well, one good thing, Landry's only got nine years left on his contract.'"

By 1964 the defense had begun to come together. Lilly continued to develop and the club had added Lee Roy Jordan and Chuck Howley at linebacker, George Andrie at end and Mel Renfro in the secondary. By that time Landry also had installed a new twist in the standard 4–3 defense, calling it the 4–3 Flex. The defense, still employed to this day only with more variations, got its name because one or more defensive linemen are a few feet off the line of scrimmage, flexed, so to speak.

Basically, Landry had refined the original 4–3 defense he installed with the Giants to combat the "run to daylight" offensive theory of his friend and rival, Vince Lombardi, at Green Bay. Lombardi's reasoning was to have a blocker hit a man and let the defender react to the block, moving one way or another against the pressure. A running back then would go to the hole created as the defender reacted to the pressure of the block. The specific hole varied, depending on the easiest direction the blocker would take the defender. Certainly, this made it easier to block because the offensive player would just take a defender the direction he was trying to go. The back then would adjust to the available hole.

Landry sought a system in which the defender *would not* react to pressure. Thus, in theory, Cowboy defenders will not react to false keys or pressure, and no holes will be created. Each has a gap responsibility and will simply go to that gap, no matter what appears to be happening.

A defender for Dallas, such as a defensive lineman, will first hold his gap, wait, and then react. The natural instinct of an athlete is to react immediately to what he sees and so it takes two or three years to teach a player to wait and then react.

Dallas was back to five victories in 1964, obviously getting closer, and then came the mid-season trauma of 1965 when Landry, once and for all, backed Meredith as his No. 1 quarterback. The Cowboys won five of their final seven games, finishing 7-7, and, as runners-up to Cleveland in the NFL Eastern Conference, were invited to the Play-off Bowl to play the Baltimore Colts, second place finishers in the NFL Western Conference. Lombardi's Green Bay Packers and the Colts had tied with 10-3-1 records during the regular season but the Packers won a play-off game, 13-10, and then beat Cleveland, 23-12, for the title.

Most felt the Colts would have won the title but they lost first Johnny Unitas and then backup quarterback Gary Cuozzo to injuries. At the end of the season the Colts had to play halfback Tom Matte at quarterback. Matte, who hadn't played quarterback since his college days, wrote his assignments on tape, wrapped around his wrists. Dallas, reaching .500 for the first time, appeared ready. Some 2,000 Dallas fans, caught up in the excitement, made the trip to Miami for the game. But Matte looked very polished, offensive tackle Jim Parker got the best of Lilly, and the Colts humiliated the Cowboys, 35-3.

It was after the game that Landry philosophically uttered his immortal words when asked which players had faltered for the Cowboys. "It was," said Landry, "a team effort."

But Landry knew the Cowboys were growing up. They would show just how grown up the next season.

IT HAD FINALLY happened and all of Dallas was caught up in the excitement of the time, the event, more so than the city in its entirety had been for any sporting event since Doak Walker's days as the Great American Hero at SMU. In the vernacular, the city of Dallas was on a "natural high" because the Cowboys had in 1966 gone through a storybook season in which they did to opponents what opponents had done to them for so many years. They won the National Football League Eastern Conference title and would play the legendary Green Bay Packers, Western Conference champions and defending NFL champions, for the league's championship in the Cotton Bowl on January 1, 1967.

The game was a match for the period. The youthful, exciting Cowboys were the team which could explode from any place on the field, the team which had gone against the grain and one which counted among its stars so many players who had been overlooked and forgotten by other clubs. And they were going against the time-tested Packers: the team of Starr, Nitschke, Taylor and Adderley, a club which did things simply, played in the trenches, and personified the NFL establishment. Most fans around the nation, as the oddsmakers, strongly felt the Packers would win, but in their hearts they were pulling for the exciting, brash underdogs, the Dallas Cowboys.

The late '60s were a staggering, eventful time. Neil Armstrong would become the first man to walk on the moon. President Lyndon Baines Johnson, a Texan who strongly pulled for the Cowboys, would continue to persevere and have a great deal of success pushing civil rights issues at home but, as those before and after him, would find Viet Nam an unsolvable puzzle. There would be movement and movements. The city proper of Dallas, as other metropolitan areas, would sit still as the populace continued a migration to the suburbs, eventually making area towns such as Plano, which once seemed so far away, almost a part of Dallas. The young would begin to speak out against the war in Viet Nam and anything else they opposed. They would burn property, lock themselves in the offices of presidents of universities, say this was wrong, that was wrong and some would drop out, let their hair grow long, be called hippies and make their surrogate capital the Haight-Ashbury section of San Francisco. What they did revolted us, made us mad. But it got our attention.

The war between the NFL and AFL reached a financial peak as teams spent a combined total of $700,000 to sign 1966 draft choices, each trying to outbid the other. So after Tex Schramm and Lamar Hunt had been negotiating in secret for months, a merger was announced on June 8, 1966. Champions of the two leagues would meet in what Hunt named a "Super Bowl" game.

This added some extra excitement to the season, and for so many fans around the country, the Cowboys had become a great escape, from themselves, from what was happening. By that season of 1966 in Dallas, Texas, watching the Cowboys had become the thing to do. It always had been said that Dallas only loves a winner and as fans flocked to and filled up the Cotton Bowl this proved to be true.

Tom Landry's great patience had paid off! As late as 1964 some of the veteran Cowboys were saying his system was too complicated, that it just wouldn't work. Critics said his 4–3 Flex Defense in which players were in a holding pattern before reacting just wouldn't cut it because it went against human nature. But the Cowboy defense led the NFL in fewest yards given up rushing. When Landry installed the multiple offense, now standard procedure among so many NFL teams, detractors suggested it would self-destruct and dissolve in its complexities. But the Cowboy offense led the NFL in scoring with 445 points and ran up single game totals of 52, 47, 56 and 52 points.

Jokes were still being made about the system, only by this time Landry could laugh, too.

Don Smith, the New York publicity director who had known Landry when he was with the Giants, came to Dallas to advance a game and remarked, "I took a page from Landry's playbook to a Chinese laundry. They gave me three shirts and a lace pillowcase."

Cowboy flanker Pete Gent, who one day would find success as an author but served in those days as somewhat of a team cynic, a rebel with long hair, watched a rookie poring over Landry's playbook in training camp. "Don't bother reading it, kid," said Pete. "Everybody gets killed at the end."

But Ernie Stautner, the all-time NFL great who had joined Landry's staff for the 1966 season, said, "I almost fainted when I saw Tom's playbook. It was all there, things that had taken me sixteen years to figure out for myself in the NFL. I mean things that just weren't taught in most places, such as keys. All the keys for the defensive linemen are down in black and white. There's no guesswork to it. Maybe I'm dumb but I didn't realize anyone taught keys to defensive linemen." Few did then. Everybody does now.

But Landry had been patient and the players had learned his playbooks and Dallas had won. That same patience had paid off for so many players. Cornell Green, a basketball player signed as a free agent, had complained after a few days' practice that his hip was sore. It was discovered he had been wearing his hip pads backwards. He struggled, trying to adapt to football, but all along Landry had felt he might develop. By 1966 Green was rated as one of the two or three best cornerbacks in the NFL. Landry had watched and waited for Mike Gaechter, a gifted, moody athlete who was known mostly for track and had little college football experience, to come around, and the same goes for Gent, who had been an All-Big Ten basketball player but had not played football in college. Landry had also seen football potential in Bobby Hayes, the World's Fastest Man. The list goes on and on.

"You take a guy like Cornell," said Gil Brandt, Cowboy vice-president who has headed the scouting department since the team's inception. "So many would have given up on him, but Tom just saw something he liked—and he waited. It paid off. The man just has a great ability to see something in a player that maybe somebody else wouldn't see. And he's patient enough to watch that trait develop and let the guy become a good football player."

Cowboy owner Clint Murchison, Jr., once agreed by saying, "Tom has the great ability to recognize potential in a player. We have kept players who would not have been around on other contending teams. Tom can see something worth keeping in a mass of humanity. Tactics dwindle in importance to that. What a coach can contribute to a team, in my opinion, is 10 percent inspiration, 10 percent motivation, 20 to 30 percent tactics, and 50 to 60 percent player recognition."

This never was more evident than on the 1966 team, although a great deal of credit must go to Brandt and the scouting system for finding overlooked and unwanted players in the first place. But no less than eight free agents started for the 1966 Eastern Conference champions, including Green, Gaechter, linebacker Dave Edwards and cornerback Warren Livingston on defense, and Gent, Danny Reeves, center Dave Manders and tight end Pettis Norman on offense. The draft also had brought in Hayes, Bob Lilly, Mel Renfro, Ralph Neely, and Lee Roy Jordan to go with already established stars like Chuck Howley, Don Perkins and Don Meredith. Meredith was 29, Lilly 28, Jordan 26, Hayes 24, Green 27, Renfro 25, and Neely 23. It was the youngest team ever to play for an NFL title.

In 1965 the defense had established itself and so prior to the following season Landry had concentrated on his offense. Possibly the best move he made was sticking by Meredith in 1965 in spite of public opinion and that of many of his peers. But it had paid off as Meredith enjoyed a fine season in 1966, winning both the Bert Bell and Maxwell Club awards as the NFL's MVP.

"The confidence came from Tom," Meredith said. "He worked with me closer than he ever had time to do. We'd meet during the week, when we were on the field. He told me I was great and you know [he grinned] Tom's never wrong. He drilled details into me. He had everything all spelled out. He said I could complete 51 percent, which would be outstanding. I hit 51.5." But Meredith also threw for 2,805 yards and 24 touchdowns, a club record for a 14-game regular season.

"Championship quarterbacks," said Landry, "are the ones who can make the big play and turn a game in your favor. I'm convinced Don can do that." And at a banquet in Philadelphia when Meredith was to receive the Maxwell Award, Landry told the audience, "You people in Philadelphia compare all quarterbacks to Norm Van Brocklin. Sure, Dutch had great leadership but, remember, he had ten years in the pros before he won a championship here in 1960. Don's getting that kind of command. He will have it." But, ironically, Don Meredith would not complete his ten years in the pros, although in 1966 there seemed to be no doubt that he would.

Landry had put more emphasis that season on winning in preseason, which he ordinarily uses as a time to test new players, for veterans to work on techniques and certain other areas.

"The basic problem you face is developing a losing pattern," said Landry, recalling that his team did not reach .500 until 1965. "The most difficult thing in coaching is to overcome the feeling that you're going to lose. You can do it only by bringing in new blood. We brought them in in 1965, people like Hayes, Neely, Morton, Pugh, and Reeves, and we became more solid, began turning things around, including the feeling that we would lose. This culminated in 1966."

Dallas won all preseason games and, after beating Green Bay, 21–3, Lombardi met Landry at midfield in the Cotton Bowl and said, "Tom, you have a damned good football team."

"Thank you," said Landry. "I hope you're right."

Landry had tried one of his great experiments in preseason, which both worked and failed. A great failing of the 1965 team had been that it couldn't run wide, causing the opposition to gang up on Don Perkins trying to work the middle. So Landry decided to move Mel Renfro, a Pro Bowl free safety and fine kick returner, to halfback. Renfro, who had played offense at Oregon, always had wanted a shot at either halfback or wide receiver, so he got it. His tremendous speed and acceleration gave Dallas a new dimension. He averaged some seven yards per carry in preseason but suffered a hip-pointer. When the regular season began, Mel had eight carries for 6.5 per try and caught four passes for 65 yards but badly sprained his ankle.

Landry replaced the injured Renfro with one of the free agents, a little-known quarterback from South Carolina named Danny Reeves. Danny was not fast, didn't seem all that quick, but continually did the things necessary to win. He went on that season to rush for 757 yards, catch 41 passes for 557 yards, and score 16 touchdowns. He also proved a tremendous asset with his ability to throw the halfback pass, as Frank Gifford had done, except Reeves was a better passer than Gifford or Paul Hornung. He turned out to be, perhaps, the best passer from the halfback position in modern-day football.

When Renfro returned, Landry moved him back to defense, explaining to Mel that he was afraid he would continue to suffer injuries as an offensive halfback and that he needed him on the field.

Dallas averaged 45.7 points in winning its first four games, but then faltered when it faced contenders St. Louis and Cleveland, tying the Cardinals 10–10 and losing to the Browns, 30–21.

"The St. Louis and Cleveland games were the low points of our season," said Landry. "We had been going so well that people were wondering if we could be beaten, and we just weren't mentally ready to meet the strongest teams."

Dallas beat Pittsburgh and then lost to the Eagles (a team they had beaten earlier in the year, 56–7) by the score of 24–23 as Timmy Brown returned kickoffs 93 and 90 yards for touchdowns and Aaron Martin ran a punt back 67 yards for a TD. The Cowboys seemed at the end to be moving for the winning touchdown but Reeves had the ball stolen out of his hands. The next week, Danny found in his locker a football with handles on it, courtesy of equipment manager Jack Eskridge.

Writers covering the team asked Landry if they could come to his office to see films of the kick returns by the Eagles, but he refused. When told this, Alicia remarked, "Oh, just come over to the house any night. Tommy has the projector running every night anyway."

But Landry continued to feel more at ease around the writers. Early that year the Cowboys had flown in prop-propelled DC-7s. When an overload of fuel had delayed their arrival in Atlanta, causing a workout prior to the game to be canceled, Landry had suggested a switch to Electra jets. This enabled him to hold Saturday workouts in Dallas and still get to road games in plenty of time for the players to rest. However, after switching to the jets, the Cowboys tied one and lost two road games. Asked before the next road game in Washington if he planned any changes, Landry deadpanned, "Well, we might go back to DC-7s."

Dallas was trailing Washington, 31–30, with 1:10 left to play and the ball at the Dallas 3-yard line with no time-outs left. What happened made it a game which Landry considers one of the club's most memorable comebacks. Meredith, using a roll-out series in which he could move outside, step out of bounds to stop the clock, or throw, was superb in taking the club in six plays to the Redskins' 13, from which Danny Villanueva kicked a winning 20-yard field goal with 25 seconds left.

"That just doesn't happen," said Landry. "You just don't pull out a game like that with no time-outs left. It was a great performance by Meredith."

The showdown for the Eastern Conference title came on Thanksgiving Day in the Cotton Bowl with 80,259 watching—the largest crowd ever to see a sporting event in Dallas.

"As long as I've been in the NFL, dating back to my days with the Giants, the Cleveland Browns have personified the best in the league," said Landry. "Cleveland always has been the team to beat to win the title.

"Before this season [1966] we just weren't good enough to cause clubs preparing to play us to go all out. The result of this is that we don't have that many big games or big game experiences from which to draw. Cleveland has. It's tough to crack that nut but, once you've done it, you're a better team. So we've got to prove we can do it."

But, with the press not around, he told his players, "I have all the confidence in the world you'll win this game."

The Cowboys overcame a 14–13 halftime deficit to win, 26–14, as Meredith and Perkins led a fourth period touchdown push which put the contest away.

"Meredith's execution on that last touchdown drive was his finest all year," said Landry. "It was the biggest game in our history because whichever team won would take the Eastern title."

Dallas beat St. Louis 31–17 but Meredith suffered a concussion and second-year men Craig Morton and Jerry Rhome quarterbacked the final two games as the club finished with a 10–3–1 record and the Eastern title and, of course, that meeting on January 1, 1967, with the heralded Green Bay Packers . . . .

Prior to that final day of 1966 fog had plagued the city, but it lifted the morning of the game and the day was sunny and brisk. Landry had dissected films of the Packers and reached the somewhat astonishing conclusion that Dallas could move the ball against Green Bay, which no one had done effectively all season. "We can," he told his players, "move the ball against the Packers. I'm confident of this, if you'll just execute. We can move the ball."

For the second time in his career Landry was involved in what people were calling the "Game of the Decade." It did not begin this way because the Packers moved the opening kickoff 76 yards for a touchdown and then scored again as Mel Renfro fumbled the ensuing kickoff and Jim Grabowski picked up the ball and raced into the end zone. Green Bay led 14–0 and the Cowboy offense had not touched the ball.

"Even then," said Meredith, "we were convinced [by Landry] that we could move the ball on them." Meredith brought the Cowboys back for two touchdowns to tie the game, 14–14, before the first period had ended.

Green Bay scored twice more on Starr's passes and Villanueva countered with two field goals. But in the final period Starr found Max Mc-

Gee with a 19-yard scoring pass and the Packers seemed out of reach, 34–20, with just 5:20 left to play. Certainly, the all-important extra point by Don Chandler would put the game out of reach and place the Packers more than two touchdowns ahead. I was walking the sidelines near the Packer bench at that time and Lombardi was screaming, "Watch it! Watch it! Don't let them block it!" But Lilly rushed through and got a hand on the ball. The man who missed the block came off the field and walked clear around the Packer bench, trying to avoid Lombardi, who would not have taken his head off, but only made him believe he would.

Dallas needed two touchdowns to send the game into overtime, but had to get one quick score to have a chance. Landry and Meredith, who called his own plays but got a great deal of advice on the sidelines, had the right play at the right time. Frank Clarke, the club's premier receiver during the formative years, was then used as a replacement for Pettis Norman at tight end on obvious passing downs. Clarke still had good speed and could get past a strongside linebacker and, more times than not, just outrun a strong safety. Hayes had done little, a pattern that was to repeat itself in the next championship game. He had caught a single pass for a single yard but, with his speed, he still was the man Meredith could use to get the Cowboys back into the game. Lombardi and his defense had duly noted this.

So when Dallas faced third and 20 at its own 32, cornerback Bob Jeter and safety Willie Wood both drifted with Hayes as he ran a route to the right sideline, opening up the middle. Suddenly, Clarke, who had delayed slightly, shot up the middle full speed ahead and was past strong safety Tom Brown before he knew what was happening. Meredith laid the ball into his arms and Clarke raced in for a touchdown to pull Dallas within seven with 4:08 remaining.

"That was Landry," Lombardi said later. "We had it all figured, everything covered, and he springs that on us."

The crowd could sense that the momentum had changed. Edwards blitzed and threw Starr for an eight-yard loss. Willie Townes batted down a pass and Lee Roy Jordan roped Jim Taylor for a loss of seven yards on a sweep. Chandler, under a big rush, flubbed the punt off the side of his foot and the ball traveled just 16 yards, going out of bounds at the Packer 47 with 2:11 left.

Meredith went to his hot receiver, Clarke. He found him for 21 yards and two plays later Frank again had sprinted by Brown and was running under a ball that was a certain touchdown. Before the ball settled into his arms, Brown grabbed his jersey and jerked him out of the way. Interference was called and the ball was placed at the Packer two, but it should have been a score.

There then began a series of unusual happenings which would almost become a trademark when Dallas played in title games. It was as if some invisible hand would show them water and then make it a mirage.

Reeves made a yard on first down to the one but something else was happening, unnoticed to those who should have seen. All year Hayes had been taken out on goal line situations and replaced by Clarke because Frank was bigger and a much better blocker. With Clarke replacing Hayes at split end, Norman, a fine blocker, would remain in the game at tight end. But with Dallas on the brink of keeping itself in the biggest game in the club's history, Hayes was still in the game. Clarke had run off the field after the interference call and Hayes had stayed in. Meredith should have noticed, sending him to the bench. Hayes knew full well he wasn't supposed to be in the game and should have taken himself out. And Landry should have noticed and sent Clarke back in.

On second down, tackle Jim Boeke jumped offside, costing Dallas a five-yard penalty back to the seven. Boeke, a good tackle, always would be remembered for the time when he jumped offside. But Meredith threw a swing pass at Reeves, who had enough daylight in front of him to score. However, on a previous play Reeves had gotten a finger in his eye and had blurred vision. He couldn't follow the flight of the short pass and dropped it. Reeves should have mentioned the problem when it happened.

Facing third and six at the six, Meredith let up on a pass to Norman near the goal line. Pettis had to come back and dive to catch the ball at the two. "If there is one thing, one slogan, Landry pounds into us, it's never give the defense more credit than it deserves," said Meredith. "The pass to Pettis was designed on the premise that the outside linebacker [Dave Robinson] would not react quickly enough to cover Pettis. I guess I just couldn't believe that. Surely, I was thinking, Robinson will be on him.

"So I hesitated before I threw the ball. That's why it was low. If I'd just had the confidence I should have in what Tom told us, I'd have thrown the ball chest high and Pettis would have waltzed in for the score."

Meredith called a roll-out on the final play, a good call. He could throw if the defensive backs came up on the play, or perhaps run the ball over if they dropped back. Meredith took the snap and faked inside to Perkins. Ordinarily, Robinson would have taken the fake, delaying his reaction to Meredith moving outside. But Robinson slanted out with Meredith and then shot inside to get him. Had Clarke been in the game, he could have, perhaps, blocked Robinson and delayed him for a needed second. But Hayes was in the game and could only brush the much bigger man. Robinson was all over Meredith before he had time to do anything. As Robinson grabbed his left arm, Meredith did the only thing he could, just throw the ball up for grabs in the end zone. Brown grabbed it. The game was over.

"We had the momentum," said Landry. "We would have beaten the Packers in overtime."

But Green Bay had won. Lombardi's team had beaten Landry's, and it left a hollow feeling inside after fighting for all those years to gain respectability, to field a winning team, and then have it all fall short by less than 24 inches.

The Packers went on to smash Kansas City, 35–10, in the first Super Bowl in Los Angeles. But it was the young, exciting Dallas Cowboys about whom everybody was talking. "We were the heroes of the country," said Schramm. "We had gone up against a poised old machine called the Packers and almost won. We were still riding on that crest the next season."

Tom Landry won more honors that year than he would win again. He was named "Coach of the Year" by the Associated Press, United Press International, and his peers in *The Sporting News,* and "Pro Coach of the Year" by the Texas Sportswriters Association. He was very proud of his team and of Meredith, who after all those years finally believed, with a lapse every now and then, in his system. But before the next season began, Landry was heard to remark, "The only caution I have about Don becoming one of the very best is that he's had a lot of injuries. They've plagued him every year and so he's always faced with the prospect of it happening again."

Later, what Landry said could be construed as a kind of subconscious foreboding.

During training camp the summer of 1967 Dallas seemed more than able to take up where it had left off and there definitely were signs that the club would be improved with the addition of Lance Rentzel, who came from Minnesota for a third round draft pick. Rentzel had tremendous ability, but never had made it with Viking coach Norm Van Brocklin. It was also noted by the club that he had once been picked up in Minnesota for indecent exposure, although charges were dropped. But Landry knew everybody made mistakes and Lance's problems were in the past.

Landry had been disappointed at the production of the flanker and Rentzel quickly took over for Gent at that position. Dial, who never had achieved the success he'd had at Pittsburgh, retired after suffering from back trouble. Gent, who became bitter with Landry and Cowboy officials, later voiced his opinions in a novel, *North Dallas Forty,* an account of the dehumanization of an athlete. He recently recalled his impressions during a visit I made to his home in Wimberley, not far from Austin:

"I was mostly a survivor. When I first joined the club in 1964 everybody just kept saying I was a basketball player and I was very determined to prove I could make it in football. It became obvious from the first that Coach Landry was very religious. When he first met the team he said something like, 'Gentlemen, I've given my life to Christ and I find answers to my problems in the Bible.' He didn't come on that strong but it was like he just wanted us to know where he stood.

"But, heck, that first year I went to church with Tom and his son, who was visiting camp. I did it a couple of times, figuring, quite honestly, that it wouldn't hurt my chances.

"The Dial thing bothered me. He'd come in as a big star and was making all that money, but I was doing a better job. One time Tom started him and told me, 'You have better moves, better hands and run better routes, but Buddy has proven he can make the big play. It's just a feeling I have that Buddy will make the big play for us.'"

Gent finally won the starting job, which he held until Rentzel came in 1967. But during the time he backed up at flanker, he became more than ever the club's somewhat caustic humorist, to the delight of the writers covering the team and to the chagrin of Landry.

Once Hayes had been injured during a road game and on the return flight, Landry decided he'd move Gent from flanker to the other side, split end, where he'd start against Philadelphia, instead of the injured Hayes. Landry walked to the back of the plane, the players' section, and found Gent.

"Pete," said Landry, "you'll be moving to the other side this week. So get ready."

"You mean, coach," said Pete, "that I'm going to play for Philadelphia?"

Landry, as he will in some moments, simply took a deep breath and walked away. It was as difficult for him to understand Gent, who had become the first of the Cowboys to grow his hair long, as it was for Gent to truly understand him. Landry probably thought only briefly about the situation and then continued to reflect and think about most all his players only in regard to their effect on his football team.

Ironically, years after Gent's book had come out he was assigned to do a story on Landry for *Sport* magazine. "Most people would have felt that he wouldn't talk to me, and I'm sure a lot of the club's officials wouldn't have," said Pete. "But I knew, in the final analysis, Landry would be fair. I felt he'd talk to me because it was the fair thing to do. And he did."

Some of the other players had noticed Landry was loosening up toward them, often not only showing more courtesy toward them but also, at times, listening to what they had to say about football. In the early years he seemed to be a closed book.

"One day during the early years I went to see Tom in his office," said Chuck Howley. "He was by the window, looking out. I must have waited for five minutes before he was aware that I was there. You used to pass him in the hall at the Cowboy offices and he'd walk right by without speaking. I don't think he ever saw you.

"But in the later 1960s he started speaking to you when he passed you in the hall."

"Tom," said Dick Nolan, "always was so preoccupied, thinking, planning. As far as personal relationships with the players, I think he just felt if he got too close, if he dealt with them on a personal basis, he might lose some objectivity. He wanted in no way for a personal relationship to get in the way of making the decisions which would be best for the Dallas Cowboys. I'm sure he felt something for a lot of the players and had to watch himself at times. But nobody can argue about what he has accomplished and that he was fair. Tom is probably one of the fairest people anywhere."

Landry did not particularly take to nonsense in regard to football and, unlike most of us, didn't particularly find it funny when Meredith, who threw an interception to Cornell Green in a controlled scrimmage, took off his helmet and started chasing Green as though he were going to bean him with it. Landry was quoted at the time as saying, "Gentlemen, nothing funny ever happens on the football field." But as I recall he added, "If we can help it." And then he smiled.

The coaches had this scoring system where the defense got points for stopping the offense, intercepting passes, recovering fumbles. At halftime, the first team defense must have been leading about 40–0 and the offense really wasn't getting any work done. So Tom came down from the press box where he'd been watching.

"Okay, Dick," said Landry. "Now play just a straight 4–3 and give the offense a chance to get in some work against it."

"Yessir," said Nolan, who then put in the second team to play the straight 4–3 against the offense.

"Hey, Dick," yelled Landry, "do what I said. Put the first team back in there and let the offense run against them in the standard 4–3. We need the work, to move the ball."

"Tom, you can run on the second team all you want," said Nolan, "but nobody is going to use my first-team defense as a bunch of dummies. When they go on the field, they're in there to win."

Landry shrugged, went back to the press box, perhaps remembering a time when he was coaching the New York Giants' defense and the great pride he had. Landry is regimented, controlled, but he can remember when he wants to remember.

Meredith cracked two ribs in the second preseason game in 1967 and Craig Morton, in his fourth year, came in and pulled a victory out against San Francisco. Morton looked great the remainder of preseason and it became obvious to everyone that he had beaten out Jerry Rhome for the No. 2 quarterback spot. Meredith detractors, hiding in the shadows since Dandy's fine season of 1966, said Craig should replace Meredith.

"Meredith is the quarterback," said Landry. "I'm not taking anything away from Morton, who has done a fine job." It was to be that kind of year for Meredith, who suffered a twisted knee, a broken nose, and had an awful time with pneumonia. He made it through the first four regular season games, three wins and a loss, but barely survived, as did Dallas, the fifth game in Washington.

With 1:10 left to play Dallas set up at its own 29-yard line, trailing 14–10. Meredith hadn't felt well but played the entire game. On that final series he was really hit and suffered a mild concussion, although nobody knew it at the time. He seemed to be a little wobbly, the way he was walking, but everyone just figured that was his loose way of doing things. He moved the Cowboys to the Redskins' 36 and on a pass play weakside linebacker Chris Hanburger, an all-pro, made a fatal mistake. He forgot to pick up Danny Reeves coming out of the backfield. So Reeves just turned and took off for the goal line, all alone and yelling back at Meredith. Meredith, in the haze, reacted and threw what looked like a dying quail toward Reeves. Danny waited, caught the ball and took off for the winning touchdown.

Later, with Meredith standing within hearing distance, Landry was asked why he didn't notice his quarterback was woozy and take him out of the game. Looking at Meredith, Landry quipped, "Well, I can't tell the difference."

When the club returned to Dallas, Meredith went into the hospital with pneumonia and lost twenty pounds within a week. He would miss three games, but Morton would step in and perform well. Craig also showed a flair for final-minute dramatics when Pittsburgh had Dallas, 21–14, with 1:12 remaining and the Cowboys at their own 23-yard line. Rentzel faked a sideline pattern, as cornerback Brady Keys bit, and then raced downfield. Morton threw the ball a mile and Rentzel ran under it and took off. But safety Paul Martha hit him at about the 15 and he fumbled, the ball bouncing crazily to his right. Reeves, the alternate receiver, had run downfield to block and tried to pick up the ball. He bobbled it, dribbled it and nudged it toward the goal line, where he finally gave up and fell on it at the Steeler five. Morton threw the winning touchdown pass to Norman from there.

We of the press were somewhat mystified at the intricacies of this particular play in Landry's multiple offense and Ermal Allen, the Cowboys' special assistant who had joined Landry's staff in 1962, explained:

"Rentzel, you see, had an option of fumbling out of bounds to stop the clock, or toward the end zone to the alternate receiver, who had the option of running to Lance's left or right. Carefully reading his keys, he went to the right and there was the ball. As you see, Tom has all avenues figured. We call that play, Vaudeville Right."

Meredith returned as Dallas won four of its final five games, losing to the Baltimore Colts, 23–17. Dallas then split its final two games, finishing with a 9–5 record and what was then called the Capitol Division title of the Eastern Conference. The Colts were one of the league's strongest teams and Landry was disappointed with the loss, especially considering his team had led at halftime, 14–10, then allowed the Colts to score 13 final period points.

"There used to be a joke among coaches," said Landry. "It was, 'What did you tell 'em at halftime to make them come back out and play so bad?'"

Meredith had suffered a broken nose in the final regular season game but was expected to be ready for the Eastern Conference title game against Cleveland, champions of the Century Division. The game was amazing, Dandy's finest hour. He connected on ten of twelve passes (one was dropped), as Dallas took a 24–0 lead and went on to crush the Browns, 52–14. Meredith departed at the beginning of the final period to a standing ovation from the Cotton Bowl crowd of 70,786. Before he left the field, he shook hands with each of his offensive linemen.

"It was our best game," said Landry, "because so much was at stake and we did everything well."

Meanwhile, Green Bay, which had struggled through an injury-ridden season, as Dallas had, won the Central Division with a 9–4–1 record and beat Los Angeles, the Coastal Division champion, 28–7. After many problems and narrow escapes, both teams seemed to be at their best and it was the match up the nation wanted for the NFL title. They had met for the crown on the first day of 1967, and now they would meet again for it on the final day of 1967.

Green Bay, Wisconsin, is a city of some 100,000 which rests on the Fox River. It is unique in the NFL because of its size and because its townspeople constitute all the stockholders. The team was shooting for its fifth NFL title, its third straight in the last seven years, and the town had another name, more popular with the natives. It was called Titletown, USA.

Dallas was still very young. The Packers had a fine defense but age was beginning to show. It was a matter of whether Lombardi could get them "up" one more time because most felt age wouldn't allow the Packers to repeat the following year.

"I don't think there was any doubt," said Nolan, "that we had the better team. Tom knew it. I think everybody did. Something really unusual had to happen for us to lose."

And so it did. After the Cowboys had arrived in Wisconsin they traveled to Lambeau Stadium to work out. Temperatures hovered around fourteen degrees above zero and this worried the players and coaches a little. But the sun was out and, after the workout, Meredith said, "It's not bad. If it gets no worse, we'll be fine."

Lombardi, talking to the Dallas-Fort Worth press, said predictions were that the weather would get no worse but, if it did, the field would still be in great shape because of the $80,000 electric heating wire apparatus he had had installed under the turf.

"Gentlemen," he said, "the field will not be frozen."

That night the entire Dallas Cowboy traveling party went to bed assured. By mistake members of the press, who usually sleep later than the players, received the same wake-up call as the team. For everybody there the call will live in infamy.

"Good morning," the operator said, "it's 8 A.M. and the temperature is 16 degrees below zero."

"Uh, 16 after what?" I said.

She laughed, "It's 16 below zero, so dress warm."

Landry tried to keep the team's mind on the game but it was impossible. "The Packers," he told them, "are playing in the same weather as we are." But nobody believed it. The Packers were more used to frigid temperatures. Five hours later, at kickoff time, temperatures had warmed to 13 degrees below, but a strong wind caused the chill factor to be 30 below. Equipment manager Jack Eskridge gave the players extra sweatsocks and sweat shirts, then noticed Landry. Eskridge, the team doctor and trainers knew Landry would be too preoccupied to dress warmly so they put a fur-lined coat and hunter's cap on him.

It was the coldest December 31 in Green Bay history. Meredith found he couldn't throw the ball normally and watched Bart Starr warm up to see if he could pick up the trick. Receivers had trouble holding the ball and Bobby Hayes seldom, before or during the game, ever took his hands out of the warmth of his waistband. You couldn't blame him, but he caught three passes for only sixteen yards. They had butane blowers on the sidelines and stoves in the press box. But the coffee they served in the press box would freeze before you could get it to your mouth. Sportswriter Frank Luksa, who now works for the Dallas *Times-Herald* but then was serving the Fort Worth *Star-Telegram,* walked over the frozen snow near a ditch outside the stadium. He slipped and fell into the ditch and had to call on two natives to form a human rope to get him out.

Fans huddled in the stadium in arctic dress. Some built small fires. There was no way the game ever should have been played but nobody seemed to know what had to be done to stop it. National television—the whole world—was ready. It had to be played. The NFL felt it must march on.

The Packers struck for the first two touchdowns, driving 82 yards and then scoring as Starr hit Boyd Dowler on a 43-yard touchdown throw. As in the previous title game, Dallas trailed 14–0.

"It was all so odd, really weird," Landry said. "In the awful cold, everything was so confused. You couldn't find anyone on the sidelines to keep up communications. You just don't play football in temperatures like that." But they did.

George Andrie got Dallas back into contention after Willie Townes tackled Starr, causing him to fumble. Andrie picked up the loose ball and skidded—almost skated—into the end zone. Villanueva kicked a field goal and Dallas trailed, 14–10, at half-time.

By the second half most of the field was frozen, more suited for hockey than football. Lombardi's heating wire system had failed. The game did not look real. The players became gray, ghostlike figures who seemed to be moving in a painful, slow motion pace.

But Dallas drove 83 yards to the Packer 13. Meredith ran nine yards to the five but fumbled when he was hit and Green Bay recovered. At best, this cost Dallas a field goal. Landry, however, had devised a special play for the Packers. Actually, it was an old play with a new twist. Throughout the two seasons in which he had started, Reeves had enjoyed great success with the halfback pass. He'd run to his right, with the option of running or throwing. But, for the Packers, who knew Reeves's pattern full well, Landry had decided to send Danny sweeping to his left. Green Bay wouldn't expect him to throw the ball going to his left. He'd have to stop, turn to throw and it would be unnatural. As the final period began Dallas was at the 50-yard line and Reeves told Meredith he felt it was time.

Reeves took the ball from Meredith and headed to his left. Cornerback Bob Jeter came up to stop the sweep and Willie Woods also moved in. Rentzel faked as though he were going to block Jeter and then turned and took off for the end zone. Reeves suddenly stopped, drew back, and threw the ball. Rentzel slowed down, caught the ball and high-tailed it into the end zone. Dallas led 17–14.

It seemed, at last, in the cards that the Cowboys would win as Green Bay took over at its own 32 with 4:50 left to play. But Starr was at his best. He continually tossed short passes to running backs Donny Anderson and Chuck Mercein. They'd take the ball, fake as the Cowboy linebackers would slip on the frozen field, and make valuable yardage.

Finally, Mercein rambled eleven yards to the Dallas one-yard line when Edwards, in position to make the tackle, slipped down. Anderson got a foot and the Packers called their final time-out with sixteen seconds remaining. Starr went to the sidelines to talk to Lombardi. Lombardi told Starr to try to sneak the ball across, forsaking a field goal that would tie the game and send it into overtime. "If we can't score from there," said Lombardi, "we don't deserve to win."

Starr took the snap as guard Jerry Kramer hit tackle Jethro Pugh, moving him ever so slightly toward center Ken Bowman, who also hit him. Starr wedged behind Kramer into the end zone with thirteen seconds left. The Packers had won, 21–17. They had been able to score at the end, whereas in the previous title game, Dallas had not. The temperature at the time of Starr's touchdown was 20 below!

Landry and his team stood frozen, both physically and mentally. Time ran out and fans poured onto the field and tore down the goal posts. They would celebrate far into the night.

"I thought Starr would roll out and, depending on what he saw, throw to an open receiver or just toss the ball out of bounds to stop the clock and give them time to get Chandler on the field. If the play they ran had failed, the game would have been over. There's no way they'd have gotten off another play," Landry said.

Two of Landry's coaches, an offensive and defensive coach, exchanged heated words in the dressing room and Landry told them to cool it. "What's said in this room stays in this room," he said. But he added, "I can't believe that call, the sneak. It wasn't a good call but now it's a great call."

On the charter flight back to Dallas the plane was like a hearse. Landry, patient as always, talked to the press, answering any and all questions as best he could. Andrie, Townes, and safety Dick Daniels had frostbite, and Pugh and Renfro also had to be treated because of the extreme cold in which they had played.

The physical damage was great but the mental damage was even worse. The long-range effects of another championship loss would eventually cause critics to claim Dallas couldn't win "the big one" and Landry to alter his approach. Fans also would say that Landry should be more emotional, like Lombardi, whose Packers beat Oakland, 33–14, in Super Bowl II. Shortly thereafter, Lombardi stepped down as coach and up to the general manager's job. The Packer era was over. It was almost the Cowboy era.

10

No MATTER what you did or what you thought, everything was paled by the events of a 64-day period, just over two short months of 1968, stretching from April 4 to June 6. Everybody from professional football to Wall Street was shocked when the madness of assassination continued as first Martin Luther King, Jr., the catalyst of the civil rights movement, and then Senator Robert Kennedy, a man who might have been president, were senselessly gunned down.

People were saddened as pictures in still life flashed across their minds . . . King, the advocate of peaceful demonstrations, standing before huge throngs and saying, "We shall overcome . . . we shall overcome!" And the people so uplifted, cheering from their hearts . . . . And Senator Kennedy, who had been Attorney General under his brother, President John F. Kennedy, reaching out to shake hands with young people on the college campuses where other politicians would not go. He seemed to be able to touch them to an extent, to give them an alternative to rebellion against everything that was the Establishment. But King's life had been taken as he stood on the balcony of a

Memphis motel, and Kennedy had been gunned down in a Los Angeles hotel.

The killings seemed to be a chain reaction that shook the very roots of the country, already disturbed by the murder of President Kennedy in 1963 and the Watts riots in Los Angeles in August of 1965, when 34 people were killed and more than 1,000 injured.

People were saddened, afraid, searching for answers as 1968 moved into the hot summer months, so prone to violence.

Tom Landry had been busy, as usual, during the off-season, as he traveled around the country making speeches, attending various affairs for the Fellowship of Christian Athletes. He, too, wondered just what was happening in this country and voiced his thoughts and opinions in late June of that year as the featured speaker of the FCA coaches banquet in Atlanta, Georgia, prior to the All-American (College All-Star) football game.

Landry, with a quiet and dignified air about him, moved to the speaker's stand amid a long and loud ovation. The narrow losses by his young Cowboys to Green Bay in the NFL title games had made his face most familiar to those of his profession. As the audience quieted he told them it was an honor to be invited. He talked briefly about what a fine game the city was hosting and then became serious and said:

"I had several jokes planned to tell, but with the events of recent weeks they don't seem appropriate now. I believe that every American who lives in these United States is genuinely concerned about the direction our country is going. Every time we pick up a paper or magazine, writers are asking the question, 'What is wrong with the United States?' Billy Graham, at the HemisFair Crusade in San Antonio, made the statement that there have been the rise and fall of 26 nations that followed the same path the United States is following today. Will God make an exception of us? Ruth Graham said, 'If He does, He is going to have to go back and apologize to Sodom and Gomorrah.'

"In the past few years we have seen a president assassinated. We have watched the Watts area of Los Angeles burn, snipers stalk and looters run rampant. The Dallas Cowboys were scheduled to open the 1965 preseason against the Rams in the Times Charity game during the height of the Watts riot. We had to postpone the game on a day-to-day basis until we finally played, after four days. There was nothing to do but watch television coverage and observe people trying to carry off television sets, furniture—stuff really too heavy to carry. It would have been comical if it weren't so tragic to see the disregard of law and order and, yes, the rights of others.

"Several months ago, Martin Luther King was struck down by an

135

assassin's bullet. Riots were touched off in many cities, the worst being in our nation's capital. Men in government and education were fearful of the next step that might be taken. A team of athletes was invited to come to Washington, D. C., to speak to the high school and junior high assemblies. The theme was, 'Fitness, Mental, Physical and Spiritual.' The officials were hopeful the athletes could influence the young students.

"You can appreciate our concern when you imagine walking on the stage of an auditorium and observing the fire damage where the drapes had been set to flames . . . and watching the principal sit on the edge of his chair while the athletes spoke, getting up three times to eject students from the assembly.

"The murders of King and Robert Kennedy finally have awakened the American public to the fact that there must be something wrong with us. Immediately, there was a furious rush to pass gun control legislation. This is okay, if it makes anybody feel better, but it is more of a conscience-easer than an antitoxin. Until a man changes what is in his heart, the solution to our problems won't be found. Christ says a wise man builds his house on rock if he wants it to withstand a storm. Murder, rioting and looting are evidence of a society that is sick.

"Not only in the area of violence is our nation decaying, but in other areas as well. There is an atmosphere of getting something for nothing. Paul Anderson spoke last week at Estes Park [in Dallas] at one of our FCA conferences. He did a wonderful job of dispelling the idea you can get something for nothing when he launched into a dramatic message on what it means to be free. He said a price must be paid. He said, you ask about free love, and said it destroys you physically and mentally. You ask about our free country? It was paid for by the lives of men. Free? Being free? Me? Yes. But it was purchased by Christ on Calvary. So you see there is nothing really free . . . someone has to pay.

"The Supreme Court confuses me; the Constitution says that this country was established under God and yet you can't pray in schools because an atheist says you can't. The Supreme Court says a prospective member of a jury cannot be disqualified because she or he does not believe in capital punishment. Yet, the law says for first-degree murder the penalty is death—capital punishment. I must admit that I am confused. Where is the rule book you're supposed to play the game by?

"I know our only lasting hope lies in Jesus Christ." Landry went on to quote UCLA basketball coach John Wooden, who said, "There is only one kind of life that truly wins and that is the one that places

136

our faith in the hands of our Savior. Until that is done we are on an aimless course that runs in circles and goes nowhere."

"For this country to survive as a powerful nation with freedom and opportunity, the hearts of men must change," Landry continued. "Only Christ can change men so drastically.

"At no time in history has the athlete wielded so much influence. This is what prompted a high school coach by the name of Don Mc-Claren to conceive of the idea of FCA thirteen years ago. James Jeffrey, the executive director of the FCA, uses a quotation from Shakespeare to express the urgency of the hour. It goes like this: 'There is a tide in the affairs of men which if taken at the crest will lead on to fame and fortune, but if missed, will return to the shallows.' What Jeff is saying to us, tonight, is to use this great influence we have to challenge our young people to follow Christ, which in time will save our country.

"Within the framework of competitive athletics, we have important values that we have learned as athletes—values that are on the decline in almost every facet of American life, namely, competitive spirit, character and discipline.

"When a rookie reports to the Dallas Cowboys' training camp our staff knows an awful lot about him. His quickness and control, strength and explosion, mental alertness and his character have been evaluated closely. The only thing we are not sure about is his competitiveness, which we define as will to win or determination to be the best. So, to me, this is the most important trait an athlete can possess because it determines whether he stays or goes.

"In our country we are destroying man's competitive spirit in so many ways. It has become fashionable to expect the government to guarantee almost anything. No longer are our young men asking for an opportunity to prove themselves, but they only ask, what are the benefits?

"I am starting my twentieth year in professional football and I have seen a change in the athlete coming into pro ball. In 1949, all the athletes were a product of the depression years and World War II. Coaches could treat them any way they wanted and the athletes would respond because to them success was important. The alternatives they had seen had not been attractive.

"In the mid-fifties, the athletes entering pro football were the products of the postwar era—plenty of everything—and we observed more independence, and motivation became an important factor. Job opportunities were plentiful in other lines of work.

"In the sixties, I have seen the decay so prevalent in other areas of

American life start to take its toll on the athlete. Competitiveness is being eroded; the will to win and determination to be the best are not so important anymore. There are easier ways to get by. Now is the time we must reestablish a competitive spirit in America that has made it the greatest nation on earth with the highest standard of living."

Landry paused, then quoted Knute Rockne, who said, "Some of you may say this will to win is a bad thing. In what way is it bad? Education is supposed to prepare a young man for life. Life is competition. Success in life goes only to the man who competes successfully. A successful lawyer is a man who goes out and wins, wins law cases. A successful physician is one who goes out and wins—saves lives and restores people to good health. A successful executive is a man who can make money and stay out of bankruptcy court. There is no reward for the loser. There is nothing wrong with the will to win. The only penalty should be that the man who wins unfairly should be set down."

Then, trying to put winning in proper perspective, Landry quoted Bart Starr: "Vince Lombardi taught me that winning is not everything but making the effort to win is. It not only made me a better quarterback but a bigger and better person."

"We must never lose the competitive spirit," Landry told the audience, "that enabled Pettis Norman to come from a tenant farm to a recent appointment as vice-president of a bank in Dallas. We must never lose the competitive spirit that enabled Lee Trevino to hit 1,000 to 1,500 golf balls a day because he knew if he became good enough he would be given the opportunity to win a National Open.

"The old cliché that 'We're building character' after a losing season is still valid. Only Christ can build character faster than the athletic field. When all is said and done, character is probably the most important value of all. Horace Greeley said, 'Fame is vapor, popularity an accident, riches take wins, those who cheer today will curse tomorrow, only one thing endures—character.' Mr. Greeley was talking about the type of character that was revealed in Jesus Christ. The Apostle Paul wrote to the Romans, 'If you love your neighbor as much as you love yourself, you will not want to harm or cheat him, or kill him or steal from him.' If we would all do that, it would take care of everything else. But until that happens, we need a third value that may be the most pressing at the moment. That is discipline."

Landry made an analogy of the rules in sports and the laws of the country. He said if the rules were broken in football, you received a penalty or might even be thrown out of the game. He said you either learned to play by the rules or suffered the consequences. "Apparently," said Landry, "the sentiment in the U. S. today is that if you don't like the rules or laws, forget them." He then, with controversy, cited Police Chief William Parker of Los Angeles, who said during the Watts riots, "I don't care what color they are or what cause they represent. They're breaking the law and there's only one place for them, in jail."

"He was soundly chastized, but his words made some sense to me because I am used to watching people play by the rules," said Landry. He quoted Darrell Royal, who said, "Athletics seems to be the last place where we have discipline, and sometimes you wonder how long is it gonna last."

And then he cited a piece written by Blackie Sherrod, nationally known columnist of the Dallas *Times-Herald,* who recalled something Vince Lombardi had said after Robert Kennedy was murdered: "It is beyond belief. We have suffered a complete breakdown of mental discipline in this country. Something has happened to our moral fabric. We confuse freedom with license. We don't have any understanding of freedom. Before you can understand freedom you have to understand duty and respect."

Landry continued to quote from Sherrod's column, " 'The other day, where a March on Poverty business sent a delegation to call on Ramsey Clark, the Attorney General, they pounded on the doors and broke windows in the Justice Department. Broke windows, honey, right there in the USA grounds. Gentlemen, this is where I would have loved to have seen a door open and a stocky man walk out and say, "My name is Vince Lombardi. I am the Attorney General of this country. Now what was it you wanted to see me about?" ' "

The audience applauded, imagining Lombardi, the man who with his countenance could strike fear in a 6 foot 5 inch, 260-pound athlete.

"It is high time we define clearly the rules for playing the game in the USA," continued Landry. "And it is high time we had the intestinal fortitude to make them stick. You might be thinking, 'Yeah, coach, I agree. We need to reverse this trend. We need to renew our competitive spirit, reestablish character and apply discipline. But, heck, what can I do?'

"Don't ever underestimate your influence as an athlete. Every redblooded American boy knows more about athletes and sports than he does about anything else. He is looking to be like you. There is a poem entitled, 'To Any Athlete' and one of the three verses goes like this:

> There's a wide-eyed little fellow
> Who believes you're always right,
> And his ears are always open,
> And he watches day and night;
> You are setting an example

Every day in all you do,
For the little boy who's watching
To grow up to be like you.

"It is not only the little guy who listens to you. When the athletes gathered in Washington, D. C., that day to speak to students, there were doubts in many officials' minds whether we would be received properly in the schools. I was asked to speak at a breakfast of local dignitaries preceding our appearance in the high schools. I could see the worried expressions on the faces of the athletic directors and school officials. I told them without reservation that the athletes would be received without incident."

Landry told how the athletes were received by a standing ovation from over 30,000 students. He said the athletes told the students, some of whom were from the toughest schools in the city, they had to get off the seats of their pants and get an education, that the United States was the greatest country in the world, and that they had to have respect for law and order.

"I'm not sure whether the students wanted to hear what was said or not," continued Landry, "but they listened and respected the athletes for what they said."

He related a story Maxie Baughan, a linebacker for the Los Angeles Rams, had told him. Baughan had recalled being upset at a call that went against the Rams in a 24–24 tie with Baltimore. As he left the field Baughan threw his helmet to the ground and kicked it. When he got home his six-year-old son met him, wearing a Rams uniform. The boy asked him to come outside. When they got outside the kid threw his helmet down and kicked it. "Look, Dad, just like you," said the kid.

"So you can see, fellows, as athletes we can influence so many people," continued Landry. "This is what the Fellowship of Christian Athletes is all about. It is the greatest organization in the U. S. because its purpose is to confront athletes and coaches and through them the youth of America with the challenge and adventure of following Jesus Christ in the fellowship of the church and in their vocation. It is not an organization of saints. FCA is made up of athletes, coaches, and businessmen who love Jesus Christ and are willing to stand up for him. The Bible tells us, 'for God so loved the world that he gave his only Son, that whosoever believes in him should not perish but have everlasting life.' That is the life that wins."

In later years, after experiencing the aftermath of the '60s, the protests, and so on, Landry softened his view somewhat and believed that the period, although destructive, had some positive ramifications because it made the older generation look more upon people as individuals, and in the process take a closer look at themselves. But he continued to believe that the violent protests contributed strongly to the negativism of the country and the destruction of necessary discipline.

Landry knew as training camp was about to begin in the summer of 1968 that the Dallas Cowboys, physically, had their best team. They were more solid at every position and Don Meredith, going into his ninth season, had matured to the extent that he certainly was more capable than ever of becoming a championship quarterback. What Landry did not know, yet perhaps subconsciously feared, were possible psychological problems in the wake of two close and frustrating losses to Green Bay in the NFL title games of 1966 and 1967.

But Meredith was more prepared than ever for the season. He seemed more serious and said, "I'm becoming more and more oriented to Landry's way of thinking. I'm glad I am. I fought it for several years but he's got the best thing going in the pros. He's right in his approach and I'm glad I've finally realized it."

Once during the off season Al Ward, then a vice-president of the Cowboys, recalled standing by an elevator at the team's offices on the eleventh floor of Expressway Towers. "An elevator near the one where I was standing opened and there was Meredith, his hair tousled, wearing a pair of loafers, no socks, a pair of jeans and a wrinkled sweater. It was obvious Don had just gotten out of bed and was heading for the coaches' offices."

Ward looked over at Meredith and said, "Hi, Don, what are you doing?"

"Well, the Man called and said he had some things he wanted me to look at," said Meredith, looking back as he walked past Ward.

"How long ago did he call?"

"About three minutes," said Meredith, disappearing down the hall.

In a particular passing drill Meredith became very frustrated when he missed a wide-open receiver. Turning toward the huddle, back of which stood Landry, he said, "Well, I'll be an s-o-b!"

"That," said Landry calmly, "wouldn't help you hit that receiver any better."

But, of course, Meredith always was Meredith and the little fun-loving man inside him always was there, waiting. Each day Landry conducted meetings with his three quarterbacks: Meredith, Jerry Rhome, and Craig Morton. At one meeting Landry was at the blackboard, making a point, while the trio watched. Meredith took a cigar out of his mouth and began twirling it around with his hand, as though he were a symphony conductor accompanying Landry's movements and words. Dandy really got carried away as Rhome and Morton covered their mouths to keep from laughing out loud. Suddenly, Landry turned around and caught Meredith, who quickly stuck the cigar into his mouth—the lighted end first. Meredith gagged and started spitting tobacco everywhere.

"Are you getting this, Don?" asked Landry.

"Yessir," said Meredith, still choking.

The Cowboys had moved their permanent training camp to the campus of California Lutheran College in Thousand Oaks, California, in the summer of 1963. Cal Lutheran, a small, immaculate college, is at the base of a small mountain range. Behind one of the two practice fields is a mountain, which Landry usually includes in his jogging territory. Thousand Oaks, some 40 miles down the freeway from Los Angeles, had some 40,000 residents during the early years the Cowboys trained there, but now the population has doubled. It is a town with, obviously, many oak trees and lies sprawling in the Canejo ("rabbit") Valley. Often, scrawny rabbits can be seen rushing across the road, up into the hills.

In training camp the visiting writers, club officials and some of the assistant coaches will go out and have a drink or so at night but Landry remains very regimented. He might go out with his coaches for dinner once a week but he spends the rest of his time away from football in his room, reading history books, westerns, and his Bible. This, of course, changes when Alicia makes her annual visit to see her husband. She usually comes and stays a week or so in a nearby motel near the conclusion of camp. Landry, when time and duty allow, will take her out for dinner at night and to church on Sundays.

If she came during early camp, when Landry is busiest, she'd have a difficult time getting his attention. I always laugh at the story about Landry taking her to a downtown Dallas Cowboy Club luncheon during one of the early seasons. It was when he had one of his poorest teams and was concentrating doubly hard. After speaking at the luncheon, he got into his car and headed back to his office. About halfway there, he remembered that he'd taken Alicia to the luncheon. He hurried back to pick her up and she said, "I won't give you a touchdown but I suppose I'll give you a field goal for remembering to come back and get me."

At training camp in 1968 I was standing by Alicia's car, parked near the practice field, talking to her before the team and coaches came onto the field. She was laughing about Tom forgetting her that day at the Cowboy Club luncheon.

Alicia had just driven in from Los Angeles International Airport and hadn't had time to see Tom. In fact, she hadn't seen him for four weeks. He came jogging onto the field, saw her and veered slightly toward her car. He slowed down ever so briefly as he passed, and said, "Haven't I seen you somewhere before?" They both grinned and he went on to practice.

"Okay," I said, "now you can go on back to Dallas."

"There is a little more to it than that," she said.

What we were to refer to as the Cleveland Syndrome first struck in 1968 and again in 1969, magnifying what had happened against Green Bay the previous two years and causing a large psychological barrier that Landry, the players and the organization would have a terrible time overcoming. From 1968 to 1969 the team would change. Calvin Hill, a No. 1 draft choice from Yale, of all places, would become the club's first big running back and Craig Morton would move in for Don Meredith at quarterback. But each season Cleveland would keep the heavily favored Cowboys from winning the Eastern Conference title. The losses to Cleveland would be the first step backward the organization had taken since the formative years and cause doubts from the highest to the lowest echelons of the Cowboys. The players would begin to doubt themselves, fans would begin to wonder again about Landry's approach and if the Cowboys would ever reach the pinnacle of professional football—if the promise of the Green Bay games had been only a mirage.

The club added new players in 1968 with Mike Clark, Mike Ditka, and Ron Widby coming in trades and draft picks Blaine Nye and Larry Cole making their presence known. Rayfield Wright also was showing signs of developing into a superstar after being moved to offensive tackle. And the veterans seemed even more solid as the Cowboys won their first six games, a streak that would be tied in 1969 but not bettered until the 1977 team won eight in a row. The Cowboys beat Detroit, 59–13, in the season opener in the Cotton Bowl.

The Cowboys, 6–0, felt they would finally get a measure of revenge on Green Bay, which had slipped to a 2–4 record and, obviously, was fading with age. Lombardi had stepped up to general manager and named long-time assistant Phil Bengtson as head coach, but the dynasty was over. Yet, Green Bay won, 28–17. Landry, reminded that his team still couldn't beat the Packers, bristled a little and snapped back, "I'm making no apologies for this team. The whole idea is that some-

143

day it will grow to the point where it can beat the Packers. Right now, I'll certainly take a 6–1 record."

The Cowboys remained a little sluggish for two weeks following the Packer loss. One reason was they lost Danny Reeves to a knee injury. Reeves's replacements, Craig Baynham and Les Shy, were inconsistent the remainder of the year and, if the club lacked anything physically, it was consistency from the halfback position. But it won five of its next six games and already had taken the Capitol Division as it traveled to New York for the formality of ending the season against the Giants in Yankee Stadium.

Meredith had been superb, throwing to Lance Rentzel and Bobby Hayes, and Don Perkins was finishing his final season by rushing for 836 yards and a 4.4 average. Roughly, all Meredith needed to win the NFL passing title over Baltimore's Earl Morrell was to hit two of ten passes. But Dallas already had the division title, would play Cleveland for the Eastern Conference crown, and Dandy and some of his teammates just didn't feel too intense as they attended a long party held by author George Plimpton the night before the game. When Meredith showed up in Yankee Stadium the next day he couldn't, in his own words, "hit the ground with the ball." He completed just one of nine passes, told Landry he didn't have a "feel" for the game and was replaced by Morton, who saved the day by quarterbacking Dallas to its twelfth victory of the season. The 12–2 mark was the best the club was to post in regular season until 1977.

Snow had begun to fall in late afternoon and we all sat on the charter during a two-hour delay at the airport. Finally, the 747 lifted us out of New York and, suddenly, there was a loud explosion and the plane seemed to rock abruptly in its climb.

A stewardess screamed. Bob Lilly said, "That's it! That's it!" D. D. Lewis, a rookie, sat next to Meredith. "Dandy, aren't you scared?" Meredith noted casually, "Naw, D. D., it's been a good 'un."

The plane straightened in its climb, gained altitude, leveled out and the remainder of the flight, as others before and since, was uneventful. Apparently, one of the engines had sucked in ice and, while the nose of the aircraft was pointed upward, it became locked in low altitude. Dave Manders and George Andrie said they'd never fly again. Landry sat through the entire episode looking calm and unruffled as usual.

Cleveland was a formality that would put the Cowboys into the NFL title game against the Minnesota–Baltimore winner. The Cowboys remembered how they had stomped the Browns, 52–14, in the 1967 Eastern title game and had beaten them 28–7 in the second game of that 1968 season.

144

Landry cautioned his team that the previous games with Cleveland had been misleading. "There is no way we were 38 points better than Cleveland last year," he said. "In a championship game like this there aren't two inches separating the teams. Because it's such a mental thing, a big game like this, sometimes the scores become lopsided because a team will get behind and see things slipping away and start making mistakes." Landry felt certain Dallas would win but wasn't underselling the Browns.

Meredith was off and also was having terrible luck. But the defense was playing well and Chuck Howley picked up a fumble and raced 44 yards to give Dallas a 10–3 lead. However, Leroy Kelly slipped past Howley, who went with the wrong man, on a pass route and gathered in a 45-yard touchdown throw from Bill Nelsen to tie the game at half-time, 10–10.

The second half blew up in Meredith's face. On the first play, Meredith threw a sideline pass to Hayes, who was open. But linebacker Dale Lindsey batted up the ball, caught it and ran 27 yards for a touch-down. Meredith's keys told him Lindsey wouldn't be in the area, but he was. The next time Dallas got the ball Meredith threw for Rentzel, who batted the ball into the surprised hands of defensive back Ben Davis, whose interception put the ball in position for Kelly's 35-yard touchdown run. Some two minutes into the second half, Cleveland led 24–10. Landry benched Meredith, replacing him with Craig Morton.

"We needed a psychological lift," explained Landry. "Morton was the only thing I had that I could use. I took Meredith out not so much for what he was doing but to try to shake things up. I told Meredith I thought I'd go with Morton and he agreed."

Meredith never forgot Landry's pulling him but said, "I could never argue with Tom. That's because it's Tom I'm talking to. I won't second-guess the call because Tom's job is bigger than mine and mine is big enough."

Dallas got behind 31–13 with 2:09 left but Morton, who hit only nine of 23 passes, did rally the team to a final deficit of 31–20. The game had begun on a dark, gray afternoon in Cleveland's Municipal Stadium and, as it ended, snowflakes began to fall on nearby Lake Erie.

Meredith boarded the return charter back to Dallas, then abruptly got off, taking Pete Gent with him. They went to New York to try to forget what had happened and Landry didn't fine either of them.

Later, Landry was to say, "All I know is Meredith was a better quarterback this season than he has ever been and this is the best team we've ever had." Some on the club felt Landry had been unfair pulling Meredith. They knew Meredith had not thrown well but also believed that other circumstances had gone against him, such as Rentzel tipping one of the interceptions. But it didn't matter. Tom Landry is not a man who second-guesses himself on decisions.

Baltimore beat first Minnesota and then Cleveland to win the NFL title and earn the dubious distinction of losing Super Bowl III to the New York Jets, led by brash Joe Namath. Dallas and Minnesota had to play in Miami in the Play-off Bowl game and Meredith hit 11 of 13 passes during one stretch to lead Dallas to a 17–13 victory. He was named MVP in the game and received a trophy with the figure of a football player on top. As he carried the trophy on the charter flight back to Dallas it was noticed that the head of the figure of the football player had been knocked off.

"That figures," said Meredith.

In early July of 1969, before training camp began, Don Meredith was doing a lot of soul-searching. He was disappointed Landry had pulled him in the Cleveland game. Also, he was getting tired of being booed in the Cotton Bowl. He had some family problems and, after nine years, just wasn't sure he wanted to play football anymore. Don went to see Tom Landry and told him his feelings. Many feel if Landry had strongly tried to talk him out of retirement that Meredith would have continued to play. But Meredith was to say later that, after he had told Landry the reasons for retiring, Landry had said, "If that's the way you feel, then it's probably the right decision."

But at a press conference on July 5, Meredith said, "Coach Landry and I have worked very hard these past nine seasons and I'm sure he has worked a lot harder than I have. If I have any regrets in retiring, it's that I won't be around to play an active part in a championship for this team. And I'm sure it'll come. I have come [he looked over at Landry] to love this man."

"Don and I were very close during the years of building the team," Landry said. "Don was a very important part of the success of the team. It certainly is a deep personal loss to see him step down. I know many still disagree but I firmly believe that my decision in 1965 to stick with Don was the most important one made in this club's history and led directly to our conference championships in 1966 and 1967."

Asked how he would like to be remembered, Meredith said, "I won't be remembered as a great passer or a great signal caller, but I hope I'll be remembered as a nice guy."

Meredith would only have been 31 in the 1969 season, still in his prime. He later would regret the premature retirement and contact

Tex Schramm about a possible return to the club. But by that time Craig Morton was the quarterback and, had Meredith come back, the club would have been forced to trade the younger quarterback, who appeared at that time to have a very bright future with the Cowboys.

Morton was different than Meredith had been around Landry. Craig was very attentive, serious. He was 26, had served a four-year apprenticeship and Landry decided to let Morton call his own plays. And in a somewhat surprising move Landry decided that a 27-year-old rookie named Roger Staubach, despite his lack of experience, would be able to back up Morton. Staubach, drafted as a future by the team in 1964, had graduated from the Naval Academy and then spent four years fulfilling his obligation of active duty. Nobody ever had been away from football that long and still made a successful pro career, but by the time training camp ended Landry knew Staubach was special, very special. Landry said whereas it took most quarterbacks four or five years to get into a position to start, that he felt Staubach, due to his maturity and hard work, could challenge in three years.

At first Morton didn't take Staubach's challenge that seriously, remembering how he had to wait while Meredith ran the team. It would not be long until it did become serious.

Don Perkins joined Meredith in retirement and thus Dallas became a different team, bearing the stamp of Morton and rookie Calvin Hill. Landry had been reluctant to pick Hill as the club's No. 1 draft choice in spite of the glowing reports from his scouts. Calvin was from Yale, the Ivy League, which was not to be confused football-wise with Notre Dame. But Calvin was 6 feet 4 inches, could play at 220 to 225 pounds, and had speed and a lot of athletic ability. Landry thought at first he might make a linebacker or a tight end. But by the time preseason started Danny Reeves again was sidelined with knee problems and Calvin was tried at halfback.

Before the second exhibition game in San Francisco, Schramm stood on the sidelines with a group of writers who were talking about Hill starting his first game. "I have a feeling," said Schramm, "that today a star will be born." Hill rushed for 106 yards that day, caught three passes and was to become a fixture at halfback for the club and a running mate for Walt Garrison, who took over at fullback for Don Perkins.

Morton studied hard and worked hard. Although Landry wasn't sure what effect the changes would have on his team, he believed Craig would do a good job. Before the first game all the strategy had been planned, talked about, but as the club was preparing to take the field Landry walked over to Morton's locker.

"I can do it," said Morton. "I'm ready, Coach."

"Yes," replied Landry, "I know you can, Craig."

And he did. Morton was spectacular, although he dislocated a finger on his passing hand in the final exhibition game and Landry had to play his rookie, Staubach, in the league opener against St. Louis. But Landry simplified the game plan and Staubach hit a long touchdown pass as Dallas won, 24–3. Morton returned after that and was unbelievable. He was completing 73 percent of his passes as Dallas went to Atlanta seeking its fourth straight victory. On a delayed screen, end Claude Humphrey crashed into Morton, who had just released the ball. Craig fell on his right shoulder and, immediately, left the game. His shoulder was slightly separated. He might be out for the season and Landry felt there was no way, at that stage, that Staubach could take over the team.

Landry and the club officials huddled with team doctors. Doctors said Morton would be in pain but could continue to play without causing further damage to the shoulder. Surgery, if needed, could wait until after the season. Morton had waited too long to be No. 1 and wasn't about to quit. He insisted that he could play.

The following week Landry, after talking to doctors a final time, asked Morton if he could play. "Coach, it's going to be this way the rest of the season," said Morton. "I've waited a long time and I'd like to give it a shot." For some unexplainable reason, Morton threw extremely well on his return, perhaps camouflaging the seriousness of the injury. He played the remainder of the season but his shoulder grew worse. He was unable to throw much at all during the week and by the final part of the season he often would lose his feel for throwing the ball and the zing and power had left his passes. But Morton was calling a fine game, utilizing Hill and Garrison behind an excellent line of tackles Ralph Neely, Tony Liscio and Rayfield Wright, guards John Niland and John Wilbur and centers Malcolm Walker and Dave Manders.

Dallas was 6–0 once again as it went again into the scene of the previous disaster, Cleveland's Municipal Stadium, to face Bill Nelsen, Leroy Kelly and the Browns. Nelsen, who seemed to make his entire season against Dallas, completed 18 of 25 passes for 255 yards and five touchdowns as the Browns took a 28–3 halftime lead and won, 42–10. Dallas came completely apart. I wrote in the Dallas *Morning News* that women and children had been evacuated from the stadium at halftime and that future Dallas–Cleveland games would be X-rated, nobody under 18 allowed to enter without a guardian. This angered some club officials but Landry never said a word to me.

"All our previous games built up to the match with Cleveland," he explained. "We were hopeful of showing a different outcome, but the results were not there. We played a game totally uncharacteristic of our team." But secretly, Landry had begun to realize that there were underlying problems in his club which seemed to show up against the Browns. These were forgotten as Dallas followed Hill's lead to an 11–2–1 record, the Capitol Division title and another meeting with the Browns for the Eastern Conference championship.

This game was in the Cotton Bowl but, strangely enough, the day was gray, cloudy and almost seemed to be Cleveland weather. In the ramp before going out for the kickoff some of the Cowboy players began complaining about the rain. It certainly was an indication that the minds of some already were searching for an excuse, if needed. Hill, with a toe injury, had missed two games and been hobbled in others the final part of the year, but still tied Jim Brown's rookie rushing total of 942 yards. But for Cleveland he was far from the back he had been and Morton simply was not physically able to take up the slack.

On Cleveland's first possession, Lilly led the Cowboys in smothering the Browns and the crowd, as well as the Cowboys, became excited. But the ensuing punt by Dale Cockroft bounced off Rayfield Wright's leg, the Browns recovered and went on to score. They padded the margin to 24–0 and after Walt Sumner intercepted a Morton pass and returned it 88 yards for a TD in the final period, Landry pulled Morton, who had hit just four of twelve passes, and let Staubach finish the game. The Browns won, 38–14, and sent the entire Cowboy organization spinning, second-guessing.

"Those two championship losses to Cleveland were particularly disappointing to me because I felt we didn't accomplish one thing," said Landry. "It can happen to you once. But when it happened again, I was even lower than the first time. It caused us all to start second-guessing ourselves. Once again, some people were saying it was the system, but I never thought that was it. But I wondered about our mental approach to the game. We just had some problems and we had to find them."

Leaders of every department in the Cowboy organization would reevaluate. Landry would step back and take a closer look at the team and he also would put his approach to coaching under a magnifying glass. Something was wrong. A championship, once so close, seemed as elusive as the Golden Fleece.

11

BY LATE AFTERNOON on Sunday, December 28, 1969, the Cleveland Browns once again had destroyed the Dallas Cowboys for the NFL Eastern Conference championship and the teams were in their locker rooms at the Cotton Bowl. Outside, mist was still falling and low, oyster colored clouds caused a premature darkness as fans walked to their cars and joined the crawling procession of traffic leaving the Fair Park area and fanning out across Dallas.

The Browns' dressing room was, of course, happy, crowded, and the cheers and yells were punctuated by the popping of corks from bottles of champagne. Across the ramp, in the Cowboy quarters, it was just the opposite. Tom Landry had spoken to his players, then to the press. Then he went into the coaches' dressing quarters, talked to his assistants and then asked them if they'd please leave for awhile, give him a few moments alone. He sat there for some time, alone and quiet. He knew it could have happened once. He fully understood that anything could happen in the NFL and so Cleveland had beaten his highly favored team for the Eastern title in 1968. But now it had happened again. It was too much, really. Just too much. He left the dressing room, the Cotton Bowl, got into his car and began the long drive to his home in North Dallas. He later was to recall his experience in a column called "Lenten Guideposts," in which he wrote:

"I drove home with an overwhelming sense of disappointment. Before going to bed that night, I sat down in my bedroom chair to review the whole day. Not a pragmatic review, but a spiritual assessment. 'Lord, what went wrong today?' I asked Him. As almost always happens during these sessions with Him, I soon found perspective. A crushing setback today, yes, but I've learned that something constructive comes from every defeat. I thought over my relationships that day with the players, coaches, officials, friends, family. Nothing wrong there. No bad injuries, either. 'Thank You, Lord, for being with me out there,' I said. And with that prayer the bitter sting of defeat drained away. Disappointment remained, but I've found that it doesn't sap energy and creativity. One football game, after all, is quite a small fragment of one's total life."

But in the wake of the loss to Cleveland the entire Cowboy organization was spinning. Club officials, coaches and players were first in the depths of depression, consternation, and began questioning themselves

150

and those around them. When some normalcy returned with time, those in charge began looking for answers.

"We reevaluated our entire organization," said Tex Schramm, "and our system of operation. This did not, however, include a reevaluation of our head coach."

In retrospect, Landry knew that injuries to Craig Morton and Calvin Hill had hurt the confidence of his team and, yet, something else was missing. Even with Morton hurting, unable to throw the ball well, and Hill hobbled, the Cowboys should have had enough. Perhaps, it was entirely mental . . . perhaps it was their approach to the game. After meeting with his staff, Landry sent out questionnaires to each player, asking their opinions about all aspects of the club—the approach, the system, the coaches, their teammates. This was a revolutionary move and something he would not have done in the earlier years. But now it was his team, not a makeshift bunch of stopgap players. The players would not be required to sign the questionnaires; in exchange for candor they received anonymity.

Some players said the team was overly prepared for games, that there were too many cliques in the club, too many prima donnas, that they felt tired of trying to finesse opponents and wanted to physically blow them out. Some criticized what was termed Landry's "puritanism" and voiced their opinions about some of the assistant coaches. Landry weighed what the players said, as did his assistants, some of whom became angry.

But Bob Lilly summed up the feeling of the majority when he said, "There was nothing wrong with Landry's system, nor his approach to the game. He's a great coach, but the team just needed some shaking up."

Landry concluded that he must take a tougher approach. Under the late Alvin Roy, a former Olympic weight coach and a man who had had great success in helping condition the Kansas City Chiefs, he initiated an off-season weight and conditioning program, which was voluntary, in a mandatory sort of way. Players did not have to attend the sessions but roll was kept and Landry and his staff would know full well who wasn't there. The program included weight lifting, running and agility drills. It interfered with some of the players' off-season jobs but Landry had reached the conclusion that to win a championship, professional football had reached the stage of being a year-round job.

Landry felt the team had been relying too much on the big play to score and so planned to use more of a grind-it-out, power attack, featuring a good, veteran offensive line and Calvin Hill. He moved backfield coach Ermal Allen to the new job of being a special assistant who scouted and rated all teams and players, including the Cowboys, and named Danny Reeves, a popular man with his teammates, a player-coach. Furthermore, he said all players, whether starters or not, would be judged by performance levels and those who didn't measure up might lose their first-team status.

Landry was gambling. He told his coaches that with the tougher program and the new performance level measuring sticks that some of the regulars wouldn't be starting the first of the season. "We'll sink to a lower level than we have been at in several years," he explained. "But eventually it'll pay off. There will be confusion for awhile but I just believe we have to shake things up if we're going to progress to a real championship team."

Hill, of course, loomed big in Landry's offensive plans for 1970 and so it came as somewhat of a surprise to him when Gil Brandt and the scouting department kept recommending the club use its top draft pick on a running back from West Texas State named Duane Thomas. Landry always has the final say on draft choices but Brandt and his scouting staff compiled files on all college talent, leaving few stones unturned. Sometimes mistakes are made but the overall success of the club over the years proves a good percentage of accuracy in the club's projections of college players into the pro ranks. All imaginable data on players is put into the computer, which ranks the talent accordingly. Of course, there always is, and always will be the human aspect, the intangibles that can't be rated, which is why people such as Cliff Harris and Drew Pearson, neither of whom was rated high enough to draft, still can become stars in the NFL.

The computer had rated Thomas among the top three players in the country and the Cowboys, who wouldn't pick until twenty-third in the 26-team draft, had him ranked third. There was some question about his attitude. Dallas, generally, will pick the top-rated player remaining when its time comes, regardless of position, but Landry kept thinking that he already had a fine halfback in Hill.

On draft morning Landry sat at a table with his scouts and watched the board as teams made their picks before the Cowboys' time came. Landry had read and re-read the report on Thomas and was sitting by Red Hickey, former San Francisco head coach who had been an assistant for the Cowboys and now scouts college talent for the team.

Thomas was 6 feet 2 inches, 220 pounds, had run a 4.6-second 40-yard sprint, and was intelligent, agile, and quick. "I told Tom all about Duane's ability, his positives and negatives," recalled Hickey. "I told him I had seen him taken out of a college game, walk to the bench, throw his helmet down and then curse at his coach. But I also told him that when Duane went back into the game he continued to rip off yardage. I told Tom that Duane worked very hard in practice, knew the assignments of all positions, but had trouble with the trainer in college over treatment of injuries. Tom would say, tell me about Duane again, and I would. Our time to pick kept getting closer."

Finally, Hickey turned to Landry and said, "Thomas is the best running back in the country, bar none."

"Does that mean," asked Landry, "that he's better than Calvin Hill?"

"If he comes here, Tom," said Hickey, "he'll be your halfback."

"Hmmmm."

"Tom, I'm telling you, if Thomas is still there when our pick comes, take him, if you think you can handle him."

"You say he's better than Calvin?"

"Yes, he'll be your halfback."

"Then, Red, I think I'll try to handle him."

This turned out to be a bigger job than Landry had anticipated but it would pay off. Thomas became the club's No. 1 pick but the draft also proved to be the best in the club's history at that time, although it would be surpassed in 1975. But that year Dallas drafted Thomas, Bob Asher, Margene Adkins, Charlie Waters, Steve Kiner, John Fitzgerald, Pat Toomay, Pete Athas, Mark Washington, Joe Williams and signed Cliff Harris as a free agent. Thomas, Waters, Washington, Harris and Fitzgerald would become starters for Dallas and the others, at one time or another, would start for other NFL clubs once they were traded by Dallas.

Before training camp Landry discussed the criticisms his team had received and obviously had found some answers:

"The most difficult championship to win is the first one. After a club knows it is capable of winning it gains a great deal of confidence in important games. Success breeds success. If we had won that first game against the Packers for the championship, there's a pretty good chance we would have won our next three. But the Packers were at the height of their game in 1966 and 1967. If they hadn't been around in those years, we probably would have dominated the league then. But they were a great team with a lot of maturity and a lot of winning tradition behind them when we hit the scene in 1966. And even though we played two great games against them, people started talking about our not winning the big game.

"When that happens to you, you begin to have a negative attitude about whether or not you're ever going to win the big one. Even though we had great overall success, we remained the team that couldn't come through in important games.

"Failure, like success, has a carry-over effect. After we lost the second title game to Green Bay our chances of winning the third were much worse than they had been before the second. After the third loss to Cleveland, we continued to be at a big psychological disadvantage in the play-offs and lost again.

"So to a great extent I think our problem all goes back to the Ice Game. That year we had a team capable of beating Green Bay for the championship. But when we lost, as we did, near the end it triggered and set in motion things that were to cause us to get beat in the Cleveland games. I must say it's psychological because football mostly is a mental game. Our situation now is tough, no doubt about that. But, once we break the spell in the big games, we'll start to win our share of them."

For awhile the 1970 season looked like the same old story, but then it would all change. Before training camp Landry had planned to tighten up and launch a new style of attack. He also planned to move former All-Pro tackle Ralph Neely to right guard because Rayfield Wright had become a premier tackle and Tony Liscio was solid at tackle. Landry also traded for Herb Adderley, hoping to get at least a couple of more years out of the former Green Bay great and shore up the team's glaring weak spot at cornerback. He was moving Cornell Green to strong safety and believed that in Adderley and Mel Renfro the Cowboys could hold their own at cornerback with anybody. A good, solid training camp was important to fit in new people at new positions, to being a new style of attack. But the National Football League Players Association called a strike and delayed the veterans' reporting to camp for two weeks. This severely hindered Landry's plans for change.

Craig Morton was still having problems throwing the ball. Off-season surgery had corrected his shoulder problem but his elbow was bothering him. Later it was to be learned that he had injured the elbow while trying to compensate for his shoulder problem. When the 1970 season was over Morton would undergo surgery on the elbow but the seriousness of the new problem didn't come to light until, once again, he had spent a year in pain. On the other hand, Roger Staubach, a 28-year-old second-year quarterback, was most anxious to play and, unlike Morton, he was very outspoken.

During a quarterback meeting, Landry was explaining, "There is no quarterback in the league with less than three years' experience who has won a championship. Joe Namath was unusual in that respect. He was the only quarterback to win a title after playing three years."

Staubach, fuming, blurted out, "Namath was *only* in his third year! [in reality Namath was in his fourth year]. Besides, how can you judge every individual by the same yardstick? If you do that, I don't have a chance because I'm only in my second year. You've got to judge each individual separately."

"Roger," said Landry, "see me after the meeting."

When the others had left Landry told Staubach, "You've got to understand my feelings about the development of a quarterback. The mental process is very important. A lot of quarterbacks have been ruined and lost their confidence because they've been stuck out there before they were ready, before they had the proper knowledge. You must be able to read and understand the defense and utilize our offense to its fullest potential."

"Coach, I know that, but I feel I can physically make up for any mental shortcomings."

Landry knew Staubach had all the physical tools, was more devoted to the game, and worked harder than any quarterback he'd ever had. But Roger was having trouble reading keys and, at the slightest confusion or provocation, he would tuck the ball and take off running. Outside of Fran Tarkenton, NFL quarterbacks just didn't do that. That left them open for shots by the defense and they just wouldn't last very long. Landry remembered how, in an exhibition game against Baltimore in 1969, Staubach had, in fact, run twelve times for 118 yards and kept the team and the crowd very excited. But he also had thrown four interceptions. When Landry had shown films of the game to his players, they had laughed at Staubach's escapades as a runner, how he'd faked tacklers off their feet, but Landry didn't think it was very funny. He had runners in Calvin Hill and Walt Garrison. He wanted a quarterback.

Logically, Morton should have been ready. He had served his apprenticeship under Meredith for four years, was a classic dropback passer, but injuries had delayed his reaching his potential and, at times, Landry wondered if these had shaken his confidence. Once I cornered Landry and asked him to compare Morton and Meredith and he said:

"Craig takes a more serious approach than Don did to the game. Don had his serious moments but not all the time. Of course, due to injuries, it still hasn't been determined if Craig will be able to perform on a steady keel.

"I think Craig's knowledge of the game is comparable to Don's. In that aspect he was more ready to play after four years than Meredith had been at the same stage. Don didn't apply himself as well as early as Craig has. But of course when Don did start applying himself the last four years of his career he became a fine quarterback.

"Personality-wise, I'd say Craig is somewhere between Meredith and Staubach. He's not in the real serious mold of Staubach but not as loose as Meredith. Before the injury to Craig's shoulder, his arm was very strong and I'm sure it will be again. In those early years with the club I remember he sometimes would throw the ball too hard on short patterns and split a receiver's hands. If he regains the strength in his arm, if it becomes as it once was, he potentially can throw the deep routes and sideline patterns with more force than Don.

"Last year [1969] Craig surprised me a little. He had an excellent knack for calling plays. He moved the plays and the formations around and kept the defense off balance. But . . . nobody works harder than Roger Staubach. He's very rare and, with his maturity, he certainly could challenge, possibly in three years."

The Cowboys opened the season by beating the Eagles but then fell behind the Giants, 10–0, at halftime of the second game. Staubach had not played well and all indications were that Landry would go with Morton. But as the teams were walking to the dressing room at halftime Landry might have been influenced by Staubach's competitiveness. "Coach, I can do it," Staubach told him. "I know I can do it. Please don't take me out in the second half." Landry left him in and Dallas won the game, 28–10, as Rentzel, on a flanker-around pass he had talked Landry into using, pulled up and threw a 48-yard touchdown pass to Hayes, who had entered the game to substitute for Homan.

Against St. Louis the following week Staubach threw two early interceptions to safety Larry Wilson, once badly misreading the defense, and Landry, who all along had wanted to get Morton in there, made his move. When he told Morton to go in, Craig literally jumped into the air on the sidelines and Staubach, his head down, went to a corner of the bench and sat by himself. Dallas lost anyway, 20–6, then beat Atlanta and traveled to Bloomington, Minnesota, to play the Vikings, one of the toughest and strongest NFL teams, but also one which had lost Super Bowl IV to Kansas City, 23–7.

It was the first game the entire season that Dallas had played on natural grass and, after the Cowboys had been destroyed, 54–13, I wrote that the grass had died. Tom Landry said films of the game were X-rated and he wouldn't bother to show them to the team.

"Cornell Green, Lee Roy Jordan and I were tri-captains," recalled center Dave Manders. "After the loss to the Vikings we were meeting on Monday and Coach Landry's opening remark was, 'I knew we weren't ready to play the game by the way our tri-captains came off the field after the coin toss.' I tell you, after that, we literally sprinted off the field after a coin toss."

The Cardinals, tired of playing in the shadow of Dallas, had a tremendous start and brought a 7–1 record into the Cotton Bowl to play

the Cowboys on a featured game of ABC's "Monday Night Football."
Don Meredith, well on his way to becoming a star of the show, would
do the color. The Cowboys, 5–3, apparently had to win to stay in the
race for what was now called the Eastern Division title (the NFL and
AFL each were aligned into three divisions, the Eastern, Central and
Western). It had become obvious by this time that the Cowboys should
start Duane Thomas at halfback. Thomas had ridden the bench early
but, although Hill had started strong, injuries had slowed him down.
In fact, Thomas had led the Cowboys to a 27–16 victory over Super Bowl
champion Kansas City by rushing 20 times for 134 yards and scoring two
touchdowns, one on a 47-yard run in which he had burst through a hole
and outran the secondary. But no one could do anything against the
Cardinals, who beat Dallas for the second time, posting a 38–0 win.

The crowd booed Morton mercilessly and then began to look toward
the broadcast booth and chant, "We want Meredith! We want Meredith!" But Dandy, remembering the same people had done the same
thing to him, said, "No way you're getting me out there."

It was over. The Cowboys, with a 5–4 record, appeared to have lost the
divisional title with five games to play. Landry told the team, "Well, I've
never been through anything like this. It was embarrassing to all of us.
You guys didn't really want to win. Maybe it was my fault. I don't know
but it was the worst performance I've seen."

Ordinarily, the day after a game, the team goes through a light but
formal workout. But Landry said, "Just go out and let's play touch football." It was madness, with centers playing quarterback and tackles playing wide receiver. But soon everybody was laughing and having a good
time, including Landry. To this day, Landry has kept up the practice
of having the touch game.

The team became very loose. One day there was a heavy downpour
before practice. The coaches have designated parking spaces against the
field house but rookie Steve Kiner, feeling he didn't want to get wet,
pulled his 1964 Volkswagen into Landry's parking spot and went inside.
Later, Landry came in soaking wet, looked over at Kiner and said, "I
admire a man with courage."

But amid the light-heartedness, something else was happening. "The
fans, the press, everybody was down on us," said Lee Roy Jordan. "Tom
seemed to indicate to us that if we did anything the rest of the year we'd
have to do it ourselves. So we got together, really got together, and decided everybody was against us and all we had was ourselves. It brought
the team closer together and what happened was one of the most amazing things I've ever experienced in my career." The Dallas Cowboys
turned the season around.

Landry did have one big decision to make. Morton had been feeling the pressure. He could either start calling plays for Craig, taking that burden off him, or turn to Staubach. Many players at the time felt Landry had given up on the team winning a division and had decided to go ahead and give the inexperienced and younger players more work. The fact that he decided to stick with Morton disproved this. But he began calling plays for Craig by shuttling tight ends Pettis Norman and Mike Ditka. Led by Thomas, Dallas stormed the Redskins, 45–21.

The following week the club was hit by another trauma—Lance Rentzel, despondent after the loss to the Cardinals and bothered by personal problems, exposed himself to a ten-year-old girl. The club had kept the news quiet as it prepared for a Thanksgiving Day game against the Packers and had hoped to keep it out of the papers while getting Rentzel psychological help. But the story broke and Rentzel played what turned out to be his final game, a 16–3 victory over Green Bay. His teammates wanted him to continue to play, but Landry, Schramm and Rentzel decided it would be too much pressure on him and the team for him to go on.

Some felt Landry had dealt coldly with the problem but his later comments would indicate otherwise. On one occasion he said to Bill Wiggins, a friend from UT days, who asked about his thoughtfulness, "I'm just very worried about Lance." Another time he said, "My prayer for Lance is that he will find the greatest victory ever, peace of mind."

In spite of the problems Dallas relied on an amazing defensive unit and the running of Duane Thomas to win its final five games, whereas the Cardinals fell apart. Dallas won its division against all odds. The defense didn't allow a touchdown for 23 periods and also was a key factor in breaking the Browns' possessive streak in a 6–2 victory in Cleveland.

Morton was still having trouble but Dallas beat Detroit, 5–0, in the first round of the play-offs and then, with Thomas rushing for 143 yards and Jordan making a key interception to set up a score, defeated Dick Nolan's San Francisco 49ers 17–10 for the NFC title to advance to the Super Bowl V and a meeting with the AFC champion, the Baltimore Colts.

The game on January 17, 1971, was the first Super Bowl in a series played in Miami's Orange Bowl in which Dallas was to have rotten luck. It was a terrible time for Morton. His arm was bothering him, he lost his voice, and *Sports Illustrated* called Dallas the "team without a quarterback." Craig had sought help from a hypnotist and that story also was being whispered around Fort Lauderdale, where the Cowboys were staying for the game. The national press was very critical of Morton, but Thomas, who had yet to withdraw into himself, was very popular and made reflective statements such as, when asked if the Super Bowl was the ultimate, "If it was the ultimate, they wouldn't play it again."

Landry had indicated to his aides, going into the Super Bowl, that he felt Dallas would win a low-scoring game. "We knew we could handle their offense because our defense was just playing so well," he said. "But their defense was the best we'd played against, yet we felt we could put enough points on the board, then hold them and win. Even during the game, with the breaks going against us, there was no time we didn't feel like we were in control, that we would win."

Super Bowl V was a series of freak plays, all of which went against the Cowboys. Dallas led 6–0 as the defense completely destroyed Johnny Unitas, sending him to the bench with an injury after he had completed just three of nine passes and suffered two interceptions. But Baltimore tied the game 6–6 on a fluke play. Unitas had thrown badly for tight end John Mackey up the middle. The ball had been tipped by another Colt receiver. Mel Renfro leaped for the ball and it settled into the hands of a startled Mackey, who raced for a touchdown to complete a 75–yard play. An official said Renfro also had touched the ball. Mel said he had not. If he hadn't, it was an illegal pass and would have had to be called back. However, Dallas took a 13–6 halftime lead and, when the Colts fumbled away the second half kickoff, Landry's team faced a second down at the Colt one, ready to put the game away for all practical purposes. As Thomas fought for the goal line, linebacker Mike Curtis hooked the ball out of his hands. There was a big mix-up and official Jack Fette's view of the ball was obstructed. Actually, as films and still pictures later showed, the ball bounced right to Dallas center Dave Manders who easily recovered. But Colt tackle Billy Ray Smith began shouting "Our ball! Our ball!" and pointing upfield. Fette, under pressure, pointed upfield, too, giving the ball to the Colts. The recovery officially was credited to defensive back Jim Duncan, who was not close enough to have a chance to recover.

Manders actually got up, holding the ball, and handed it to the referee. Landry, seeing what had happened, went some 10 or 15 yards down the sidelines, yelling that Dallas, not Baltimore had recovered.

"We could go ahead at that time 20–6 and, the way we were playing defense, I don't see how they could have caught us," he said.

Colt defensive end Bubba Smith later said, "We ought to give the game ball to Billy Ray. He conned that official right out of the Super Bowl." Billy Ray Smith later was to tell friends that there was no way the Colts recovered. Instead of seven points, three at the very least, Dallas had nothing.

But with the game tied 13–13, Morton was moving the Cowboys in position for what could have been the winning field goal until a holding penalty against Neely, plus a loss, left the Cowboys in a position of second and 35 at their own 27 with 1:09 to play. Morton threw for Danny Reeves downfield. The ball was high but certainly catchable. But it glanced off the fingertips of Reeves and into the arms of Curtis who ran back to the Dallas 28, where moments later Jim O'Brien kicked a 32-yard field goal with five seconds left to give Baltimore a 16–13 victory. When the ball crossed through the uprights Bob Lilly jerked off his helmet and slung it 30 or 40 yards downfield, vividly illustrating the frustration of the Cowboys.

"We're disappointed but not ashamed," said Landry. "You just can't play better defense than we did. Three tipped passes gave them all their points [Mackey's catch, another tipped pass in the Colts' second TD drive and Reeves's tip of Morton's pass]."

There were eleven turnovers in the game and, for the first time a losing player, Chuck Howley, won the MVP award. Most of the writers were saying, with all the turnovers, it was a sloppy game, but Landry noted, "Very few people understand what happened in the game. The reports were colored by writers' preconceived notions. I think it was the greatest Super Bowl game ever played, even though we lost. The close calls the officials were forced to make seemed to work against us. Whether our luck ran out or not, I don't know."

Landry also was later to admit that Manders had, indeed, recovered Thomas's fumble near the goal line. But he realized what a great turnaround the 1970 team, once 5–4 and seeming to be hopelessly out of the championship race, had made.

"The lowest point in the existence of our team came when St. Louis wiped us out that Monday night," Landry explained in recent years. "There had been tremendous pressure on us to win and we had sunk to the depths. But we came back and made it all the way to the Super Bowl. That was due to the character of the players we have and it had a lasting effect, showing future teams that we always could come back during difficult times."

"I think," said Tex Schramm, "that Landry's great strength, along with the great faith we have in him, enabled this team to pull itself off the floor after all those disheartening blows and come back with renewed purpose."

The Cowboys had come back from great adversity and lingering psychological problems to make the Super Bowl. There would be other setbacks the next season but nothing would stand in their way to do even more.

160

12

Tom Landry didn't particularly care for what he had to do but it was a part of his job. He thought about Pettis Norman, not as a number on the football field, but as a man who not only had suffered through the early, frustrating years of the club and certainly contributed to its rise, but also as a worker in the community. He was proud of Pettis and often related in speeches how his tight end had shown the fortitude, drive, and character to work his way up from very humble beginnings to gain a college degree and then become vice-president of a bank in Dallas. Pettis, thought Landry, certainly was an inspiration during times when young people needed someone positive with whom to relate.

Still, the Cowboys were in business, too, the business of winning, and Landry had done what he felt was best for the team. During the summer of 1971 he had okayed a trade which sent Pettis, Tony Liscio and Ron East to San Diego for Lance Alworth, a much needed flanker who could fill the void left by the departure of Lance Rentzel. Rentzel, in a move which Landry felt was best for all concerned, had been traded to Los Angeles for tight end Billy Truax. Dallas already had Mike Ditka at tight end so Norman became expendable.

Landry had been trying to reach Pettis and finally located him by phone at the Oak Cliff State Bank. "Pettis," he said, "this is Coach Landry. I'd like to talk to you."

"Okay, Coach, I'll come right over to your office," said Pettis, who later admitted he felt he had been traded.

"No, that's all right," said Landry. "I'll come to your office."

"That's too far, Coach. I'll just come by to see you."

"I'll be there as soon as I can make the drive."

Landry drove from his North Dallas office to Oak Cliff and told Pettis what he was expecting to hear. He said the Cowboys, as Pettis knew, badly needed a flanker and that to get one he'd had to trade him to the Chargers, a solid team.

"I tell you," said Pettis, "maybe the man isn't very emotional, like they say, but he cares. He certainly cares about you."

Years later, in 1978, Landry traded Golden Richards to Chicago because of the advent of Tony Hill, and Richards was to recall, "He called me into his office and took the time to carefully explain why he'd traded me. He said I was a fine player and didn't believe it would help me, as a former starter, to be a backup. He said I'd be starting in Chicago.

"Sure, I was disappointed leaving Dallas but he was very straightforward in explaining the situation and seemed to have my best interests in mind, too. I had respect for him while I was in Dallas and respect for him after I left."

But in the summer of 1971 the acquisition of Alworth seemed to make the Cowboys a team in place, one which could take that final step in ascending to the National Football League throne, the Super Bowl championship. Yet, Landry would face some serious problems—there were always problems when you were in charge of a group as large as a football team. The most crucial thing Landry would face would be the dark side of Duane Thomas, the rookie sensation of 1970.

They were very different people. Duane had grown up in the black ghetto just a few minutes from the glass and concrete panorama of downtown Dallas. It is a place where you learn survival and, even if you make it and become successful, the underlying bitterness and resentment are often latent but still there. When Duane was a boy he had been shuffled around from relative to relative and could not in any way relate to the consistency and security with which Landry grew up in Mission, Texas.

Duane had problems with agents. When he was drafted by Dallas he'd signed with a group which took more than the usual fee from him and he'd had to come up with $7,500 to buy out of that contract. Then he signed with another agent and still had money problems. He was in debt and needed money desperately. He'd also had a tremendous rookie season and wanted the Cowboys to tear up his original three-year contract and, at least, double his base pay.

Tex Schramm told him no, the Cowboys had not torn up Calvin Hill's contract after he'd been Rookie of the Year and they wouldn't do it for Duane. "But I'm not Calvin Hill," said Duane.

Duane's basic contract, give or take a little, called for base salaries of $18,000, $20,000 and $22,000 over three years. He received a $25,000 bonus for signing and had a number of incentives in his contract. For instance, if he became a starter, he would get an extra $5,000, another $2,500 for making Rookie of the Year and still more if he rushed for 1,000 yards. With his base salary, incentives he reached, and play-off bonuses, he received some $75,000 for his rookie year.

When Schramm wouldn't tear up the old contract, Duane brooded, then became angry and went to visit friends in the Los Angeles area, some of whom had rebelled or dropped out of society and urged him to do the same. He said he wouldn't report to training camp if he didn't get a new contract.

So Duane Thomas wasn't among the veterans reporting to Thousand

Oaks in mid-July; but Calvin Hill looked extremely good and seemed capable of taking up where he'd left off before being hampered by injuries. However, in late July Duane showed up at camp with an unusual friend. The man wore a *dashiki* and said his name was Ali Ha Ka Kabir, although Gil Brandt put his investigators to work and found out the man also was called Mansfield Collins. Duane said he wanted Ali Ha Ka to stay with him in camp and be given a tryout with the team. Again he was refused and, figuratively, retreated once again into the trees.

Still getting a lot of advice, Thomas returned to Dallas where he called a press conference, apparently hoping to gain public sympathy. He rambled a great deal but, basically, demanded an $80,000 base salary, plus incentives; saying Dallas had never made the Super Bowl before he came and would never do so again without him. He indicated he was being treated badly because he was black, and called Landry "a plastic man, actually no man at all," Gil Brandt "a liar" and Tex Schramm "sick, demented and completely dishonest." When we kidded Schramm about what Duane had said about him, Tex grinned and noted, "That's pretty good. He got two out of three."

"Everybody is entitled to his opinion," Landry said. "But I don't notice whether a player is black or white." Later when Landry was asked about Duane and other enemies he had made while coaching, he said, "I don't think I make enemies. I don't consider people enemies and I don't look at them that way. Players are like other people in the way they sometimes react to a situation. They say things on the spur of the moment that many of them usually regret or apologize for later. It's just the nature of the game. I don't think it's a lasting thing. In football you have responsibilities and you have to make decisions that affect people's lives. Therefore, you can't avoid situations where players might dislike you for decisions you had to make. And they might dislike you even though the decision you made might have been the right one."

When it became obvious that, indeed, Duane wasn't going to report, the Cowboys traded him to New England. Schramm, with Landry's consent, sent Duane, offensive lineman Halvor Hagen, and wide receiver Honor Jackson to the Patriots for running back Carl Garrett and a No. 1 draft choice.

Garrett arrived at Thousand Oaks, all smiles. Andy Anderson of the Fort Worth *Press* and I cornered him and he told us, on the record, how glad he was to get away from the offensive line in New England and be able to run behind a fine group like the Cowboys had. Shortly thereafter, the trade was nullified and Garrett had to go back to New England . . . to face the offensive linemen he said he was glad to get away from.

Thomas caused the trade to fall through. When he reported to the

Patriots he would not complete his physical exam, refusing to take the blood test and urinalysis, fanning rumors that he might be on drugs. On the practice field he refused to get in a three-point stance, as suggested by coach John Mazur, saying the Cowboy running backs lined up in a stance with their hands just above their knees. Mazur told him to get off the field. Thomas again disappeared and Landry stopped worrying about the situation, said Calvin Hill was his No. 1 halfback, and went about the business of preparing his football team for the season.

One of Landry's priorities was to settle the No. 1 quarterback issue between Craig Morton and Roger Staubach. After the Super Bowl V loss Landry began to think more seriously that, perhaps, Staubach might indeed be able to do the job and give the Cowboys a winner. In fact, on a charter taking some of the players and their wives from Miami to Dallas after the loss to Baltimore, Landry approached Staubach and said, "I think you can make your move this coming year, if you're ever going to make it." Staubach had indicated if he wasn't given a shot at No. 1 he wanted to be traded. He felt at twenty-nine years of age, he had no more time to waste on the bench.

Morton, coming back from his second straight off-season operation on his throwing arm, was throwing well again. Craig was quietly upset about the situation, recalling how Landry once had handed Meredith the No. 1 quarterback job regardless of what he did. But Craig said if he had to go out and prove again he was the top quarterback he'd do it. There always will be a question as to what Landry might have done had Craig been the winning quarterback in Super Bowl V. Had Dallas beaten Baltimore, there certainly is a possibility that Landry would have left Morton at quarterback and, if he had done so, Staubach would have demanded to be traded.

Landry made plans to let Staubach and Morton play equally during preseason, let them call their own plays, and before the regular season began, he would get with his offensive coaches and evaluate their performances, with the No. 1 job going to the man who had the edge. For Morton and Staubach, preseason wasn't a time to work out the kinks, it was a time to fight for a position.

Both Staubach and Morton, whose arm obviously was as strong as ever, were superb in preseason as the Cowboys won all six games. When it was over Staubach had a slight edge in statistics but Landry also liked some intangible things that Morton had done. Landry wasn't sure what to do. Things were just that close. He made his decision early in the week before the regular season opener and, generally, kept his own counsel about it. Apparently, some of his assistant coaches didn't even know his choice.

He announced it at his weekly press conference.

"When we opened training camp each quarterback had something to accomplish. Morton had taken a lot of criticism last year because he couldn't throw [due to a bad elbow]. He had to reestablish his confidence and I'm very satisfied that he has. On the basis of the confidence he regained and the way he's throwing, his production has been excellent, certainly good enough for us to win. I couldn't be more satisfied with Morton.

"Staubach had to make great strides in experience and know-how to offset Morton's experience. And he has made great strides. He doesn't have Morton's overall grasp but he has enough for us to win. He can read a defense, doesn't scramble as much and shows poise.

"On a competitive basis, Roger has a slight edge in the categories we consider most important. This is not a put-down of Morton but an acknowledgment that Roger is slightly ahead. But he does not have a clear-cut advantage and so this is why we're going with the two-quarterback situation.

"I just feel this is the best thing for the Cowboys at this time. It is, certainly, important we establish a No. 1 quarterback for the future but, at this point, it can't be done because they're so close. So at this time, anyway, we'll go with them on an equal basis. One will start one game and the other, the next one.

"I don't like to do this because I know there will be a lot of criticism and people always will be second-guessing. But it's just something that must be done before we can establish a No. 1 quarterback for the future. Sometimes a quarterback doesn't play well and I'll be criticized but that's just the way things must be at this time."

Other positions had solidified, including Lance Alworth at flanker. Alworth had rib injuries and would miss some early games but it had become obvious that, even at 31, the former AFL all-time great still had a couple of good years left in him. Everyone had marveled at his great concentration when he began to work out in training camp. Landry always had felt that concentration was such a big part of success on the football field.

"Concentration," he once said, "is when you're completely unaware of the crowd, the field, the score, other than how it might affect strategy. You're concerned only with your performance, playing well at your position. Golf is an excellent example of concentration. You see a golfer blow a hole, then bogey the next two holes. You know his concentration has been broken. When my concentration [as a play caller and head coach] isn't broken, I'm never on the defensive. When you start thinking defensively, you think such things as, gee, this field's bad, and we're behind and we're not gonna be in the championship game. It's difficult to recover then.

"Most people don't realize it, but a great measure of a football player is his ability to concentrate. This is why any team in the NFL can win any game if a superior team isn't concentrating, and this is why Vince Lombardi's teams at Green Bay did so well. Lombardi is a driver who keeps his teams concentrating.

"For instance, concentration is what we lacked when we lost to Cleveland in 1968 and 1969. But last year when we made the Super Bowl and had a chance of winning it, we concentrated very well as a team."

Morton started the first regular season game in Buffalo and Staubach opened in Philadelphia, although Craig had to come into the game early in the first half when Staubach was knocked out. Both games were victories and, prior to the third game against Washington, Landry told the players, "We have a two-quarterback system now, as you know, but Craig will start against the Redskins. We need his experience and this is a big game." Landry knew Staubach, who hadn't received equal playing time the first two games, didn't think this was fair but he felt the multiple defenses used by the new Redskin coach George Allen might confuse Staubach. The Redskins won, 21–16, with Staubach coming in near the end and getting the Cowboys a late touchdown.

Landry told Staubach he'd start the following week against the New York Giants in the Cotton Bowl, but something else had happened that took over sports headlines in Dallas. Duane Thomas had quietly reported to the team and begun to go to practice again. Landry wasn't sure when Duane would be ready to play but pointed out it would be sooner than most expected because Duane was such a natural. It came a lot sooner than even Landry imagined. Hill suffered a knee injury against the Giants early in the second half and Thomas entered the game. He had missed all of training camp, all the preseason games and three regular season games. He had worked out only a few times and yet, it was as if he'd never been away. Thomas got the ball nine times and rushed for sixty yards. "Duane," said Landry, "is just an amazing fellow. He is a great natural runner and doesn't make mistakes."

While everybody talked about the unbelievable return of Thomas, Staubach sat in the corner of the dressing room fuming. With Dallas leading just 13–6 at halftime and the offense playing as if it were dreaming, Landry benched Staubach and put in Morton. Knowing how Roger felt, Landry walked over to him after the game but, before he could speak, Staubach said, "Coach, don't say anything. Whatever you say, you'll never understand me. What you just did by pulling me out there wasn't called for. You'll just never understand me."

Meredith would have been hurt in the same situation but would have joked it off. Morton would have felt he'd been unfairly treated but would have remained quiet toward Landry. Craig was that way, suffering in silence. (Pete Gent once called him "Billy Budd.") But the great fire within Staubach, the great restlessness and competitive desire, continually caused him to speak out. Landry liked his fire, felt it could be a positive factor when properly channeled, but he also wished Roger would let him run the quarterback situation without reacting so vocally when a decision went against him. Anyway, Dallas beat the Giants, 20–16.

Morton opened the next week in New Orleans but Dallas, playing badly, got behind and a late Staubach-led rally fell short, 24–14. The Cowboys stood 3–2 and returned home to officially open Texas Stadium October 24 against the New England Patriots, with Carl Garrett and the line from which he said he was glad to get away. Thomas scored the first touchdown on a beautiful, darting, yet fluid run for 57 yards and Dallas won, 44–21.

When Duane had returned to the club the only way he communicated was in his running. He refused to talk to any of the media and almost all his teammates. It was a bad situation which got worse for the Cowboys because of their self-styled sphinx.

Landry had a rule that players had to wear a coat and tie on charter flights. So Thomas would do such things as wear a regular jacket, with his shirt unbuttoned and a tie, untied, thrown over his shoulder. Landry let this ride. Duane also refused to answer roll call, which greatly angered player-coach Danny Reeves. "He sees me, he knows I'm here," said Duane, whose only constant companion was a toboggan cap, pulled down tightly over his head. Landry continually tried to talk to Thomas, to reach him, and when he failed, he tolerated Duane's actions, something he had not done for anybody before.

The players complained about double standards but, in reality, accepted the quirks of Thomas and the tolerance of Landry, as long as Duane helped them win. A split on the team also was developing over the quarterback issue. Both Staubach and Morton had not done badly but each had his followers. Some felt Morton should be in there all the time and others wanted Staubach.

"Sure, some guys wanted one of them and others wanted the other," recalled center Dave Manders. "But I think, mostly, we just wanted one clear-cut No. 1 quarterback."

Over national television Don Meredith said, "It's Landry's responsibility as a head coach to pick a quarterback. Now, after all this time he still has no idea which one is the best. Then get another coach. I'm somewhat disappointed but I'm sure not nearly as disappointed as Morton and Staubach, not to mention the other 38 players who are involved in this wishy-washy decision."

Certainly, the criticism had merit but, at that time, it is far from clear whether Meredith had been feeling some latent bitterness against Landry over the way his career had ended or was simply stating what he believed about the quarterback situation.

Most agreed Landry should choose one or the other, including the majority of the media. The favorite parlor game around Dallas was picking a quarterback and arguing the positives and negatives of each. So Landry added even more fuel to the fire when, prior to the club's trip to Chicago for a game against the Bears, Landry said he would call plays for his team by *shuttling* the quarterbacks, using each one on alternate plays. Secretly, he had felt this was the ideal way to call plays, telling the quarterbacks themselves what the next call would be, but it constituted even more of a robot system and caused even more unrest about the situation. Landry had once used the tactic with Eddie LeBaron and Don Meredith and, later, with Morton and Jerry Rhome when they were rookies. But Staubach and Morton were not rookies and did not like the idea in the least.

"I've decided to alternate our quarterbacks on each play and call those plays myself," Landry told a shocked press. "As long as I'm calling the plays it's much easier for a quarterback to have the play early so he can go to the keys and determine exactly what he's going to do on a particular play in each situation.

"I don't have any reservations about my decision this week. It's a matter of pooling all the information and all the efforts of everybody—quarterbacks, coaches in the press box, me, everybody. I'll catalog the information I receive on the sidelines and decide whether a play is to be used or how to counter a move. I'm usually two, three plays ahead. The quarterbacks will have more time to think exactly what they must do and their alternatives.

"I'm very satisfied with Morton and Staubach. Quarterback has been the strong part of our team. It's just that sometimes a change picks things up. I just felt we must do something and that we needed everything we could possibly muster to beat the Bears."

Again, Landry truly favored the idea, even with dissension mounting around him. And Dallas did, indeed, move the ball extremely well against Chicago, totaling 480 yards on offense. But the club had problems putting the ball across inside the twenty and lost, 23–19, putting itself in a terrible hole with a 4–3 record, somewhat reminiscent of the 5–4 tailspin it had experienced in 1970.

Over the years I developed a theory that Landry, although he certainly preferred winning, wasn't overly concerned if his team didn't play particularly well the first half of the season. At times I had the feeling it didn't really bother him that much if the team was one or two games behind in the divisional race at the halfway mark. When the team didn't play well and got behind midway through the schedule, had its back to the wall, it seemed to get together better psychologically, concentrate more and thus streak the final part of the season. Over the years, Landry often has said that divisional races are won or lost in the final half of the season and that it's impossible for a team to stay at a top-level performance for the entire year. If a team can streak during the final part of the season, reach its peak, then this usually will carry it through the play-offs. Often a team which starts out strong, at its best, tends to trail off at the end, such as the Cowboy teams of 1968 and 1969. Landry could well have learned a lesson from this and since then held his team back, so to speak, the first half of the season. In four of its five appearances in the Super Bowl Dallas had not been in good shape around the midway mark; the team had a 5–4 record in 1970, a 4–3 mark in 1971, a 5–3 record in 1975, and in 1978, with the expanded sixteen-game schedule, was 6–4, and after eight games trailed the Washington Redskins by two full games in the divisional race.

I discussed my theory with one player who agreed: "I think he wants us to play badly at first and get ourselves into a corner because he knows we'll get mad and fight our way out."

And safety Cliff Harris said, "I think the reason we always seem to come on so strong when we get our backs to the wall is that it presents a personal challenge for Coach Landry. He's at his best when he's challenged. Sometimes I don't think he calls as good of a game when we're 9–1 and way ahead of the other teams. He becomes much more conservative."

After the Chicago game Landry, when told that the system of shuttling his quarterbacks hadn't worked, did point out the club had gained more yardage than at any previous time that season. But, he realized in order to quiet things down on the club and in the community, he must pick a No. 1 quarterback.

He spent restless hours trying to do so. Because Landry had turned to Morton during crucial times, many believed Craig would be his choice, although if he felt the team needed a change to play up to its potential, Staubach would be the one. Finally, he reached his decision during the week before the game against the Cardinals in St. Louis. His choice was Roger Staubach. Staubach was a tremendous competitor and also a catalyst, a guy who could turn a game around on individual effort. He might not play according to the book but he had the great ability to find a way to win. Landry felt badly for Morton. He thought about the great disappointment Craig would feel after being groomed all those years to replace Meredith and then having the job go to someone else. But Landry had examined all angles and felt, if, as it had become apparent, a decision must be made, that Staubach would be the one.

"Both quarterbacks have played well," said Landry. "They've been a strong part of our team, which I've said before. But I will go with Roger just in case some of the indecisiveness about the situation is truly upsetting to our team. Roger will make mistakes but I'm confident he'll do the job we need and keep improving."

On Tuesday of that week, Landry phoned Staubach at home and said, "Roger, I've made a decision. I've decided you're going to be the starting quarterback for the rest of the season."

"Coach," said Staubach, "I really appreciate that. I won't let you down."

But Staubach later recalled, "You could tell he felt badly for Craig. I did, too. It's tremendous the way the man came back off those two operations. But I think Coach Landry made sure Craig had every opportunity to keep the number one job."

"Sure, I'm disappointed," said Morton, ever the diplomat. "I'm sure it was a difficult decision for Coach Landry but it's his decision to make. All I can do now is be ready and help the team in any way I can."

Immediately, there were more second-guesses. "I don't second-guess myself," said Landry. "I take all the facts available and make decisions based on what I think is right at the time. I think the real mistake is to look back. It's already done . . . there's not much you can do about it. I'm never one to replay things."

It proved the correct decision. Dallas didn't lose another game that season, although it was hardly smooth sailing. Prior to a crucial game against St. Louis, Landry replaced kicker Mike Clark with the little Austrian Tony Fritsch, who spoke very little English. With the score tied, 13–13, Fritsch lined up for what could be the winning field goal from 26 yards out and less than two minutes to play.

"Look out! Look out, you little *&#*, you're gonna choke," yelled Cardinal linebacker Larry Stallings.

"You're wasting your time," said Cowboy linebacker Dave Edwards, a blocker on the field goal team. "He can't understand a word you say." Fritsch kicked the field goal and Dallas won, 16–13.

The Cowboys beat Philadelphia, 20–7, and headed into Washington for a showdown with the Redskins. But there developed an unexpected hurdle for Landry. Starting tackle Ralph Neely, who had taken up motorcycle riding as a hobby, was in an accident on his bike, suffering a badly broken ankle. Backups Don Talbert and Forrest Gregg also were sidelined and the Cowboys had no one to play left tackle against the Redskins. But Landry had an idea, a far-fetched one, but an idea just the same . . . .

Tony Liscio, since being traded to San Diego, had been in turn shipped to Miami and then retired. He was back in Dallas in the real estate business. The Monday before the Redskin game he answered the phone and, to his surprise, it was Tom Landry.

"Tony, how would you like to play this weekend and block Verlon Biggs for us?"

"Uh . . . Coach, I don't think my legs would hold up. I'm completely out of shape. I . . . ."

"Tony, I think you can do the job and we need you."

"Let me think about it a couple of days."

"Tony, I'll give you thirty minutes. I have to make a decision."

Liscio agreed he'd try and, although he spent many days in the whirlpool, he probably had his best season with the Cowboys and, certainly, was a key factor in the Super Bowl drive.

Dallas beat Washington, 13–0, with Staubach doing the unusual to put the game away. Roger set the club up at the Redskin 29 to run a deep in-route to Alworth, a play Landry had called. But Roger, noticing the left sideline open, tucked the ball and took off on a touchdown run that won the game.

"No," said Landry afterward, "we don't have any plays where Roger is supposed to run. Gosh, he runs enough as it is."

Dallas beat Los Angeles, 28–21, and the following week Calvin Hill was ready to play again. For a long time Landry had envisioned a big backfield, featuring Hill and Thomas. Thomas had played fullback in the past so Landry told backfield coach Danny Reeves to work him there, too, in practice.

"Duane," said Reeves, "we want you to get in some work at fullback this week."

"No, I'm not going to play fullback," said Duane.

"Duane, go ahead," said Staubach.

"You shut up," Duane told him.

But Duane and Hill played in the same backfield as Dallas crushed the New York Jets, 52–10, beat the Giants, 42–14, and finished the regular season with a 31–12 win over the Cardinals in which Hill and Thomas were superb.

Perhaps in earlier years it would have made a difference, but when the Cowboys went to Bloomington, Minnesota, to play the Vikings in the divisional play-offs and found temperatures hovering around ten degrees, they didn't seem to mind. The team had become determined, almost clinical, and crushed the Vikings, 20–9, after taking a 20–5 lead late in the final period.

Dick Nolan's San Francisco 49ers beat the Redskins, the wildcard team, in the other divisional play-off game, 24–20, and moved into the Cotton Bowl to play Dallas once again for the NFC title and a Super Bowl berth.

It would turn out to be the toughest play-off game ever for the Cowboys. Nolan had geared his Flex Defense, a system he'd learned from Landry, to stop Duane Thomas and was very successful, holding him to forty-four yards on fifteen carries. But 49er quarterback John Brodie experienced an off day and made a crucial mistake in the second period, trying to dump off a screen pass deep in San Francisco territory. He failed to see Cowboy defensive end George Andrie, who intercepted and returned nine yards to the 49er two, setting up the Cowboys' first touchdown.

By the final period San Francisco, trailing 7–3, seemed to have regained momentum. Dallas, facing third and seven at its own 27, needed a big play, so Landry called a pass play in which Staubach was supposed to drop the ball off to running back Danny Reeves. A big rush, led by end Cedrick Hardman, was on and as Staubach faded he had little time to do anything but scramble. He ducked a tackler, dodged another one and retreated all the way to his three-yard line before starting back upfield. He ran toward Reeves, who was covered by linebacker Dave Wilcox. Wilcox wasn't sure what to do. If he stayed on Reeves, Staubach would run for the first down; but if he covered Staubach, the quarterback might drop the ball off to Reeves. Wilcox came after Staubach, who passed to Reeves for nine yards and a first down. This was the highlight of an 80-yard drive which won the game for Dallas, 14–3, and put them into Super Bowl VI against AFC champions, the Miami Dolphins.

Landry did not like to see Staubach scrambling, although he never said anything directly to him about it. After the win over the 49ers he did comment, "The big play for us was that third and seven. If Roger hadn't made the first down we would have had to punt and San Francisco could have gotten the ball and won the game." And on Staubach's running, he added, "Roger will keep running until he keeps getting hit and then he'll slow down. The more he learns, the less he'll run."

The attitude of the Cowboys was strange after they had beaten Minnesota and San Francisco. There was no celebration, no cheering in the dressing room. The Cowboys were like surgeons who had just completed a successful major operation. They were deftly clinical. As much as anything the team seemed to reflect Tom Landry. But there were other reasons. From the first day of training camp winning the Super Bowl was the major goal, the only goal. The club didn't think about winning divisional or conference titles because it had done that before, the footsteps already were there. It wasn't interested in just going to the Super Bowl but *only* in winning it. The disappointments, narrow losses, and bad calls by officials would not stand in their way because an almost cold-blooded approach would eliminate variables that had hurt them in the past. They were not emotional on the field and they were not emotional after winning the play-off games.

But Landry never had felt a player should be overly emotional on the field. Once discussing the subject, Landry said, "If you are prepared, then you will be confident and you will do the job. Emotion can cover up a lot of inadequacies but in the end it also gets in the way of performance. An emotional team cannot stay that way consistently over a full season or even a few games.

"Of course, a defensive player is not motivated like an offensive player. An offensive player's motivation may be what he hears, reads or feels. A defensive player has a certain temperament. He faces a challenge and this motivates him accordingly. If he doesn't have this, then he won't be a good defensive player.

"But at these times you don't let the emotional factor overrule your style of play. We play a coordinated, disciplined style so we've had more success with less emotional types of players. Our success proves that you don't have to have a guy who tees off every time the ball is snapped. Nor does it mean the type of player we use is any less motivated to succeed.

"For one thing, I don't believe in team motivation. I believe in getting a team prepared so it knows it will have the necessary confidence when it steps on the field and be prepared to play a good game. Players can sense this and they respond to it.

"It's a long year and there are a lot of highs and lows. Sometimes it's difficult to get ready to play but if they are not ready, they know it. If you can cause them to be ready, and be prepared for all situations they'll have to face, they'll be motivated."

Landry never prepared a team better than he did the Cowboys for Super Bowl VI on January 16, 1972. The club had two weeks in which to get ready, one in Dallas and one in New Orleans, site of the game. Landry worked hard before the club left for New Orleans because he knew that he had to make his plans, solidify them before facing Super Bowl week. There would be too many distractions then. Of course, there was a distraction in Dallas that he hadn't planned on facing. Duane

Thomas didn't show up for a practice session and no one knew where he was. There were rumors that his new advisor, Jim Brown, the former Cleveland Browns' All-Pro, might feel the ultimate in rebellion would be for Duane to skip the Super Bowl game. But Duane, apparently, had been ill or something because he was at practice the following day. He huddled with Landry, who said when questioned, that he had no reason to believe Duane wouldn't play in the Super Bowl.

Landry still had hopes of helping Thomas. He knew that the team needed him and that Duane needed the team whether he knew it or not. The Cowboys had come this far and Landry felt if he could hold things together through the Super Bowl, many problems would solve themselves.

There had been some amusement prior to the game. President Richard Nixon, whom Landry had strongly supported, had suggested plays that might work against Dallas to Washington Redskin coach George Allen. He had strongly recommended a flanker around, which Allen tried against the Cowboys, but it lost yardage. President Nixon also had phoned Miami coach Don Shula and said, "I'm a Washington Redskin fan but I'm a part-time resident of Miami and I've been following the Dolphins real close. I think if you use [Paul] Warfield on down-and-in patterns in the Super Bowl it'll be very successful against the Cowboys."

"I think the President hedged a little on Coach Shula," said Landry. "He gave them a play they've been running all year."

"How can you vote for a guy like that?" I chided Landry, who only smiled and went about his business.

However, before the club boarded a flight for New Orleans Landry received a telegram from former President Lyndon Baines Johnson, who had seen the club beat San Francisco in the NFL title game. In the telegram Johnson said, "My prayers and my presence will be with you in New Orleans, although I have no plans to send in any plays."

"At least," said Landry, "we have one President on our side."

The players boarded the charter and it prepared to take off. They were dressed in suits, sport coats and ties. Finally, Duane got on, wearing his toboggan cap, light jacket and an unfastened tie. The players were glad to see him. They would take him as he was and so would Landry, at least one more time.

There is no place more unlike Tom Landry than New Orleans and yet, it is a place in which Landry has won two Super Bowls and so, although he cannot relate to many aspects of life in that city, some of his fondest memories are there.

Landry gave the team the first night off and most went to the French Quarter but, thereafter, it was all business. Apparently, that first night trouble developed between Walt Garrison and Margene Adkins because, in the dressing room the next day at practice, they exchanged words and a scuffle started. It quickly was broken up but it angered Landry, who told the team, "If something like this happens again or anything else occurs which might disgrace this team I'll fine those involved $5,000."

The team practiced in the afternoon and each night Landry called quarterbacks Roger Staubach and Craig Morton into his room to look at films and go over again the plans already made in Dallas.

"Miami is a zone team," he kept telling them, "and you've got to hit the backs. Notice how the linebackers drop back pretty deep. So this leaves our backs open short. Hit them. Let them make the yardage."

Seven years before Super Bowl VI there had been no Miami Dolphins. But in six seasons the team had made the biggest of games, becoming the youngest franchise ever to do so, even younger than the 1966 Cowboys who had challenged Green Bay for NFL supremacy. The Dolphins reminded one of those 1966 Cowboys, full of young, good talent but without championship experience from which to draw. Certainly, Don Shula's team had not experienced anything like the atmosphere surrounding the Super Bowl game and the pressure it caused.

"Well," said Miami quarterback Bob Griese, "I feel we're even with Dallas. We haven't won a Super Bowl and neither have the Cowboys."

But veteran Herb Adderley, who had been to two Super Bowls with Green Bay and was in his second with the Cowboys, cautioned, "The Dolphins have never known pressure like this week, with all the press around and everything. When you get to the city where the Super Bowl game is held, the atmosphere is so different than in the regular season and it gets worse, the closer you get to the kickoff. We've been here before. Miami hasn't."

Landry had a masterful game plan. He knew that the Dolphins, because they were young, would have trouble coping with his attack.

Larry Csonka and Jim Kiick had had fine seasons running the ball but Landry felt Bob Lilly and the Flex Defense could stop any runners. He worried about Warfield but devised a plan to stop him. At times he would use both cornerback Mel Renfro and strong safety Cornell Green to double Warfield inside out, and at other times, he would let Renfro, one of the league's best athletes, take him man-to-man. Landry also had picked up a consistency pattern. When the wide receiver lined up six or seven yards closer to the ball, it ordinarily meant the Dolphins were going to run. Shula felt the wide receiver could get a better shot at blocking the defensive end or linebacker in close. But Landry wanted his outside linebackers, when the wide receiver came in, to shoot into the Miami backfield.

Offensively, he told Staubach and Morton, he wanted them to throw short into the spaces left vacant by Miami's retreating linebackers. And the key to any running game against Miami, he knew, was neutralizing middle linebacker Nick Buoniconti. Buoniconti was quick and had tremendous pursuit. The Dolphin defensive linemen tried to keep the blockers off him so he would be free to go for the ball-carrier. Landry decided he could counter this, actually take advantage of Buoniconti's aggressiveness in pursuit, by having his running backs—Thomas, Garrison and Calvin Hill—make a false step as though they were going wide and then cut back up the middle. Guards Blaine Nye and John Niland and center Dave Manders (especially Niland and Manders) would contain the defensive tackles at the snap, then slip off their blocks and butt Buoniconti into the direction he'd already started. By the time Buoniconti recovered, the running backs already would be through the hole in the middle he'd vacated. Landry figured Buoniconti would take a step, start toward the outside when the Cowboy running backs made a false move in that direction and, when he would try to come back as they veered back toward the middle, Niland or Manders would be there to hit him.

"The year before," said Ditka, "Craig was having trouble with his arm before we played Baltimore in the Super Bowl and, deep down, I don't think we had any confidence in our game plan as far as our passing was concerned. This wasn't Craig's fault. His arm just was a physical problem. Now we have complete confidence in our game plan, that we'll beat the Dolphins."

Before the game Landry said, "We're just very calm and taking a very businesslike approach to the game. We are not as excited or tense as we were last year when we played the Colts. The players seem to be taking a matter-of-fact approach. But don't misinterpret this. We're up for the game, maybe even more so than last year. It's just that we've been here before [to the Super Bowl]. If we win, you'll see some excitement."

Still, the stigma had hung in the air all week. It was always there, somewhere, although at times obscured by the cool, almost clinical confidence the Cowboys displayed in their preparation. But sometimes people whispered . . . sometimes said aloud, "The Cowboys can't win the Big One." Of course, in 1970 and 1971 they had won many big play-off games to get to the Super Bowl but the label would always be there until they had won it all, taken the National Football League championship.

Yet no ghosts of championship games past so much as crept into the minds of Landry and the Cowboys as they boarded the team buses and joined the early crowds moving slowly toward the early afternoon kickoff in the Sugar Bowl. Landry was very much aware this wasn't the youthful Cowboy team which had submitted to Green Bay on a brisk day in Dallas, nor the team which had lost an Ice Bowl game to the Packers in Green Bay, nor the one which had finally been edged by Baltimore in Super Bowl V. It was a new team, a new dawn and, although he did not admit it until later, Landry knew, just knew, the Cowboys would win. He had never had more confidence in a victory and said, "The team had a chip-on-the-shoulder attitude. The players were very short tempered. They were ready and you knew that they were going to do it."

A couple of days before the Super Bowl rains had fallen on New Orleans in the early morning hours, chilling what had been a sluggish, humid atmosphere. The weatherman had said there was a possibility of rain on game day but the rains never came. On Super Bowl Sunday temperatures stayed in the high 30s, with little wind, and bright sunshine shone on the throngs who converged on the Sugar Bowl like armies of ants.

The game began slowly, as though the teams were two boxers feeling each other out. Staubach's first few passes went high, causing some alarm among Cowboy fans, but Landry had hoped to stay even with the Dolphins the first half and win the game after halftime, that is, unless the Cowboys got a break. On Miami's second possession this happened. Kiick and Csonka had fumbled only once the entire season but Csonka lost the ball and Howley recovered at the Dallas 48. Methodically, Dallas moved to a third and two at the Dolphin two and Landry called a play in which Staubach was supposed to go to tight end Mike Ditka if both the safety and outside linebacker moved toward Thomas, who would swing out of the backfield. Staubach missed the key and threw to Thomas, who was smothered. Mike Clark, who had become the kicker again after an injury to Toni Fritsch, put Dallas on the scoreboard with a nine-yard field goal.

It was only a temporary setback, although Landry did point out to Staubach that both the linebacker and safety had gone with Thomas and thus Ditka was wide open in the end zone, as the play had designed him to be.

Midway through the second period, Landry's plans for Buoniconti began to work and the Cowboy ground game started grinding out the yardage in bursts up the middle. Before the day had ended Thomas, Garrison and Hill would amass a Super Bowl record of 252 net yards rushing and a tremendous 5.3 per try, Thomas would get 95 yards on 19 carries and Garrison 74 yards on 14 carries. Hill, who rushed for 25 yards, explained the situation: "My knee was so sore I couldn't cut

177

sharply but the linemen were doing such a good job on Buoniconti and there were such big holes that anybody could have gotten through."

Dallas controlled the ball a full five minutes before the half and scored as Staubach found Alworth, who cut just inside cornerback Curtis Johnson at the flag for a nine-yard touchdown pass with 1:15 left in the half.

The frustration of Bob Griese and the Miami offense was personified in a play in the first half. Griese was supposed to pass to a wide receiver but saw penetration into the pocket and began to retreat because he knew he wouldn't have time to get the ball off. He kept going backward, then tried to come back upfield. He started one way and then the other but saw his paths cut off by George Andrie and Larry Cole. Finally, Bob Lilly smacked him down for a 29-yard loss.

Just before the half Griese finally found Paul Warfield for a 23-yard pass that set up Garo Yepremian's 31-yard field goal. That would be the only points scored by Miami and also the only big pass Warfield would catch all day as the defensive plan blanketed him with Mel Renfro having one of his best days ever. Outside of the 23-yard completion Warfield would make only three other catches totaling 16 yards.

At halftime Don Shula told his defensive tackles to pinch in closer to the middle, hoping to shut down the freeway that was coming up for the Cowboy runners. Landry, expecting this, told his offense that it would begin running wide in the second half.

On the second half kickoff, Staubach, who would complete twelve of nineteen passes for 119 yards, two touchdowns and receive the game's MVP Award, guided the Cowboys seventy-one yards in eight plays for a touchdown, completely blunting the spirit of the Dolphins.

Buoniconti, a fine linebacker, was still reacting too vigorously and seemed confused from getting batted around by the Cowboys. Once on the sidelines backup linebacker Bob Matheson recalled, "I talked to Nick and told him they were cutting back on us and that was how they were making yardage. But I knew Nick wasn't going to hang back and play the cutback. He goes to where he thinks the point of attack is going to be. That's the kind of player he is and he told me, 'There's no way I'm gonna change my style of play for one game. We have other players out there on defense who can stop that.'"

As the final period began Dallas led 17-3 and Chuck Howley, the team's oldest player at thirty-six, made a tremendous play, again showing why he was one of the game's best linebackers and why Landry, unlike many, preferred the smaller, quicker linebackers to the bigger and stronger ones. Miami faced third and four at its own 49 and Griese attempted to throw to Kiick on the right sideline. Howley had tried to knock down wide receiver Howard Twilley and was on the ground as Griese released the ball to a wide-open Kiick. But Chuck leaped up, intercepted the ball, and ran all the way to the Miami nine before he tripped and fell. Three plays later Staubach threw a seven-yard touchdown pass to Ditka, on the same pass play he'd misread earlier, making the score 24–3 with 11:42 to play. The Cowboys could have scored another touchdown but Hill, diving for the end zone from the one, lost the ball and Miami recovered. It didn't matter. Dallas had left no doubts, no room for second-guessing, by registering the most thorough Super Bowl victory to date.

As the game was ending Craig Morton, the man Landry had benched, walked over to the Cowboy coach, shook his hand and said, "Coach, I'm very happy for you." John Niland and Rayfield Wright raced to Landry and lifted him on their shoulders and began carrying him off the field. Landry broke into the biggest smile anybody could remember and Bob Lilly, who had experienced all the frustrations, jogged to the dressing room and suddenly leaped straight up into the air.

The Cowboy dressing room was bedlam. Lyndon Johnson came in and shook Landry's hand. President Nixon called, said the Cowboys had looked great and the offensive line had done a tremendous job. "Thank you, Mr. President," said Landry. Schramm and Clint Murchison were tossed into the shower.

Jimmy Brown had promised Tom Brookshier that Thomas would talk to him on national television so Duane stepped up onto a makeshift stage in the dressing room as the cameras turned. Brookshier, obviously nervous as he attempted to interview the man who wouldn't talk, said, "Uh, Duane, are you as quick and elusive as you look?"

"Evidently."

"You, uh, your weight seems to fluctuate. You weigh 205 for some games and less for others."

"I weigh what I need to."

"You enjoy football?"

"That's why I'm a pro. It's what I like to do."

Everybody was cheering, howling and, just as Landry had predicted, the emotion came out for the Cowboys after they won the Super Bowl. A great weight had been lifted, a curse had been laid to rest. The Dallas Cowboys, for all to see, had won the biggest game.

January 16, 1972, had been a day of total happiness for Tom Landry and the Dallas Cowboys, a landmark time. Tex Schramm talked about a Cowboy "dynasty" and even Duane Thomas was smiling, forgetting his anger over things real and imagined, the bitterness seemingly gone from his face.

Certainly, the Dallas Cowboys were at the top of the world of pro football and Duane, in only his second year, was being compared to the great runners of all time.

But a key injury and other problems would strike Landry and the Cowboys. It would be four long years before they returned to the Super Bowl and that afternoon of 1972 in New Orleans would be the last hurrah for Duane Thomas.

13

THE 1970s had begun much as the 1960s had ended—with an epidemic of violence and dissent rampant. Arab commandos hijacked three jet planes leaving Europe for the United States, and four students, protesting Vietnam, were killed by National Guardsmen at Kent State. A small, meticulous, polite-speaking young Marine lieutenant named William L. Calley, Jr., was found guilty of premeditated murder in the My Lai massacre, and the face of Charles Manson stared at us from newspapers throughout the country. By mid-decade we would face Watergate and the decline and fall of Richard Nixon, the ascendance of Gerald Ford to the presidency, and 18-year-olds, who had the duty to fight and perhaps die in war, would be given the right to vote. But the pendulum would seem to be swinging back to some of the old American trends and ideals, as well. Americana was in vogue again.

And, of course, in January, 1972, the Dallas Cowboys had finally reached the pinnacle of professional football and won the National Football League title. Tom Landry had taken criticism for some moves he had made and because of his double standard regarding Duane Thomas, although he had held everything together for the championship.

But by the summer of 1972 the Super Bowl championship had died down to a trophy in a glass case and hard, cold type in the record book. Landry had made it clear to his team that the previous season had passed, that times had changed and everybody would be dealt with under the same rules, the same set of standards, including Duane Thomas.

"To me," said center Dave Manders, "the best job Tom ever did was in his handling of Duane Thomas. It was like a powder keg."

"Some of the things that went on in the late 1960s and the Duane

180

Thomas situation went against most anything Tom was brought up to believe," said Tex Schramm. "I tell you, he was more tolerant of Duane than nine-tenths of the coaches would have been. He really made every effort possible to help straighten up Duane. But, in the long run, I think his dealings with Duane also helped him get a broader perspective in his relationship with players in later years."

"It was a unique situation," said Landry. "I varied my treatment toward Duane because I felt I could help him and because of what I felt the other players were thinking. They seemed to be saying, 'Yeah, we'll tolerate something different like that for the best interests of the team.' Winning the Super Bowl that year was our only goal. All of us were willing to put up with anything to achieve that goal. But once we had won the Super Bowl you couldn't expect a team to go through that again.

"It took a team like the Cowboys, who had been through so much adversity, to get through something like that. Adversity is what builds character. If the team hadn't had a great deal of character it would have been 3–11 instead of 11–3.

"I believe in people. My job is more than just winning but also dealing, in a way, with people's lives. My main hope in the Duane Thomas case was that I could have found some way to save an individual. I strongly believed in him and that caused a lot of criticism. But I didn't listen to the critics. I've always tried to take a player who is not of my mold and hope he changes his character or personality. This is because of my background as a Christian. I guess I haven't been very successful because, at times, I really don't believe you can change a person's character. But I'm always willing to try because I know the only One who can change a person's character is Jesus Christ. As coaches, we're really not successful in changing character, just in molding it. Heaven knows, I've tried hard with a lot of players, probably at my own expense as a coach.

"I try to understand. I've spent long hours in conversation with players, trying to show them why they're moving in the direction they're heading and what they must do to move in the direction they really, down deep, want to go. Ultimately, all of us want to get to the same place—but some have a misconception of how to get there. I try to get them to think in the right direction. I guess any success I have usually comes later, after they're finished with football and look back."

"Tom Landry is the only coach who got two consecutive great seasons out of Duane Thomas and Lance Rentzel," said Red Hickey. "That has to tell you something about the man's great patience and understanding. Maybe it doesn't show to the general public, but it's there."

The end came for Duane Thomas in training camp, 1972. When he reported he had become a vegetarian and often he'd only check in at meals, then grab a few pieces of fruit and go back to his room. He went by the rules but walked a thin line. Duane got through the Cowboys' 20-7 victory over the College All-Stars but didn't look very good. He seemed weak but it was a long preseason and everybody felt he'd come around.

Then one day in camp Thomas missed a meeting and failed to show up for practice. Assistant coach Ray Renfro went to his room. Duane refused to talk to him. Finally, Landry went to Thomas's room.

"Duane, this is Coach Landry. Are you in there?"

"Yeah, can I help you?"

"Well, yes, you weren't at practice."

"Like, uh, I didn't feel like it."

Landry then went into Thomas's room and they talked. When Landry emerged his face seemed even more stern and determined as he walked from the players' dorm to the one which housed the coaches and officials. Landry found Tex Schramm and said, "That's it. Trade him."

That year the Cowboys had hired Sid Gillman, the longtime San Diego Charger coach who was considered somewhat of an offensive wizard in his own right. At San Diego, Gillman had two young players he felt could be outstanding, running back Mike Montgomery and wide receiver Billy Parks. Schramm made a deal to send Thomas to the Chargers for this pair.

Landry felt he had to explain the Thomas situation to the team and said, "Last night we traded Duane Thomas to San Diego for Billy Parks and Mike Montgomery. I talked to Duane for hours, telling him what he must do to become a part of society, of our team. I took him each step of the way and I felt he was making progress. But then he missed the morning meeting and the afternoon workout. I went to see him in his room to find out the causes. He told me he wasn't paid to attend meetings. He said he was paid to play on Sunday. I told Duane that he had to follow certain rules to be a part of the team and he refused. I had no choice but to trade him."

Thomas was active for only one game for the Chargers, when they played the Dallas Cowboys. In pregame warm-ups he went to the end zone, put his hands on his knees and stood there for fifteen minutes, looking at the ground. He wandered around, stared at the crowd, sat alone on the bench. He didn't play.

Duane ended up with the Washington Redskins in 1973 and 1974, playing as a backup to Larry Brown. Sometimes he would show spurts of his old self but never consistently. In the two years with the Redskins he gained about half as much yardage rushing as he had his rookie season with Dallas. In 1975 he went with the World Football League and played for awhile in Hawaii but the league folded. And in the great irony of ironies, he talked to Landry and asked him to give him a chance to play in 1976.

"He was very cordial," said Landry. "Duane, I believe, is a good man and if he can return to the running and pass-catching form he showed when he was with us before, we certainly can use him."

"A man grows," said Duane. "I have grown. I made mistakes. I feel I've learned the things necessary to move ahead now."

Everyone pulled for Duane when he came back, although the coaches said quietly that he had lost the speed he once had. Landry indicated Duane would have to adjust his running style, that the game had changed now and a runner, when challenged, had to duck his head and butt for the extra yardage. Duane missed much of training camp with a pulled hamstring. He didn't make it. He was cut at the end of preseason, 1976. As he left the Cowboy locker room for the last time he shook hands with Landry and they wished each other well. When last heard of, Duane was trying out with the Green Bay Packers for the 1979 season, at 32 years of age.

After Dallas beat the College All-Stars in preseason and was edged by the Houston Oilers, 26-24, the team went to play its third exhibition game in the LA Coliseum against the Los Angeles Rams. The game didn't count, but what happened in it would change the entire season and, once again, cause the quarterback job to be up for grabs in 1972.

It was uncharacteristically warm for an August night in Southern California but a shirt-sleeve crowd of 80,000 didn't mind. As usual the Cowboys had their own fans. A large group had come from Thousand Oaks, the team's home away from home, to watch the annual game. With the score tied 3-3 the Cowboys had driven to a third and nine at the Los Angeles 12. Roger Staubach faded to pass, ducked under a rusher, saw an opening and took off for the goal line. Middle linebacker Marlin McKeever came over to cut him off but, instead of stepping out of bounds or falling after making the first down, Staubach ducked his head like a fullback and tried to ram through McKeever, who met him head-on. There was a bone-rattling collision and, before Staubach ever hit the ground, he felt a burning sensation in his right shoulder. As he got up he had no control over his right arm. He trotted off the field. His right shoulder was badly separated and would require surgery. He was through. Landry felt bad about Staubach but was thankful he still had Craig Morton, who had been relegated to the No. 2 quarterback job.

183

Morton stepped in and did a good job for the Cowboys, although the drive, the fire that had taken the club to two straight Super Bowls, was missing from some elements of the club. Landry had cautioned the team that once it had achieved its goal, the championship, a natural let-down would follow. "It's an unconscious, relaxation-type thing," he said. "You really aren't aware that it's happening but it kind of creeps in and you let up a little. The teams in the NFL are so close that, when you do that, somebody can move ahead of you."

The letup wasn't Morton's fault. He wasn't as mobile as Staubach and thus couldn't come out of the pocket and run for third-down yardage, but he had a good year. However, there were problems among the wide receivers.

Gillman was right about Parks; he had a lot of talent. But Billy was a very sensitive, idealistic guy who was strongly liberal. Sometimes he just didn't have the gut feeling, the competitive instinct for football. For instance, sometimes he'd become moody because he started in place of Alworth, whom he liked. Billy was supposed to open the Green Bay game but said he didn't feel like playing because his friend, Tody Smith, had been deactivated. Before another game when a special pregame program was held in which Melvin Laird, secretary of the Navy, inducted recruits, Billy, anti-Vietnam and antimilitary, had to be restrained in the ramp as the club prepared to go onto the field. Sometimes he wouldn't practice, standing around complaining of a pulled hamstring. Landry took note of all this; Parks would be gone before the next season.

Landry began to use Alworth mostly as a blocker and Hayes, sidelined with injury problems, dropped some crucial passes when he returned, so Morton just stopped looking for him. Craig's favorite target became another newcomer, Ron Sellers, who had come from New England for a draft choice. Sellers made some big plays on passes from Morton and so he was the one Craig wanted to throw to in crucial situations.

Part of the problem with the wide receivers was Landry's fault. He continually changed his wide receivers, using all four, which led to the discontent of all. Hayes, who made a career low of fifteen catches in 1972 with no touchdowns, said, "Everybody is wrong sometimes and Tom was wrong in his handling of the receivers. All of us were messed up that year. You never knew if you were going to play or not."

"I never could settle that situation," admitted Landry.

But something else also was happening and a statement Landry made, perhaps, was a foreboding of what would happen to Bobby Hayes, who once had been the most feared receiver in the NFL. With his speed, he could outrun defenders on deep routes.

"Wide receivers," said Landry, "must be different than they were three, four years ago when their job was to beat a guy man-to-man and catch the ball. The game has changed. Now outside receivers must contribute to the success of the team in any way they can. They have to block. They have to catch the ball in a crowd. There's no place now for an end just running patterns and beating his man. The thing I want at the position of wide receiver now are men who'll do anything to help us move the football."

The situation at wide receiver definitely hurt the club. Gillman kept plugging for Parks. Alworth, certainly one of the best ever at catching the ball in his prime, didn't like the idea of becoming mostly a blocker. Hayes was most unhappy and vocal about it and Morton wanted Sellers in the game.

But the running game did not suffer with the loss of Thomas. In 1972 Calvin Hill became the first Cowboy ever to go over 1,000 yards rushing and Walt Garrison would exceed 1,000 yards running and catching the football. "Hill and Thomas are different type runners," said Landry. "But Hill gives us the same kind of production as Thomas. No, we don't lose anything with Calvin in there. And Garrison is just one of the toughest players I've seen. I've watched him play outstanding games when other players as banged up wouldn't even go onto the field."

So, although the offense wasn't what it had been in 1971, it was still more than adequate. Oddly enough, the club began to have defensive troubles and ended up allowing 240 points, the most since 1967. Bob Lilly suffered leg and back problems and did not play as he had in previous years. Mel Renfro had foot troubles and Landry became so displeased with the overall play of Herb Adderley that he replaced him in the starting lineup with Charlie Waters, a natural safety who did not have the necessary tools, such as speed and acceleration, to play cornerback.

Time, simply, had caught up with Adderley, one of the all-time greats. Herb was a big play man, not particularly noted for his tackling ability. When he stopped making the big plays, the big interceptions, Landry felt he had to replace him. Waters was extremely smart and a good tackler. Sometimes Waters would get beat because he didn't have the physical assets to run with the faster and quicker wide receivers, but he also came up with big plays, leading the club with six interceptions, one of which he ran back fifty-six yards and another he returned for a touchdown.

However, Adderley was a very popular player and when he was replaced it angered some of the Cowboys. And there also were problems among the assistant coaches. Landry gave Gillman the added duties of running the offensive backfield and, in effect, took that assignment away from Dan Reeves, making him a backup quarterback after Staubach's injury. Reeves didn't like Gillman, feeling that Sid had come in and tried to force his ways on everybody when the Cowboys had been getting along fine doing things the way they were.

In spite of everything Dallas and Washington stayed in a close battle for the NFC Eastern title. In the first meeting between the two clubs in RFK Stadium the Cowboys had the Redskins down, 20–7, in the third period, only to lose, 24–20, when Hill dropped a touchdown pass and Chuck Howley missed Larry Brown on a blitz to allow the Redskin running back to go thirty-four yards for a score.

The worst defeat suffered by Dallas came at the hands of the San Francisco 49ers, who again were winning the NFC West under Dick Nolan. On Thanksgiving Day, the 49ers beat Dallas, 31–10, causing Landry to tell the team:

"It's just pitiful that you'd go out and play a game like that. I tell you, I'm just not built like that. I've got too much pride to sit back and be humiliated like that. When you lose like that the only thing I know to do is work harder. Heckfire, we're right in the middle of a championship drive and we're playing like a second division team. You've got to work and you've got to fight for what you get. We're not doing anything. I guarantee you that's going to change. Anybody in here who is not prepared to fight and work with everything he's got for three more weeks can leave right now. I'll be more than happy to put his name on the reserve list for the remainder of the season. I don't need you. Look, one of the big difficulties in life is to become a man. I've seen thirty-five-year-old men who are still children. Some of us make it, some of us don't. It's going to take men to win the championship."

Landry came up with a new tactic to beat Washington in the second meeting between the two clubs. As usual, Alworth would start in motion or line up wide. But on a running play to his side, or the side in which he was going, Lance would come back toward the middle and, from the side, block linebacker Jack Pardee, who was so unaccustomed to this happening from a wide receiver that he had problems all afternoon. Dallas won, 34–24, and after the game George Allen and Pardee both claimed Landry had used an illegal crackback block. But this was the usual smoke screen Allen threw up after a defeat because the block was legal. Actually, Redskin wide receiver Charlie Taylor had cracked back on Chuck Howley from behind, tearing up the veteran linebacker's knee, in a much more questionable block.

The Cowboys finished the regular season by losing 20–3 to the New York Giants. Washington won the NFC Eastern title but Dallas made the play-offs as a wildcard and had to go to San Francisco to play the

49ers in the first round of the play-offs. This time, Nolan believed he had it. Dallas was at full strength. Staubach, who had started throwing again nine weeks after his shoulder operation, only had about 90 percent of the strength back in his throwing arm but, in a pinch, Landry could use him.

Landry felt the play-offs were a new season for Dallas, that as long as you made them you had a chance. Some believed Landry had pushed for too many changes too soon. Others reasoned that he had replaced aging starters just in time. But when the team went to San Francisco there were nine new starters from the Super Bowl championship club. Morton had replaced Staubach and Hill was in for Thomas. Alworth and Hayes were relegated to part-time duty, dividing time with Parks and Sellers. Tony Liscio had retired, leaving left tackle to Ralph Neely. Defensively, Lilly had so many injury problems that he'd only make a token start in a game, then retire to the sidelines, being replaced by Bill Gregory. Waters had moved in for Adderley and D. D. Lewis had replaced the injured Chuck Howley.

And, after being in and out in 1971, Toni Fritsch had replaced Mike Clark once and for all as the Cowboy kicker. Toni was in his second year and still having problems with the English language but, as Pat Toomay recalled in his book, *The Crunch,* everybody pitched in and tried to help. The coaches once were trying to get Toni to learn how to make an onside kick.

"Toni," said Dan Reeves, "I want you kick onside kick. Okay."

He got a blank stare from Fritsch. "Toni," continued Reeves, "Onnsidddeeee kick. Onnnnnside kick."

Nothing. So Ernie Stautner came over. "Ve vant jew keeeek onside keeek." Nothing. Blank stare. Finally, Landry walked over to Fritsch, his face very deadpan, and said, "Toneeeee, weeeee waaaaaant youuuuuu toooo keeeeeek ooooooonsiiiiide keeeek."

Anyway, Fritsch obviously got the message as he would so well display in the play-off game against San Francisco.

As he often does, Landry got Billy Zeoli to give the devotional the morning of the 49er game, which was held in Candlestick Park two days before Christmas, 1972. Zeoli's topic was, "Never Give Up."

Landry had worried about the Cowboys' inconsistency throughout the season and this seemed to crystallize as San Francisco held a 21–6 lead late in the second period. Morton had been having his problems but found Alworth for a 28-yard touchdown pass which at least put Dallas back into the game by halftime, 21–13. When Hill lost a fumble at the Dallas one-yard line in the third period, the 49ers went ahead 28–13 and all seemed lost. The Cowboys were just floundering around.

"I had stuck with Morton because we were beating ourselves," said Landry. "I had just felt we'd start clicking sooner or later. But when the trend continued near the end of the third period I felt our only chance was to change the mood of the game. Roger has a way of turning things around so I sent him in, although I knew our chances were extremely slim."

Staubach entered the game with 1:48 remaining in the third period and also had his problems. Certainly, the game seemed lost as the Cowboys set up at their own 45-yard line with 1:53 left.

"Hey, now you guys know how it feels to lose a game like this!" yelled 49er linebacker Dave Wilcox, a veteran of the frustration Dallas had caused the 49ers in two previous NFC play-off games.

But Staubach got hot against an all-out rush. He hit three passes in a row and Dallas had a first down at the 49er 20-yard line. Staubach had been calling his own plays during the two-minute offense but time-out was called and on the sidelines Landry told him, "The post to Billy Parks will be open. Let's use that."

Landry knew that cornerback Bruce Taylor sometimes bit to the outside, so Parks made his move downfield, then turned back inside and took a 20-yard touchdown pass to put Dallas 28–23 with just 1:10 left. All the 49ers had to do was get the ball and run out the clock.

"Our hopes were very slim," said Landry. "Everybody in the park knew we'd have to try an onside kick. You just don't expect what took place to happen."

Nolan inserted all his receivers and running backs on the front line for the kickoff. They were more used to handling the ball and, unlike linemen, weren't apt to fumble it. Fritsch, just before he nudged the ball, slung his right foot behind his left to kick the ball in a most surprising and unorthodox manner. Still, it rolled the necessary ten yards to wide receiver Preston Riley, who grabbed it. But as he was falling Cowboy rookie linebacker Ralph Coleman hit him and the ball spurted loose. Mel Renfro recovered at midfield for the Cowboys.

"When this happened," said Landry, "I felt it must be our day. The 49ers knew we had to pass but they were revolving their defenses to the weakside and, because of the nature of the defense, we knew our wing [flanker Parks] would be open. And, of course, Roger will surprise you at times."

And he did. On first down, with just 1:03 left to play, Staubach faded but didn't even look for a receiver. He took off running and made a nice 30-yard gain to the 29-yard line. Then, as Landry had told him, he found the wing, Parks, open for nineteen yards. Parks took the ball and stepped out of bounds at the 49er ten, stopping the clock.

On the sidelines Landry again talked about going to Parks. But, as the huddle broke on the field, Ron Sellers, a wide receiver who came in at tight end on passing situations in the game, told Staubach that he would be open on a hook route, a pattern in which he ran straight upfield, then turned and came back for the ball. The 49ers had an all-out blitz and Staubach had no time to look for Parks. He remembered what Sellers had said and then threw the ball toward him. Ron turned, the ball arrived, and he caught it for a touchdown. Unbelievably, Dallas had scored two touchdowns in the final 1:10 and beaten the 49ers, 30–28, to move again into the NFC title game, this time against the Redskins, who had beaten Central Division champion Green Bay.

"That was one of the greatest moments in our history," said Landry. "I've never seen our team so excited. Everybody was doing crazy things on the sidelines. Larry Cole was turning cartwheels.

"I've watched this game a long time and I know anything can happen. But I guess the win over the 49ers is the one I'll remember most."

It would remain so until the 1975 play-off against Minnesota when something even more miraculous would happen. But that comeback against the 49ers in 1972 would overshadow and even diminish the great frustration of the NFC title game the next week in Washington.

Hindsight is a great advantage, but it could well have been that Landry made a mistake by starting Staubach against the Redskins. After all, he had sat out most of the season. Roger had been tremendous in the comeback against San Francisco but would be rusty against Washington. Under the circumstances, Morton had played the entire year and would have been more ready to play against the Redskins. But, again, that is hindsight, and Landry and all of us at that time were caught up in what Staubach had accomplished and he was the odds-on favorite to start.

Dallas played Washington on Sunday and Landry didn't announce his decision until Thursday. He called Morton and Staubach over after practice and said, "Craig, you've performed well all year. You put us into the play-offs. But I've decided to go with Roger, which is certainly no reflection on you.

"The primary reason is that Roger brought us into this game. I saw us put things together in those last few minutes of the 49er game like we haven't all season. I believe we have momentum going now. If what I saw was right, then Roger will continue this trend against the Redskins."

He was wrong. Allen had the Redskins sky-high, at an emotional peak. Landry had planned to beat them with a running game but the

Redskins shut it off. Staubach was off target; Billy Parks, who had been up and down, was confused over the formations and, as Roger later said, "Billy sometimes was running pass routes in never-never land." The Redskins destroyed Dallas, 26–3, the worst defeat an Allen team had ever handed the Cowboys. Unlike his handling of Morton the week before, Landry left Staubach in until the finish.

"I left Roger in because we didn't move the ball at all," explained Landry. "If we had been in a different situation, moving the ball but having the breaks go against us, I would have put Morton in. Roger didn't have a good game. But under similar circumstances I'd go with him again."

Dallas had made the NFC title game again in spite of all the injuries but, after winning a Super Bowl, even this was considered a disappointment, a failure, so during the off-season there was discontent among the players and also on the coaching staff.

Nobody really knew how much Danny Reeves had been stewing until he quit Landry's staff after the 1972 season. The previous year he had been angry about the Duane Thomas situation and the way Landry had let Thomas get away with not answering the roll call, handled by Reeves. Danny also had been forced to alter his approach as the offensive backfield coach. He'd usually asked questions of the offensive backs during meetings but had to stop this because Thomas refused to take part. Landry and most of the players tolerated Thomas, but Reeves was very angry.

Then he became bitter when Sid Gillman came in 1972. Gillman had been hired as a special assistant to work with Ermal Allen in the scouting and research department, but when Sid took on assistant coaching duties, Reeves was vocal about his feelings.

Dan, then only 28, badly wanted a head coaching job but when his name came up in regard to the vacancy at Southern Methodist University, Landry told him frankly that he didn't think he was ready or mature enough to assume the job. Reeves had also heard that Landry had expressed the same feelings to SMU people, which he later found out wasn't true.

Danny quit and went into the real estate business. He had been a big star in the Cowboy organization until bad knees forced him into part-time duty as a player and he had become the youngest assistant in the league. Everybody talked about what a bright future he had but it seemed to be pointed in other directions. In an interview with Sam Blair of the Dallas *Morning News,* Reeves was very outspoken about

Landry, although this must be put into the perspective of the times. George Allen had just unseated the Cowboys in the NFC East and taken the Redskins to the Super Bowl to play Don Shula's Miami Dolphins. Allen had traded away the Redskins' future by giving up draft choices for older players and paying them more money than they ever had made. This worked for awhile but in the later 1970s Allen's empire would crumble. He would be hired by the Los Angeles Rams, then be fired after the preseason. To this day, the Redskins are still trying to overcome the loss of draft choices Allen swapped away.

"Dealing with people is the toughest thing in coaching," said Reeves in the interview. "Don Shula and George Allen have been highly successful and to me that is the main reason. They're players' coaches. They're not management coaches. Whatever the players want, they try to get it for them. That's the biggest thing with the Cowboys. They're not player-oriented. They're management-oriented.

"Today you've got to appreciate the players' problems, look at them intelligently and come up with the answers. You've got to really know people to be a real success. These guys are aware of what's going on in society and they don't want to be considered different from anybody else.

"You've got to be able to motivate them. You say, well, they ought to motivate themselves. But you've got to give them a purpose for playing. You say they ought to play for the Super Bowl. Well, the Cowboys have won the Super Bowl. You've got to make them want to play for a certain reason, and, last year in particular, we didn't have that. I think that comes right down from the top.

"Coach Landry is a genius in the football knowledge he has. But he never has had the outward personality that makes a person feel close to him. I guarantee you that with 100 percent of our players, if they had a personal problem, Coach Landry is the last guy in the world they would go to.

"But I guarantee you if one of Washington's players had a problem, he'd feel close enough to George Allen to talk to him. Understand, our players respect Coach Landry. He's a genius as far as football is concerned. But I don't think he handles people the way they should have been handled the last couple of years.

"He just never has people's feelings in mind. When he does something, it's strictly a business proposition. He does what he thinks best, no matter what people's feelings are. If he would just go a little bit out of his way to explain things, it would be a . . . lot clearer. It's not that he doesn't care. It's just that it slips his mind that he could make a decision that could hurt your feelings."

191

Reeves was right and wrong. At times, Landry had very much considered people's feelings in moves he made. In the case of Roger Staubach and Craig Morton he probably did so to the extent that it delayed his decision on which one was to be No. 1. Certainly, he went out of his way for Duane Thomas, and Lance Rentzel and when a player such as Pettis Norman was traded. But in other ways he had not, including when he benched Herb Adderley, a very popular player. The players felt an explanation was due and Landry gave them none. Others felt they were slighted, or dealt with coldly, such as the four wide receivers shuffled around in 1972. But, in Landry's defense, if he tried to deal with the feelings of each person there would have had to be three days in each twenty-four hours.

When Reeves's duties changed from coaching to becoming a backup quarterback in 1972, Pat Toomay observed in his book, *The Crunch,* "The last thing Landry wants on his staff is a young, bright coach with ideas. Reeves is benefiting accordingly."

Of course, Toomay had no way of knowing that Landry would rehire Reeves in 1974 as coach of the special teams. Danny would then move up the ladder and, in recent years, he has become offensive coordinator. Landry recommended him for the Atlanta, Los Angeles and New York Giants head coaching jobs. Danny could have had the Falcon job but turned it down and Leamon Bennett was hired. He lost the LA job to George Allen and the Giants job after the Super Bowl in 1979 to Ray Perkins. Landry told Reeves he felt he was mature enough, ready for a head coaching job, which doubtless will come. In fact, many believe Reeves one day will be the man to replace Landry as head coach of the Dallas Cowboys.

Certainly, Reeves appears almost certain to be the second man (Dick Nolan was the first) to become a head coach out of Landry's staff. But considering the great success Dallas has had, and the large number of assistants from other successful teams who have secured head coaching jobs, the Cowboy record is poor.

"Sometimes," Landry pointed out during Super Bowl XIII, "I think we tend to overplay our organization and not look specifically at the people who contribute. Our overall success is based on good organization but those who contributed to that often were overlooked. Sometimes this is true of our assistant coaches. Maybe people outside look at me too much and not them, but they deserve the credit. I'd hate to lose any of them to head coaching jobs but I hope I do. There is no doubt they're capable."

Over the years there has been a somewhat guarded criticism of Landry by some of his assistants, who feel that he doesn't delegate enough authority to them. Certainly, they in no way have the authority that Landry had as the defensive coach for the New York Giants. He called all the shots for the Giants' defense, made the game plans, judged the personnel, had sole authority.

"When I was with him he left me alone with the defense," recalled Nolan. "I thought that trend would continue after I left but it hasn't particularly happened. Now, I suppose, Ernie [Stautner] pretty much calls the shots for the defense but Landry stays close. I think the reason he left me alone is that we were together with the Giants and I already had been schooled in what he was trying to do."

Landry is a dominant figure who likes to make final decisions regarding almost all aspects of coaching and, although in recent years he has delegated authority more, his dominance, even subconsciously, has moved assistants even more into the background.

"The thing about Tom," said Ed Hughes, who replaced Landry at cornerback for the Giants and later was an assistant for the Cowboys, "is that he does dominate an organization because few people know as much about the game as he does. He just dominates an atmosphere.

"You give him ideas and sometimes he'll accept them and sometimes he won't. Once I was teaching something and Landry said it was in the playbook another way. I was a little embarrassed but he came up to me and said, 'Ed, I'm sorry. I have a bad habit of doing that.'"

"Sure, you'd like to have more authority," said Gene Stallings, former head coach at Texas A&M who joined Landry's staff in 1972, "but it's the team Tom built. And when things go wrong he's the one who gets criticized. He's the one under all the pressure."

"He's changed a lot over the years," said Reeves. "He's more relaxed. I'll argue with him about something and he'll listen to my side of it. But once he makes up his mind, it's set. He's not opposed to making changes, like putting in the Spread Formation in 1975. I think he's more flexible than he's ever been, which [he smiles] isn't too flexible."

"Tom doesn't lose too many assistants," said Nolan. "It's a great learning experience for an assistant to work under him. He just knows more football than anybody. And you look how stable his staff is and so you have to figure most of them remain pretty happy there."

Raymond Berry left or was asked to leave Landry's staff after two years (1968–69). The reason given was that he wanted more time to pursue a film he was making on receiving. Due to the two men's strong religious convictions, many felt Landry and Berry would form a long relationship, but there is also some indication that Berry was too stubborn and strong-willed to work out on Landry's staff. Ray Renfro and Bobby Franklin were allowed to resign after the 1973 season. Both were fine men but Renfro, a top coach, had personal problems which had begun to detract from his job, and Franklin had problems in the Landry system.

Landry never tries to force his religious feelings on his assistants. But, as with the players, he never tries to hide his beliefs.

Red Hickey, who became a scout for the Cowboys in 1966, recalled when Landry hired him as an assistant coach in 1964 that Tom told him, "Red, I want you to know that the main thing in my life is my religion. Then comes my family and then football. That's the way I live. I'm not expecting my coaches to live that way. I don't tell them how to live their lives. But I want them to know how I feel.

"You have an excellent background in the league [as head coach of the San Francisco 49ers] and if you don't like something you see in our playbook, please mention it to me. Depending on how I feel, we will or will not change it."

"I always was a very emotional type guy," said Hickey. "I remember once in practice Bobby Hayes kept missing something and I yelled at him. Tom quietly came up to me and said, 'He'll get it right, Red. Just be patient. He'll get it.'"

Not only with his players but also with his younger assistant coaches Landry sometimes has to come to grips with the more lax (at least on the surface) sexual standards. In recent years a young assistant took his girl friend, whom he later was to marry, on a road trip to Houston. Landry tried not to become involved but did tell the assistant he didn't think he should be doing that until they were married. He did not tell the guy he couldn't do it but the hint was enough.

On the current staff Jim Myers and Ermal Allen have been with Landry since 1962. Jerry Tubbs, who came to Dallas as a player in 1960, became a full-time assistant in 1968. Stautner joined Landry in 1966 and Mike Ditka in 1973, after retiring as an active player. Bob Ward, the conditioning coach, came in 1977 and trainer Don Cochran has been with the team since 1965. Assistant trainer Ken Locker has been with Dallas since 1973 and equipment manager Buck Buchanan, since 1973.

And, of course, Reeves has been with the club since 1965 as a player, a player-coach and a full-time assistant, except for the season in which he quit, 1973.

In 1973 there was a great unrest over the Dallas Cowboys, an air of uncertainty. Sid Gillman had left for Houston, where he took over the Oiler organization, and Danny Reeves had resigned to go into the real estate business. Ron Sellers, the club's leading receiver, had been traded for a Miami Dolphin backup receiver named Otto Stowe. Nobody could understand this but the Cowboy staff said Stowe was faster, could block better, and had the potential to become one of the top receivers in the NFL. Billy Parks and Tody Smith, the somewhat abortive No. 1 draft pick in 1971, had been traded to Houston for a No. 1 draft pick, which in 1974 would be Ed (Too Tall) Jones. Chuck Howley, George Andrie, Lance Alworth and Mike Ditka had retired. The club had brought in good young talent, drafting Robert Newhouse and Jean Fugett in 1972, then Billy Joe DuPree, Golden Richards, and Harvey Martin in 1973. Dallas had also signed an unknown free agent named Drew Pearson, but it would be difficult to replace those who had departed.

Bob Lilly, Lee Roy Jordan and Dave Manders vocally expressed unhappiness over the way the club dealt financially with the players. Of course, they had heard of the huge salaries George Allen was paying. But when camp started Jordan showed up, unsigned and mad, and proceeded to have the best season he ever had with the Cowboys. Lilly jumped on a plane to training camp but was so unhappy about the state of the club that when he got to Los Angeles International Airport he turned around and went back to Dallas. Tex Schramm immediately went after him and talked him into coming back. When training camp opened, Craig Morton, who again was supposed to battle Roger Staubach for the No. 1 quarterback job, walked out of camp over contract problems and didn't return until just before the first preseason game.

Manders retired and the club's snapping of the ball on extra points and field goals became something out of the Keystone Kops.

"I live in crisis," said Landry. "I face it as I see it."

A friend of Clint Murchison phoned Manders with an idea for the Cowboy owner's birthday party. Everybody was aware of the awful problem the team was having on snaps and so the guy asked Dave if he'd hide inside a giant box, all wrapped up as a present. The box arrived and out popped Manders dressed up in a tux. Everybody laughed. At the party, Landry walked over to Manders grinning and said, "I thought you retired." However, Manders returned to snap the ball after the first regular season game.

We were calling training camp "The Shambles" that summer, as Landry was becoming very upset about the way things were going and the way some of the Cowboys had played the previous year. As a player, Landry hadn't had the speed or quickness to play cornerback in the NFL but was successful because of his great dedication and hard work. This dedication and hard work carried over into his coaching career, so he found it difficult to truly understand those who wouldn't give 100 percent.

"Basically, we had the talent and skill to get into the championship last year," he said. "Once you have this, it is only a matter of dedication and persistence to win the Super Bowl. These things we lacked. That's one of the main things about winning the Super Bowl. It's your goal, you struggle for years to reach it, then react in one of two ways. For us, there were a certain number of players who came back just as hard to try to win it again. Others looked at that ring on their finger and thought it was the ultimate.

"That sort of thing takes the edge from their play. They're no longer dedicated and persistent. They turn their interests in other directions. When that happens, you're no longer a Super Bowl team. And last year [1972], that's what I saw take place. . . . Individuals make the difference. Either you're satisfied or you're not. A man must dedicate himself to a goal. He won't be a success in pro football unless he persists toward that goal. If you don't do it, somebody else will and you'll watch the Super Bowl on television.

"I see a number of players I can go with to win the Super Bowl. But we can't do it with twenty. It takes forty. We had twenty in last year's NFC championship game against Washington. There are players I know will win again. But there are players who haven't proved to me yet that they can help win a Super Bowl. I want to see some evidence, not conversation. I want to see some work being done, some enthusiasm.

"There is a possibility that some people here have achieved their goals in pro football and started looking elsewhere. Then they lose their capability as a contributing force toward winning a Super Bowl.

"Me? I'm always positive. I know we're going to do it again. I know we'll be back in the Super Bowl. If not this year, then the next or the next. That's my goal and my ambition. All my moves are made according to that."

Landry again had said preseason would determine whether Craig Morton or Roger Staubach would start. Staubach had led the team to the championship in 1971 and Morton had done a good job after Staubach's injury in 1972. This time, Landry reasoned, the question would be settled once and for all. I believe by 1973 Landry actually preferred Staubach as his quarterback but wanted to make sure Morton had an equal chance to win the job.

Staubach finished preseason with an edge in statistics but Morton came on strong in the final exhibition game against Miami and some broadcasters had mistakenly said Craig had won the job.

Landry met with Roger and went over the positive and negative points he felt Staubach possessed and then asked him how he felt about the situation.

"Coach, I've given this all a lot of thought," said Staubach. "I think you need to make a decision and stick by it. If you aren't going to start me I want to be traded. If I have any choice in that matter I'd prefer you trade me to Atlanta."

"You're going to be the starter," said Landry.

Landry asked Morton to come to his home that same night and, as he had with Staubach, went over what he felt were the positives and negatives. He told Morton he appreciated what he had done but that he was going with Staubach. For the first time, Morton said, "I want to be traded." But this would not happen until mid-season 1974.

For the second time (the first was 1971) Staubach led the NFL in passing and Calvin Hill again rushed for over 1,000 yards, gaining 1,142 for a 4.2 average per rush, and also led the club in receiving with 32 catches for 290 yards. Stowe was an immediate star at flanker and D. D. Lewis, who had been waiting in the wings for five years, did a good job replacing Howley.

Again, it was Dallas and Washington in a dogfight for the NFC Eastern title. The Cowboys won their first three games, including a victory over New Orleans in the second contest which marked Landry's one hundredth win.

"It's very difficult for someone in our field who's lost a head coaching job to get another one, like in baseball or even in college football. There seems to be a stigma that goes with nonsuccess. A lot of good men with head coaching potential are destroyed in poor situations. They couldn't display their talents, were fired, and never came back.

"The significance for me to have 100 victories is that I've been able to stay as a head coach so long. I've been very fortunate in working for good management," said Landry.

In the first showdown meeting Dallas was outplaying Washington but led just 7–0 at halftime after Toni Fritsch missed two field goals. After being hit, Staubach was a little fuzzy in the head and Landry replaced him with Morton. The Redskins rallied for two fourth period touchdowns, one an interception of a Morton pass which Brig Owens ran back twenty-six yards for a score, giving the Redskins a 14–7 victory.

Dallas then lost two of its next three, including a 37–31 defeat at the hands of the Rams in which Harold Jackson, a 9.2 sprinter, caught touchdown passes from John Hadl of 63, 67, 17 and 36 yards and made another 44-yard catch to set up a field goal. Charlie Waters, the man Landry had asked to try to play cornerback, took most of the blame.

197

The team lost Otto Stowe, who broke his foot in the eighth game of the season and then his backup, Mike Montgomery, also was injured. Landry put Drew Pearson, the rookie free agent, into the lineup and he turned out to be the best one of all. He played as though he'd always been there, and was to become an All-Pro.

After Dallas lost 14-7 to Miami on Thanksgiving, Landry called Staubach into his office for a conference. Landry knew that Staubach was troubled about his mother, who was slowly dying from cancer. He had allowed Staubach to call his own plays but told him, "Your play calling has been good but we haven't won the close games and seem to be missing some big plays. So I've decided to call the plays again. We'll shuttle our tight ends, Billy Joe DuPree and Jean Fugett." When the press questioned him about the actions, Landry said, "In no way do I mean to imply Roger isn't capable of calling the plays. He's as capable of doing it as anybody in the league and has done a good job. I just feel if we pool all our resources we'll be better off. I think my calling the plays is the best way for us to go." Landry has been calling the plays ever since. At that time Landry, at Roger's request, didn't mention to the press the illness of Staubach's mother. It wouldn't be given to the press until she died prior to the final regular season game in St. Louis.

As Dallas prepared to host Washington in the next to the last regular season game, one which likely would decide the NFC Eastern title, Landry, who, as many of us, isn't above a misnomer, was talking about the aggressiveness of Redskins' cornerback Pat Fischer. "Now," Landry told the team, "when he starts his carousement. . . ." He paused, seemed puzzled, and said, "Where did I get carousement?" Somebody said, "You mean harassment, Coach." And Landry continued, "When he starts his harassment. . . ."

Dallas crushed the Redskins 27–7, then beat the Cardinals in the final week 30–3 to win the East, and would host the LA Rams in a rematch in Texas Stadium during the first round of the play-offs.

Dallas jumped out in front of the Rams by 17–0, taking advantage of an interception and a fumble recovery. Staubach was shaken up and Landry kept asking him, "Are you clear? Is your head clear?" Staubach would say he was fine, then sneak off and hit the smelling salts. The Rams came back to trail by one, 17–16, and Dallas lost Calvin Hill with a badly dislocated elbow. But Staubach and Drew Pearson won the game, combining on an 83–yard touchdown pass on third and 14. The final score was 27–16 and Dallas, once again, moved into the NFC title game, a step away from the Super Bowl. This time the Cowboys hosted Minnesota, which had beaten Washington, the wildcard team, in the other play-off game.

Without Hill and with Garrison trying to play with a broken clavicle, Dallas operated far below par. Staubach also had his problems, suffering through what was perhaps his worst game. He was intercepted four times, although two were not particularly his fault, and passed for only 89 yards. Fran Tarkenton led the Vikings to a 27–10 victory as the Cowboy offense managed just nine first downs. Viking coach Bud Grant said he thought the Cowboys were just too battle-weary, having played so many "must" games to beat out Washington for the divisional title. But Dallas had missed the Super Bowl by one step again. Minnesota played Miami in SB VIII, losing 24–7. The Dolphins, after being thoroughly beaten by Dallas in Super Bowl V, joined Green Bay in having won two Super Bowl games.

On Monday, December 31, the day after the Viking loss, the Cowboy offices in Expressway Towers were almost empty. Tex Schramm stood by the window behind his desk and said, no, he wasn't going to jump but added, "You know after we beat Los Angeles in the first game of the play-offs, the Rams left town feeling bad. But they came a long way to get to the play-offs and I bet by the time their team charter landed in LA they'd started talking about what a fine season they'd had.

"It's not that way for us. We've won the Super Bowl. So when you fail to do so again there's a great disappointment. It lingers."

Down the hall I found the coaches' offices completely empty, except for one man, Tom Landry. He sat alone behind his desk and smiled as I walked in. Again, watching him, I was reminded that Landry is the pillar of the Cowboy organization at such times. When I asked him what was going through his mind he said, "I was just sitting here trying to analyze what happened to us. I still feel very, very disappointed. I had hoped we'd play better. That's the biggest disappointment . . . that we didn't play a better game against the Vikings.

"But I was thinking, too, that this has been an excellent year for us. We had all the problems going into camp but the players did such a great job and played so well to win a number of key games down the stretch. So, it's just a shame that it had to end this way because that's what people tend to remember—the way something ended.

"You can't take anything away from the Vikings. I've been looking at the films. They were razor sharp, like we were in our last game against Washington. When two good teams go into a game evenly matched and one has that slight mental edge, it tends to dominate. The play-offs usually have been that way. The Vikings have a lot of older players and maybe they feel this might be their last chance. I just know I've never seen the Vikings play any better. Their offensive line was really firing out of there and the front four on defense reacted so quickly. I saw Carl Eller [defensive end] blocked out once and he reacted so quickly he got right back into the play."

Landry said how proud he was of Garrison, who played with a lot of pain, and how, although Staubach didn't have a particularly good game, there were a lot of contributing factors. "I just feel proud of this team," he added. "It tried. The Vikings were just better on this particular day. But . . . it's been a good year for us."

I told him I had to go and asked him if he were leaving. "No," he said, "I'm going to sit here for awhile." He seemed so very alone.

14

Not since the early days of the Dallas Cowboy franchise had Tom Landry entered a season that was more out of focus than in 1974. Dallas, again, had been close to returning to the Super Bowl the previous year and Landry felt good, had begun to see the positive signs which he felt necessary to produce a winner. Oh, he was mildly concerned about age creeping into his defensive unit because Bob Lilly was 35, Cornell Green, 34, Lee Roy Jordan, 33 and, before the season was over, Mel Renfro would be 34 and Dave Edwards, 35. But he felt they could hang on for another season. However, Landry had not expected to see his best laid plans go up in smoke due to circumstances far beyond his control. First, the World Football League swept through NFL cities much like the proverbial headless horseman on a fire-breathing horse. And then the squabble between the National Football League Players Association and NFL Management Council became so heated that the entire preseason schedule was threatened and, perhaps, it might even get worse. To a lesser extent there also had been some drastic rule changes, which would alter some time-tested stratagems.

To slow down the trend toward defensive domination and add more scoring to the game, the Rules Committee had passed legislation to help the offensive team get better field position. Kickoffs would be made from the 35-yard line, not the 40, and players, with the exception of two outside men, had to stay on the line of scrimmage until a punt actually was kicked. Field goals tried outside the 20 would be brought back to the line of scrimmage if missed, which encouraged more gambling. Holding penalties would be reduced to ten yards and defensive backs were allowed to bump a receiver only once. But each team faced this and each team equally would be affected by a possible NFLPA strike, so although these things bothered Landry, he felt nobody could get an unfair advantage. The thing that hurt was the World Football League. Once, when asked what he would do if the veterans didn't show up for preseason, Landry said, "Then we'll play with rookies." But the World Football League did especially hurt.

At first nobody took the WFL seriously. Unlike the old American Football League, the new organization lacked the big money men, such as the Hunts, Hiltons and Adamses. Yet, with some money and sleight of hand, the WFL became, for awhile, a reality. The NFL began to take it seriously when all WFL teams chipped in to sign Larry Csonka, Jim Kiick and Paul Warfield of the World Champion Miami Dolphins. Soon, it became obvious that the brains of the league were pointing their guns at two of the NFL's better clubs, Miami and Dallas. While it played hit and miss with other clubs, the WFL clubs signed to future contracts from Dallas Calvin Hill, Craig Morton, Otto Stowe, Pat Toomay, Mike Montgomery, Jethro Pugh, Rayfield Wright, D. D. Lewis and Danny White, the Cowboys' third-round draft pick in 1974 after Ed (Too Tall) Jones and Charles Young. Some, such as Hill, had one year remaining on their contracts with Dallas and others, two. Thus was created the Lame Duck player, a term which Landry didn't like but found very appropriate.

The way it turned out, only Hill and White would have their contracts honored by the WFL, but the disruption and distraction of the signings was evident. Hill had phoned Landry, telling him that he was considering joining the WFL. They discussed the situation and indications were that Calvin would consider both sides. However, it was later learned that before Hill phoned Landry a possible cover shot already had been taken for *Sports Illustrated* in which Calvin posed in a WFL uniform.

Those who signed claimed they, as professionals, would play just as hard during their Lame Duck seasons and most of their teammates seemed to agree. However, Landry did not:

"When they signed with the WFL it created an almost impossible situation from my standpoint," he said. "As a team sport we must have a joint effort in a championship drive. There can be no doubts about any player putting out everything he has. Every player must be rewarded if we win, or suffer if we lose.

"I just don't believe the players who signed future contracts will suffer if we lose. They'll be rewarded regardless."

Landry, of course, came up in a generation of football players who had great loyalty to their teams and, for a time, it was difficult for him to relate to a player who would go elsewhere for more money. But finally, in later years, he began to understand better that security for oneself and one's family often takes the place of loyalty.

Although he diplomatically remained neutral over the NFLPA–NFLMC problems, I think he also grew impatient, deep down, with the players who agreed to strike. I think he was too fair a man to hold it against them but, again, it was something those in his generation would not have thought about doing. The NFLPA was good to the extent that it certainly gained the players better benefits, but difficult in that it unleashed some militant elements who sought to become the all-powerful dragon they were trying to strike down.

In 1974 players boycotted training camps and wore T-shirts which said, "No Freedom, No Football," and showed the figure of a clenched fist, the sign of revolution. Indeed, for awhile, there was no football. The College All-Star game was canceled. The veterans finally reported late and the strike ended August 14, but rookies did have to play the early preseason games.

Landry's patience was running thin by the time the veterans got to camp. So he not only extended the length of camp but for awhile instituted, in effect, three-a-day workouts. He had players up before breakfast, running the trail leading up the mountain behind the practice field. The veterans were calling it the "Ho Chi Minh Trail." Then there would be midmorning and midafternoon practices. The players continually complained of fatigue as Landry kept training camp open for eight weeks, trying to get the veterans through two full-scale weeks of workouts despite the strike and the fact they were already playing preseason games.

The strange case of Otto Stowe emerged, which was slightly reminiscent of the fall of Duane Thomas, in that Landry reached the end of his patience and told him to leave camp. Otto was coming off a broken foot, injured at mid-season the previous year. Assistant coaches told Landry that Otto, a WFL defector, was not attempting to get into condition and that they could not tolerate his attitude. Some of Stowe's teammates agreed. Some did not. Otto said his foot still was bothering him but doctors said it would be a little sore and that it was something he'd just have to work through. He was not on the team's injured list but suited up for practice, became very moody and participated very little. Landry decided he had to go.

Landry was very blunt in his evaluation. "He doesn't seem happy any place," said Landry. "He won't be happy in the WFL either. When he wasn't happy in Miami, it was because he wasn't starting. He was starting in Dallas and he wasn't happy because he felt he wasn't making enough money."

Stowe never actually played in the WFL and, as far as I know, never played professional football again.

The team then lost Toni Fritsch, who tore up a knee in the pre-season game against New Orleans, and this caused a long procession of kickers to come and go before Dallas finally settled on Efren Herrera, a free agent who had been cut by other teams. Things had been so bad that when Herrera joined the team for the Minnesota game and kicked an extra point, fans in Texas Stadium stood up and cheered.

Roger Staubach had problems much of the season, mostly due to a slow start. He underwent surgery on his foot during the off-season, slowing down his usually avid conditioning program and then in an early preseason game he suffered cracked ribs. Dallas won the first regular season game in Atlanta, 20–0, but then lost four in a row as Staubach suffered nine interceptions. He'd gone through the entire 1971 season throwing only three interceptions.

Dallas was in a position to win all the games, losing by narrow margins games that could have been won. The Cowboys dropped their games, 13–10 to Philadelphia, 14–6 to New York, 23–21 to Minnesota and 31–28 to St. Louis. Many felt the Viking game typified the tailspin. It could have been, with a victory, a pivotal point to turn the season around.

Dallas had fallen behind 20–7 after three periods, but came alive on a touchdown pass from Staubach to Walt Garrison and an eight-yard touchdown run by Calvin Hill, giving the Cowboys a 21–20 lead. With just over two minutes left Fran Tarkenton began to rally the Vikings. However, on one play, Tarkenton faded to pass and was smacked hard by second-year defensive end Harvey Martin. Pictures showed the ball popping loose as he was going down and Dallas recovering. However, an official ruled the ball was dead, that Tarkenton already had been down when he fumbled. With new life, Tarkenton finished taking his team 68 yards to the Cowboy's 10-yard line where Fred Cox attempted a 27-yard field goal with seconds left. The kick was not true, going off the right side of Cox's foot, and the ball seemed to sail directly over the upright, neither inside nor outside. After a pause, back judge Stan Javie signaled the kick was good.

Landry later said the field goal was very questionable and that Tarkenton had, indeed, lost the fumble but he also added, "If we'd been playing football as we should have, we wouldn't be in a position where a call settles a game."

Landry, and the entire team, became terribly frustrated with the continual plague of narrow losses. Once on the sidelines when a call went against Dallas, Landry yelled at an official, "Dammit, watch the play!" Then he paused, thought about the situation for a minute and turned to Danny Reeves. "Did I say what I thought I said?" he asked. Told that, indeed, he had, Landry sighed and started watching the game again.

"That," said Lee Roy Jordan, "is about the extent of Tom's profanity. But, listen, he gets as upset and excited as the rest of us. He's just not as verbal. You can look at him and see agony or joy on his face, if you know how to read him. If we thought he was throwing tantrums and screaming, we might lose control ourselves. He projects confidence, poise and composure to us. It doesn't bother us that he's not always yelling or patting somebody on the back."

But if Landry ever had cause to show agony or mutter mild profanity on the sidelines, it was in 1974.

In late October, just before the halfway mark or seventh game in the season, Craig Morton forced the issue. He demanded to be traded and failed to show up at practice. Dallas swapped him to the New York Giants, its opponent that week, and Craig actually was able to play, although Dallas won, 21–7. After losing four straight, the Cowboys won four straight, dropped a crucial 28–21 game to the Redskins, beat Houston, 10–0, and then hosted the Redskins in Texas Stadium on Thanksgiving Day in what turned out to be the highlight of a dismal year.

At that time Dallas stood 6–5 with only extremely slim chances to make the play-offs. With the Cowboys trailing 16–3, Staubach was hit and knocked out on his feet, and had to leave the game with 9:57 left to play. Clint Longley, the free-spirited rookie from Abilene Christian College, had not played a down since preseason but had been moved up to the No. 2 quarterback job when Craig Morton had forced a trade. He had to go in . . . nobody else was left.

"The plays we set up against Washington were good, sound plays," said Landry. "But there was a great deal of tension among our regulars and Roger was not sharp. He wasn't seeing the plays. When Clint went in, he wasn't even concerned about keying the defense. All he was doing was fading and hitting a receiver he saw open. It just so happened that Washington was in a prevent defense a lot of the time and keying wasn't that important. If the Redskins had played all types of defenses, Clint would have had to key and this would have been difficult for him."

Longley's performance has been called a victory for the uncluttered mind. He was magnificent, passing the Redskins silly. But his performance seemed to have fallen short as Dallas set up at midfield trailing 23–17, and facing second and ten with 35 seconds left in the game and no time-outs. George Allen had employed his Nickle Defense in which an extra back, Ken Stone, replaced a linebacker, Harold McLinton. Teams had completed only about 20 percent of their passes against this particular defense, which had five defensive backs, and nobody in memory had gotten behind it.

"We knew we couldn't get behind them so we figured to hit a play across, underneath the zone," said Landry, "and, hopefully, Drew [Pearson] could outrun it, maybe split it because they were doubling him inside out."

But unbeknownst to Landry, Pearson was working a little strategy with Longley on his own. "I'm going to fake inside and then go deep," Pearson told Longley. Landry recalled, "Drew obviously had felt he could start in and the inside guy would be waiting. Then he felt he might turn back and go deep when the back switched back on him. What happened was just amazing."

Pearson did fake inside and cut back deep. Ken Stone took the fake and let Drew get behind him and the Cowboy receiver then got into a foot race with Ken and Mike Bass for the goal line. Longley hung the ball out there and, in a final burst of speed, Drew got a step behind the two defenders and took the pass for a touchdown. Dallas had won, 24–23.

"We couldn't hit the long bomb but we did," said Landry. "Nobody on our team could believe it and the shock of winning was a tremendous thing. It was the highlight of the season."

Longley, a free spirit who liked fast cars and boats and had a hobby of wearing twin six-shooters and hunting rattlesnakes, backed up again in 1975, but his attitude changed during training camp of 1976. Danny White had come to the club that year, after the WFL folded, and was battling Longley for the No. 2 spot. One day during training camp Longley and Staubach exchanged heated words and met after practice. Longley threw the first punch, then Staubach was all over him and had him on the ground, with the option of pounding away, when Danny Reeves raced over and broke up the fight.

Landry told them in no uncertain terms that any recurrence would cost them more money than anybody had been fined before and things seemed to quiet down. But Longley was still simmering when he read in the newspapers that Staubach had bested him. Finally, one afternoon he waited in the locker room as Staubach came in to dress for practice. When Roger was putting on his shoulder pads Longley busted him, knocking him up against a weight scale, gashing his face. While Staubach was trying to get his pads off so he could fight back, Randy White, a rookie, grabbed Longley and held him. While Roger was being treated, Clint left the locker room and hurried to the dorm, where he got a ride into Los Angeles. After being treated in the hospital Staubach came back looking for Clint. But Longley was gone and his days with the Cowboys were over. Under the circumstances Landry decided to trade him to San Diego. Clint played there for awhile but his career didn't last long and, at last count, he was out of the NFL.

But Clint Longley was a highlight of a dismal 1974 season in which Dallas, losing the close ones, finished with an 8–6 record and failed to make the play-offs for the first time since 1966.

The team had age problems and the prognosticators forecast the Cowboys would be like the New York Giants, the Green Bay Packers and the Baltimore Colts; after being on top for a long time these teams slumped and fell to the bottom of the NFL as their stars aged. But to paraphrase Mark Twain, the news of the Cowboys' death was greatly exaggerated.

It seemed unusual, really. The Dallas Cowboys had dropped back into the pack and were faced with crucial retirements and the loss of defectors to the WFL such as Calvin Hill, the heart of the running game, and yet, during the off-season Tom Landry seemed very loose. He had more bounce in his step, seemed to be joking and talking more and, generally, was more relaxed than he had been in years. Landry appeared to be a man who knew a great secret nobody else knew. But what was exciting him was the great challenge of rebuilding a championship team, of beginning to reshape the Dallas Cowboys. Great teams before Dallas had fallen and taken four, five years to again become a winner, if they ever did at all. However, Landry is at his best when challenged because he becomes more innovative, unlocking secrets in his mind that perhaps he'd never have looked for when the club was stronger.

"When he's faced with a big challenge, then you really see his great competitive spirit come out," defensive lineman Larry Cole observed. "It's interesting to see the fighter in him emerge. He's smiling more, mainly having fun in a competitive way. He loves it."

Before the 1975 season began John Niland, an All-Pro guard during the Super Bowl years who had not played as well in 1974, asked Tom and Alicia over for dinner.

"When he accepted I was shocked," said Niland. "But then I got to thinking that Tom probably was receptive to such things, but none of the players ever thought to ask him. My wife, Iree, likes to be innovative for such occasions, so she decided to have Chinese food, decorations and even use chopsticks to eat.

"I can still see Tom sitting at the end of the table trying to eat with chopsticks."

Landry would try to hold the food with the chopsticks and then it would drop back onto the plate before he could get it to his mouth. But he kept trying to get the knack of it. Here was an extremely intelligent man, an intellect, but he couldn't solve the mystery of the chopsticks and finally asked for a fork.

Before the 1975 season began Landry asked Niland to come to his office. "John," said Landry, "these things are extremely difficult to do but . . . we've traded you to Philadelphia."

"Coach, listen, I fully understand," said Niland. They talked for a while and as John started to leave he said, "You *really* didn't like that meal, did you?" Landry seemed puzzled at first and then they both laughed. "I really respect and love that guy," said Niland, now retired and in business in Dallas.

During training camp Landry also dealt Bobby Hayes to San Francisco. Hayes was in the twilight of his career and had lost his starting job in 1974 to Golden Richards. However, during the off-season Landry had said he felt Bobby could have one more surge. Bobby left the Cowboys feeling he'd been treated unfairly by Landry. He played for Dick Nolan in San Francisco for a while but early in the season was placed on waivers and not claimed. In 1979 when Hayes went to trial and pleaded guilty to selling drugs, Landry came to court as a character witness. He said Bobby was a fine man but was easily misled, and that he hoped the court would be lenient on him.

Walt Garrison tore up a knee bulldogging during the off-season, and decided to retire. Cornell Green went through part of camp and then ended his career and joined the club's scouting department. Charlie Waters became the starting strong safety, a much more natural position for him, and was an immediate success, becoming one of the very best at the position in the NFL. Calvin Hill, who had in consecutive years gained 1,036, 1,142 and 844 yards rushing, departed for the WFL's franchise in Hawaii.

But the most significant retirement was that of Bob Lilly, the brightest of the Dallas Cowboys stars. Landry called Lilly a player who comes along once in a coach's career and the best defensive tackle he'd ever seen play the game.

Lee Roy Jordan recalled how Landry always seemed to have praise for Lilly during the Monday film sessions, which most of the players feared. Landry has been known to embarrass players during such sessions.

"It was always like Tom really got psyched up for the film sessions," said Jordan. "But, man, you'd sit there and it would be Lilly-this and Lilly-that, what a great play Bob had made here and another one there. Bob, of course, *was* a great player but sometimes you wanted to say, hey, we were out there, too."

"That Lilly," recalled Dave Manders, "he always sat right next to the projector, which was buzzing right along. After we'd played an awful game, Tom would be pretty critical of us and Lilly would just talk right back to him. I thought, this really is Lilly's team. Then one time it occurred to all of us that, because Lilly was sitting next to the projector, Tom couldn't hear a word he said."

"There have been some really great people on this team," Landry recently reflected. "For instance, Bob Lilly. What a great guy. I think I'd really have liked to have gotten closer to Lilly, become friends, but sometimes you just can't do that when you're a coach."

"Tom Landry," said Lilly, "is a fine man, a very high caliber person and he did an awful lot for me. But I don't think anyone really knows him personally, except his family. We respect him an awful lot but don't really know him.

"Tom never interfered with the way we lived our lives and I assume he doesn't want anyone to interfere with the way he lives his. He lives his life the way he sees it.

"I do think he's been a tremendous influence on certain individuals and strongly contributed to the good, clean, wholesome image of the Dallas Cowboys.

"Tom is a very complex person. He doesn't mince a lot of words. He didn't inherit the gift of gab, like Vince Lombardi. He has strong points and they easily outweigh his weaknesses, which I don't think he has many of. I think probably one is lack of communication. That's a vital part but he seems to overcome it with hard work. He does get his point across.

"No, I wouldn't say I ever got to really know Tom. Again, I have tremendous respect for him. And I just know he's a fine person. We've talked a few times but basically it's been about business. There hasn't been a lot of association outside of football. He has been concerned when things have happened to me down the line. So I know he's very concerned about individuals on the team and their children.

"I guess a man today in business can't get too involved in the personal lives of his employees. Things are so darned complex."

For the first time in ten years nobody really expected the Dallas Cowboys to be a championship contender in 1975 and, as Landry said, "The pressure's off. Nobody will be picking us to do anything. They'll be talking about how we're on the way down. A lot of negative things will be said. They'll say we're leveling off, that other top teams before us went down and now so will we. We'll just have to fight to prove we're not going down and I'm personally very excited about the reshaping of this football team."

Landry had a new toy. He had given a great deal of thought to ways to combat the popular new trend in pass defenses, used by Dallas and others, in which one or two extra backs enter the game, replacing linebackers or linemen on obvious passing situations. The extra backs made defenses more difficult to read and Landry also was concerned with the fact that Roger Staubach had been trapped ninety times in the past two seasons. Landry did not come up with something new . . . he came up with something old, the Spread Formation.

Landry reasoned that when you face a second and long, a third and long, your opponents know you are going to pass, so why not just go ahead and line up in a passing formation, such as the Spread. By lining up five yards back of the center, Staubach would have more time to see what was happening, to read the pass coverages. The formation also spread out the defenses because of the positions of the receivers.

Landry had used the formation briefly in the early years but Red Hickey employed both the Spread, more of a passing formation, and the Shotgun, a running formation, when he was head coach of the San Francisco 49ers in 1960.

There were a number of chuckles around the league when Dallas unveiled the formation as part of its offensive arsenal in preseason, but the formation was to leave the people who were laughing behind.

Dallas needed more than a new formation. With retirements and defections, the Cowboys were a team with tired blood. The draft looked good but even Landry had no idea just how good it would be and the effect the newcomers would have on the team. Dallas had fine drafts before but the 1975 group was the best in the club's history and one of the best ever in the league. Landry had been pleased with the work of Gil Brandt and his scouting department before but he never was more happy than with the group which came to training camp that year.

They were Landry's kind of football players. Often during camp he would remark that they were the hardest-hitting bunch he'd had.

"When they scrimmage or have contact drills, you can hear the pads popping all the way to the other end of the practice field," said Landry.

An unbelievable number of rookies, twelve, made the team and would be called "The Dirty Dozen." It wasn't just their physical presence that helped the club, but also the new spirit they brought. They were Randy White, Thomas Henderson, Burton Lawless, Bob Breunig, Pat Donovan, Randy Hughes, Kyle Davis, Rolly Woolsey, Mike Hegman, Mitch Hoopes, Herb Scott and Scott Laidlaw. Hoopes became the club's punter. Lawless was the only other one who became an immediate starter, moving in to replace John Niland, but some of them were used on obvious passing situations and they added a new dimension to specialty team play.

Experts say it takes four or five years to really make a judgment on a draft but in 1975 the dividends were immediate and, using the accepted yardstick, phenomenal as White, Henderson, Lawless, Breunig, Donovan and Scott became starters. Laidlaw, Hegman and Hughes also have started at times.

"The draft we had in 1975 helped point this team in the right direction again," said Landry. "I'm not sure what would have happened without it but we'd have had a lot of problems."

The club surprised nobody in preseason, posting a 2–4 record. Landry knew he needed another running back. Of course, none was available, but then strange circumstances took place. As preseason ended Pittsburgh cut nine-year veteran Preston Pearson. Nobody claimed Pearson when he was cut except Dallas. Nobody wanted him except Dallas. So the Cowboys picked him up and he became the final missing link for the surprise team, the Cinderella team of 1975.

Landry used Preston beautifully. He wasn't a big running back, a guy you could give the ball to twenty times. But he was a good route runner, an excellent receiver and superb on screens when he was out of the congestion of tacklers and had room to weave and maneuver. What Landry would do was run him nine or ten times a game, insert Doug Dennison for short yardage plays and utilize fullback Robert Newhouse as the key down-to-down runner.

"The man [Landry] used me perfectly, let me do the things I do best," said Preston. "I'm best in one-on-one situations, where I can beat one man at a time and that's the situation he tried to get me in. Nobody ever has utilized the things I do best as Coach Landry did."

"Tom did his best job of coaching that year," said Lee Roy Jordan. "We had a great, exciting feeling on the team and a lot of enthusiasm.

I know it made me feel like a rookie again with the way all those young guys came in there and played so hard. There wasn't the great experience and super talent that we'd had on the championship team in 1971 but Tom would try things, move people around and take advantage of what each person could do best. What happened was that Tom was in a situation which challenged his mind. He really responded, gambled a lot, took chances and it was the most exciting year I can remember."

The early schedule was not kind to Dallas. Experts were picking the Los Angeles Rams, a team with everything, to win the Super Bowl and the St. Louis Cardinals, who had solidified under Don Coryell, an offensive genius, to win the NFC East over the Washington Redskins. The Cowboys were a very dark horse. So Dallas had to open the regular season against the Rams, a team which had beaten them, 35-7, in preseason, and then play the Cardinals.

It was obvious from the first that Landry was going to get a fine defensive effort. The fact was that Landry had the Rams' number on offense. Under Chuck Knox LA ran a very simplified offense, predicated on first downs. The Rams wanted four, five yards on first down and then could get the defense in a pass-run guessing situation. But Landry seemed to know exactly what the Rams would do; the Cowboys stopped them on first down and all afternoon Jordan, Waters, Harris and the defense appeared to be in LA's offensive huddle.

However, LA had a great defensive team but it was not so great that it couldn't be outsmarted by Landry. Roger Staubach was a natural in the Spread, which the team used 17 times against the Rams. Staubach ran seven times for 50 yards and, on crucial third-down plays, took off on passing plays for gains of 15, 17 and 13 yards. Twice Landry completely fooled the Rams by calling shuttle passes in which Staubach would take the snap out of the Spread, fade, then just toss the ball underhand to a back running a few yards in front of him but still behind the line of scrimmage. The plays netted 21- and 17-yard gains. There also was another key upon which Landry had not planned. New rookie punter Mitch Hoopes always had fantasized about being a triple-threat running back. So once on fourth down he took off for a 13-yard gain to keep a drive alive. All the elements spelled a shocking 18-7 win for Dallas.

Ram linebacker Isiah Robertson, frustrated, mad and unhappy, as were most of the Rams, said about the Spread, "It's a rinky-dink formation. It'll catch up with them before the season is over." Oddly enough, it would catch up with the Rams once again that year and even today Landry often uses the Spread on obvious passing downs.

People downgraded the formation, but by the end of the season the third-down success rate of the Spread was 44.5 percent, whereas the usual success rate on third downs is 33 percent.

Landry knew if Dallas could split its first two games he'd be happy. So after beating LA he just didn't believe the team could handle the Cardinals. If the Cowboys had a chance they'd have to outscore St. Louis, because nobody could stop Jim Hart, Mel Gray, Terry Metcalf and Co. from putting up points. But with Staubach passing for 307 yards and three touchdowns, Dallas did outscore the Cardinals, posting a 37–31 overtime victory.

"When we upset Los Angeles and St. Louis," said Landry, "we gained momentum that was necessary to catapult us the rest of the season. None of us dared think about making the Super Bowl at that time but we just were concentrating on having a better season than we'd had in 1974."

But with Staubach at his best and Landry finding success on everything from fullback passes, featuring Robert Newhouse, to reverses on kickoffs, starring Thomas Henderson, the Cowboys posted a 10–4 record to finish a single game behind the Cardinals in the NFC East and gain the wildcard spot in the play-offs. Actually, had it not been for a 30–24 overtime loss to the Redskins, Dallas would have matched the Cardinals' record. Dallas had the Redskins beat in regulation play but Toni Fritsch badly missed a short field goal attempt.

As the wildcard team Dallas couldn't be at home during the play-offs so in the first round it traveled to Bloomington to play the defending NFC champions, the Minnesota Vikings.

Landry had confidence the team could play with anybody. "It kept surprising me and then, finally, the things that happened were no surprise," he said. Dallas actually outplayed the Vikings but trailed 14–10 as Minnesota got one gimme touchdown when a Viking punt touched a Cowboy blocker and was recovered at the Dallas four.

The crowd, much as the one had done in San Francisco in the 1972 play-off game, began to go to the exits, holding up their hands and signifying the Vikings were No. 1. The Cowboys set up deep in their own territory in the final minute but seemed stopped when they faced a fourth and six from their own 25 with 44 seconds left. Staubach threw for the sidelines and Drew Pearson, the club's great clutch receiver, made a fine catch, stepping out of bounds at the 50. Two plays later the Cowboys were still at the 50 with 24 seconds left, perhaps time for one more play, maybe two. From the Spread, Staubach faded, waited as long as he could and then arched a long pass toward Pearson, speeding down the sidelines step-to-step with cornerback Nate Wright. As the ball came down Pearson and Wright both slowed down to wait but somehow, miraculously, Pearson maneuvered and caught the ball just off his hip around the five-yard line as Wright fell. Drew then lunged into the end zone. The Cowboys, who had been beaten, won 17–14 on what became known as the "Hail Mary" pass.

"It was amazing, unbelievable," said Landry. "I can't believe the ball stuck on Drew's hip like that. It was a thousand-to-one shot but, I tell you, I'll take it. The game was out of my hands. Roger called the play and he and Drew executed it."

Los Angeles and Minnesota had the best regular season records in the NFC (12–2) and most had conceded they would meet for the conference title in Bloomington. The Rams crushed St. Louis 35–23 in the divisional play-off, and had expected to watch the Vikings beat Dallas on television the next day.

"Psychologically, our victory over Minnesota worked against the Rams," explained Landry. "They had expected to have to go north to Minnesota for the championship game. They were more concerned over playing Minnesota than they were having to play us. The Ram players had written off our regular season victory over them as a fluke. I'm sure Chuck Knox tried to tell them we had a pretty good football team but the Rams already were talking about playing in the Super Bowl."

Los Angeles that season had allowed just 135 points, the second lowest in a 14-game schedule in NFL history. Quarterback Jimmy Harris had been injured but Ron Jaworski had moved in and led the team to a victory over the Pittsburgh Steelers. Some of the Ram players talked about how they'd beaten Pittsburgh once and they could do it again, if the Steelers went on to win the AFC. They had not calculated the team Dallas had become nor the effectiveness of Landry's "rinky-dink" Spread Formation.

On a fine sunny day in the Los Angeles Coliseum a SRO crowd of 84,483 watched the Cowboys totally fool and dismantle the Rams. Landry had geared his Flex Defense to stop Lawrence McCutcheon and it was never more effective, holding the fine Ram running back to 10 yards on 11 carries and the entire Ram offensive to a net 118 yards.

Meanwhile, Roger Staubach and Preston Pearson, the halfback nobody wanted, were going wild. Before the afternoon had ended Staubach would have completed 16 of 26 passes for 220 yards and four touchdowns, three of which would be caught by Pearson. Dallas had taken a 21–0 halftime lead with Pearson making a tremendous, diving stab on his fingertips for the first score from 18 yards out. As the second half began the Rams felt they still had a chance. Dallas moved to a third and nine at the LA 19 in the third period and Landry called for the old shuttle pass out of the Spread. Only this time, he decided to run it to the weakside, taking advantage of end Fred Dryer's aggressive pass rush and linebacker Isiah Robertson's great pride in pass coverage. The play moved from the drawing board to the field without a hitch. Staubach took the snap and started to his left. Dryer shot in after him and Robertson chased a back coming out of the backfield on a deep route. Suddenly, Preston, lined up far to the right, came galloping across field behind the line of scrimmage. Staubach just tossed him a basketball-like pass and Preston went right up the alley, vacated by Dryer and Robertson, and scored. If the game had not been over already, it was then, as Dallas won 37–7 to move into Super Bowl X in Miami. The clock had never struck midnight for what they were calling Landry's Cinderella team. It had become the first wildcard club ever to win a conference championship and advance to the Super Bowl.

"I had thought," admitted Landry, "the final score might be in the 13–7 area but everything we tried worked."

The Pittsburgh Steelers had won Super Bowl IX over Minnesota, 16–6, to give Art Rooney, one of the great old men of the NFL, his first championship ever. In Super Bowl X on January 18, 1976, the Steelers were favored to join Green Bay and Miami in having won two Super Bowl games. The strength of the team was a tremendous defense, featuring a front four of Joe Greene, Ernie Holmes, Dwight White and L. C. Greenwood, a hard-hitting secondary led by Mel Blount and an offense featuring Terry Bradshaw, Franco Harris and Lynn Swann.

Landry knew he could not match the Steelers so he again planned to open things up and try to catch them by surprise. The thing he did not expect was that the Steelers would be able to rough up his receivers without receiving a single penalty. There is no doubt Pittsburgh was better than Dallas but it was unbelievable that the Steelers, the most penalized team in the NFL, could go through the entire Super Bowl game without being penalized a single time.

On the opening kickoff Dallas tried a reverse to Thomas Henderson, who almost broke all the way but, even though he was stopped, set up a 29-yard scoring pass from Staubach to Drew Pearson. Dallas held the lead until the final period but the Cowboy receivers, Golden Richards and Drew Pearson, both on the small side, were being bounced around by the Steelers. Richards finally was knocked out of the game with broken ribs after taking an elbow. Lynn Swann was killing Dallas by making fine catches with Mark Washington draped all over him. One catch set up a touchdown but Dallas still led 10–7 in the final period when Mitch Hoopes went into his own end zone to punt. Veteran Dave Edwards failed to pick up Reggie Harrison, who blocked the punt out of the end zone for a safety. Pittsburgh, with good field position, scored a field goal after Hoopes's free kick from the 20, giving the Steelers a 13–10 lead. Roy Gerela hit another field goal making it 16–10 and then Bradshaw and Swann combined on a tremendous play to put the game away despite a furious finish by the Cowboys, who never quit.

With third down from its own 36, Dallas had a blitz on. As Bradshaw faded, linebacker D. D. Lewis went in too high and missed him, allowing him to arch a long pass down the middle of the field. Swann went up, took the ball from Washington at the five and scored with 2:54 remaining. Staubach took Dallas 80 yards to bring the count to 21–17 but his final desperation pass for Drew Pearson in the end zone was intercepted as time ran out. The Cowboy magic had ended.

"We didn't play a bad football game," Landry said, after watching game films. "The fact that Pittsburgh didn't get any penalties was very unusual. It also looked like some of our receivers were being held and couldn't get downfield. But we played well. We were a team.

"Had we known the way the game would be called [the tactics allowed by defensive backs] we might have been more ready for it. But, still, we had our chances and we lost to a great team."

Staubach didn't lead the NFL in passing, finishing second in the NFC to Fran Tarkenton, but Landry said, "Nobody in the league did more for his team than Roger."

And, as far as the season was concerned, the unexpected success, Landry said, "This was the most satisfying year I've had as a coach. It was very exciting in 1966 when we became a top team for the first time but I enjoyed this year even more. This team never thought it was going any place until it got there. That happened all the way to the end. Therefore, it was a most gratifying year for me. Goodness, what was so delightful for me was the type of players, the best group I've had from the standpoint of character, morale, spirit and teamwork. They're the type who give you your greatest reward from coaching, who really make it enjoyable."

The 8–6 record of the previous year had not been, as most had predicted, a first step in the demise of the Dallas Cowboys. It only had been a mirage. The Cowboys were back.

15

CONSIDERING the accomplishments he'd made in his profession and the great influence he'd had on the community for such a long time, it seemed very belated in coming, but in mid-March, 1976, the city of Dallas finally got around to honoring Tom Landry with an appreciation dinner. The affair was held at the plush, downtown Fairmont Hotel and a capacity crowd of 1,400 paid $100 a plate to jam into the Regency Ballroom. Proceeds went to benefit Trinity Christian Academy.

Frank Gifford and Sam Huff flew in from New York to honor their former coach. Phyllis George was there to help with the program and Mrs. Vince Lombardi, whose late husband had coached with Landry in New York and against him at Green Bay and Washington, was a surprise guest.

Dick Nolan, who had made the trip from San Francisco to honor his friend, surveyed the packed house and called to Landry, "Hey, Tom, there are more people here than used to come to our games in the Cotton Bowl."

A format reminiscent of the old television program, "This Is Your Life," was used to reunite Landry with relatives, former coaches and friends from his past. It was declared "Tom Landry Day" in Dallas and congratulatory telegrams were received from President Ford and Texas Governor Dolph Briscoe.

About an hour before the banquet began I cornered Huff in the hospitality room where, instead of alcoholic beverages, Dr. Pepper was being served, and asked him what most impressed him about Landry.

"He has the most beautiful woman in the world," said Huff, grinning. "Man, Alicia is beautiful. She has to be the best draft pick Tom ever made."

And then Huff, the original middle linebacker in Landry's first 4-3 defense in New York, added, "Tom Landry is good people. People take him for granted. Nobody's been as consistent as he has coaching. Year after year after year he goes out and does a top job. Players come and go but Landry keeps the team one of the best. Look at last year [1975]. No way that club makes it to the Super Bowl but, yet, it does."

And as Huff took his place behind the podium during the formal festivities at the dinner, he told the audience, "It's about time somebody around here realized what Tom's done and honored him. I think people just take him for granted. They don't appreciate him like they should."

"Tom Landry is the best coach in the NFL," said Frank Gifford.

Bob Lilly, who had retired in the summer of 1975, was very moved and said, "I regret my true feelings about Tom Landry never have become a matter of public record. But he's one of the finest men I've ever come in contact with and I can honestly say he's had more of a positive influence on my life than anybody."

Preston Pearson also was on hand from his home in Pittsburgh. When someone expressed surprise that Preston, who had been with the club just one year, would make a long trip for the dinner, he said, "The man gave me my life. No way I would miss this."

Baylor University coach Grant Teaff, who emceed the banquet, said, "Tom Landry is the type of hero we need in this country."

"I taught him everything he knows," said Nolan, adding a light touch to the festivities.

Jerry Tubbs, who had been Landry's middle linebacker in the early days with the Cowboys, Lee Roy Jordan, the current middle linebacker, and Huff were asked to pose for a picture with Landry. Huff and Tubbs already were there when Jordan began walking toward them.

"Well," said Landry, looking first at Huff and then Tubbs, "here comes the one with speed."

Landry thanked everybody and seemed very humbled, almost mesmerized by the honor. "It means so much more to me," he said, "because it happened in the town where I've made my home."

"They could," said Gifford, "honor him every year like this and it wouldn't be inappropriate."

Besides boating, golf, jogging and working out with exercise equipment such as the Nautilus machines at the club's practice facilities, Tom Landry also enjoys playing racketball and tennis whenever he gets the chance. One day he joined Dave Manders, who finally had retired for good after the 1974 season, in a doubles match against assistant coaches Mike Ditka and Danny Reeves. Ditka and Reeves certainly rival Roger Staubach in fiery competitiveness and would make a game of checkers a matter of life and death.

So what began as a friendly game suddenly became very heated, at least for everybody but Landry, who remained calm. With things not going too well for them, Reeves and Ditka began smashing the ball as hard as they could, with little preference where it went. Manders recalled it was like being in a shooting gallery. Dave also picked up the tempo and, once racing to return a shot, crashed into Landry, sending him sprawling on the ground. Typically, Landry didn't say a word, but just got up and resumed the game. Finally Ditka, angered, swung his racket into the air after he missed a return shot. The racket slipped out of his hand and went whizzing right past Landry's head.

"Whew," said Landry. "This game is rougher than I thought."

Prior to the 1976 season Paul Brown, the great innovator of the Cleveland Browns and the man who had helped form the new franchise in Cincinnati, retired, making Landry, going into his seventeenth year, the dean of NFL coaches. Landry, due to his intellectual approach and the way he controlled his emotions, often had been compared to Brown. Brown had brought about many changes in the game and so had Landry. And each was a dapper dresser, seldom seen without a hat. In fact, Landry was named as one of America's twelve best-dressed men in 1976, although there should have been an asterisk after his name because Alicia picks his clothes.

"Tommy just doesn't have time to shop," said Alicia. "But he'd look good in anything."

For the second time Landry also had been honored as "Coach of the Year" for 1975 in the NFL by United Press International and, yet, with the great success he'd had and no pressure whatsoever as far as his job was concerned, he said, "I go to training camp every year scared to death. That keeps me on edge. It makes me careful about evaluating what has happened in the past. I don't look at past records, because they mean nothing to me. But there's always the temptation and it's one you've continually got to fight. During those seasons when we kept going to the play-offs, people would tell me the law of averages was going to catch up with me. That scared me, too. It made me work harder and the result is that the players also worked harder.

"This won't be like last season [1975]. We won't surprise anybody this time. It'll be extremely tough to obtain the same success. We still have a lot of young players who need more seasoning."

Veteran Dave Edwards retired but second-year man Bob Breunig moved into the starting strongside linebacker position. Lee Roy Jordan, who had contemplated making 1975 his final season, decided to come back for one more year while Randy White, an All-American lineman at Maryland, became schooled at middle linebacker. Many, including some on Landry's staff, believed White's natural position was in the defensive line but Landry kept seeing him as the ultimate middle linebacker, a man who was 6 feet 4 inches, 245 pounds, and with the speed and quickness to play the position—a Dick Butkus with speed. It turned out to be a mistake on Landry's part, although some disagree. In 1975 and again in 1976, White was used on special situations as a down line-

218

man and proved an excellent pass rusher. But he remained a backup and had problems when he was put at middle linebacker. Landry reasoned he would adjust in time. In 1977 it became apparent that it would take another year or so for White to become a middle linebacker so Landry moved Breunig, who had played the position in college, into the middle to take over for Lee Roy Jordan. Still stubborn about White's future as a linebacker, Landry put him in the strongside position. He did all right, but three games into the preseason of 1977, Landry finally moved White to weakside tackle, the position Bob Lilly played. Almost immediately White became one of the great stars of the club, making the Pro Bowl and becoming co-MVP with Harvey Martin in Super Bowl XII. In 1978 White was named Defensive Player of the Year in the NFL, made all the All-Pro teams and people had begun to compare him with Bob Lilly.

It just makes you wonder where he might have been had not Landry tried to make a linebacker out of him for his first two years in the league. In effect, he was out of position for two years. However, many, including Dick Nolan, argue that the experience White gained by playing the other positions make him a better lineman because he had a better over-all picture of the defense. But the results of White's move from line-backer to weakside tackle was certainly as successful and dramatic as Bob Lilly's had been when he was switched from defensive end to weakside tackle in 1963.

In 1976 Dallas again had some problems at running back due to in-juries to Preston Pearson and Robert Newhouse. Doug Dennison, making just 542 yards, carried the brunt of the running game with Scott Laidlaw coming on and doing a good job in Newhouse's spot. But there was no Duane Thomas, no Calvin Hill. All-Pro tackle Rayfield Wright and Jethro Pugh also were trying to play with injuries.

These things did not go unnoticed by the opposition. "It was obvious in films that Wright and Pugh were hurting and so were the Cowboy running backs," said one coach. "So we tried to take advantage of these situations."

But what opponents had not counted on was the magnificent per-formance of Roger Staubach. Staubach, throwing mostly to Drew Pear-son, Billy Joe DuPree and Scott Laidlaw, was unbelievable during the first seven games of the season. He was hitting some 70 percent of his passes and threatening to set new standards for an NFL quarterback.

"Staubach isn't All-NFL anymore, he's All-World," said Chicago Bear coach Jack Pardee. "He's doing the best job anybody has ever done."

Dallas won its first five games, lost a cliff-hanger to St. Louis, 21–17, when Mel Gray caught a tipped pass off the arm of Jim Hart for a touchdown. That day, Staubach was good on 21 of 42 passes but had seven dropped, including one which skipped off DuPree's hands in the end zone at the final gun.

For all practical purposes the Cowboys' hope for another Super Bowl ended the next week when they hosted Chicago in Texas Stadium. In the second period Staubach ran four yards for a touchdown but had his right hand stepped on. This not only bruised his hand but chipped a bone. This ended the greatest season he might ever have had.

Craig Morton was gone. Clint Longley was gone. The only backup quarterback Dallas had was Danny White, who, because of the time he spent in the WFL, was a rookie with Dallas. He just didn't have the experience in Landry's system to play. So Staubach, despite the chipped bone, tried to play the following week against Washington. Dallas won, 20–7, but Staubach reinjured his hand. It bothered him the remainder of the season as his passing totals dropped drastically.

However, the defense came alive and Dallas finished with an 11–3 record, the NFC Eastern title and a first-round spot in the play-offs against Western Division titlist, Los Angeles. The game was played in Texas Stadium and became a battle of fine defensive teams. Again, Dallas seemed to have LA's offensive number and led 10–7 in the final period. However, the Rams drove to the Cowboys' one-yard line and Lawrence McCutcheon dove for the end zone on fourth down. An official signaled a touchdown and Lee Roy Jordan and the defensive team went wild, claiming McCutcheon had not crossed the imaginary plane of the goal line.

Strong safety Charlie Waters had kept Dallas in the game. In one of the best defensive performances of the year he had intercepted a pass and blocked two punts, setting up one touchdown and giving Dallas a shot at winning the game late in the final period. After the second blocked punt, Dallas seemed stopped on a fourth and ten at the Ram 17 with 1:37 left and LA leading 14–10. Landry called a play designed to clear the area for a turn-in by tight end Billy Joe DuPree. Staubach, who had a bad day by hitting just 15 of 37 passes and suffering three interceptions, hit DuPree in the numbers on what appeared about the seven-yard line. DuPree was hit and pushed back. An official ruled his forward progress had been the ten, a yard short of the first down. As the clock was running out Pat Haden took a safety in his end zone and LA won, 14–12.

Landry, again, was very blunt after watching films. "We got the short end on two controversial calls," he said. "But, under the circumstances, I thought we played a good game." Landry felt films showed Mc-

Cutcheon had not scored from the one and that DuPree, indeed, had the first down.

He later added that sometimes you get calls and sometimes you don't but that, over the long haul, they tend to even out. But he did admit that sometimes, the timing wasn't too good on such decisions.

"The first seven games we were just outstanding," he said, summarizing the season. "Injuries hurt us and when Roger injured his hand we lost our momentum and never regained it. Roger is as good as anybody playing the game today. In 1975 he literally took us to the Super Bowl and he might well have done it again this year had he not been injured. His knowledge of the game is much better now than at any time. What it boils down to is experience and maturity, two things that can only be gained with passage of a certain amount of time."

Even with Staubach healthy, everybody in the league knew Dallas needed a steady running back, one who could handle the ball twenty times a game and produce. With Landry's blessing, Gil Brandt was hard at work on a deal that would give the club just such a man.

Dallas Cowboy vice-president for personnel development (head of scouting, signing of players) Gil Brandt once said, "I've been around Tom so long I know exactly the kind of player he wants, what his thoughts are in that regard."

As the 1977 draft approached it took no genius to know exactly what Landry needed, but Dallas was not likely to get a top running back when its first-round pick, second to last, came around. So Brandt dealt, conjured, hustled and made a deal with Seattle in which Dallas would trade first-round draft positions, twenty-fifth for second, with the Seahawks and also give Seattle three second-round draft picks Brandt had accumulated. After Tampa Bay made the first pick in the draft—USC's Ricky Bell—Dallas, without blinking an eye, chose Tony Dorsett, the Heisman Trophy winner from Pittsburgh who had set all-time NCAA rushing records. As a footnote, Brandt then turned around and traded the Seahawks Duke Fergerson to get back a second-round draft choice and Dallas picked Glenn Carano.

But Dorsett was the one. He was not big at 5 feet 10 inches, 190 pounds, but had tremendous speed, explosion and everything the Cowboys had not had in a running back. Danny Reeves had been smart and versatile. Duane Thomas had been fluid, had a good feel for running, and Calvin Hill had been strong and consistently ground out the yardage. But Dorsett would easily give the club its greatest breakaway threat.

With the retirement of Lee Roy Jordan and the fact that a number of young players would move into the starting lineup, the 1977 team was a puzzle at first but the pieces were there, and Landry would put them together.

Unlike many would have done, unlike most of us who covered the team believed he would do, Landry did not open the door to the starting team and invite Tony Dorsett to step inside. Dorsett was hampered by minor injuries most of training camp and wasn't the most attentive of players in team meetings, where he might have picked up a point or two about a most complex and confusing system. But anybody would have been blind not to see that the talent was all there. Yet, when the season opened Landry named Preston Pearson as the starting halfback. Preston had had a good camp, and certainly was a fine, valuable player, but there was speculation each week that Dorsett would move in as the starter. Landry didn't so honor Tony until the tenth game of the regular season. Oh, Tony was getting in his playing time and piling up yardage but Landry just wouldn't start him. The feeling is that he wanted Tony to see more clearly what was supposed to happen on plays, where the blocks and tacklers would be coming from, rather than just turn him loose and, perhaps, risk an unnecessary injury. There also was diplomacy involved because some of the veterans resented to a degree Tony's somewhat lackadaisical attitude in meetings and practices. Landry kept saying he would play Tony by "feel" and that he'd turn him loose when he felt the time was ready, not when it appeared so to somebody else.

Tony Dorsett, the most heralded college star to come to the Cowboys, would have to wait. Others would not. The 1977 championship team did not just show up at training camp intact. Landry had not expected to lose two starting offensive linemen, All-Pro tackle Rayfield Wright and guard Blaine Nye. But Nye, who often retired as training camp began only to return after two or three days, this time retired for keeps. Wright reported but his knee kept bothering him and he had to undergo further knee surgery. Landry filled the holes by moving in Pat Donovan for Wright and Tom Rafferty, a fourth-round draft pick in 1976, for Nye. He had to make some gambles on defense. Lee Roy Jordan had been wanting to retire and the club finally decided the time was right to try to get along without him.

Jordan was tough to replace because he'd been a fixture for the Cowboys for fourteen years. Lee Roy had been very fortunate in his career in having played college football at Alabama under Paul (Bear) Bryant and as a pro under Landry. Both were already legendary coaches.

"Landry and Bryant were totally different, alike only in that they both were winners," said Jordan. "Bryant was the greatest motivator

I've ever been around. He wasn't a genius like Landry as far as the technical aspect of the game. But he could really get you excited about playing. He'd get you to a high emotional pitch and sometimes you'd play over your head because you were conditioned to win, physically and mentally. You just thought you were going to win because Bryant made you believe that.

"I don't think there's any doubt Landry is a brilliant man. He isn't a guy who motivates you. He leaves that to the players themselves. But he tells you what it takes to win and does so without emotion. He just states the fact. He's so intelligent that he can coach offense and defense at the same time and I don't think there's anybody else who can do that.

"Playing under Landry and Bryant I learned that there are two different ways, two different approaches to winning. Both are their own men, do things their own way and are very successful at it."

Jordan's retirement caused two position changes. First, Bob Breunig was moved from strongside linebacker to Jordan's position in the middle. Secondly, Thomas Henderson, a backup for D. D. Lewis at weakside linebacker, was moved into the starting strongside linebacker spot. Mel Renfro had too many injury problems to be expected to play week after week so Landry okayed the moving of Aaron Kyle, the No. 1 draft pick in 1976, to the starting right cornerback spot. And the other change, as mentioned before, was putting Randy White at weakside tackle. So, in effect, the 1977 defensive unit had four new starters playing different positions. However, with Harvey Martin posting twenty-three quarterback traps, becoming Defensive Player of the Year in the NFL, the defense was about as strong as ever. Martin, Charlie Waters, Cliff Harris and White all made the Pro Bowl.

The offense was also playing well as Dallas set a team record by winning its first eight games and causing speculation that the club might equal the mark established by the Miami Dolphins of 1972 by going through a fourteen-game schedule and the play-offs undefeated.

"Dallas," said St. Louis coach Don Coryell, "is the best team I've ever seen since I've been in the league."

Others agreed. But after Dallas lost its first game, 24–17, to Coryell's Cardinals, Landry said, "What Miami accomplished was remarkable. But Miami was a very seasoned football team. When people started talking about us being undefeated it was almost ridiculous. We're not a seasoned team. We have excellent potential but going undefeated almost would have been impossible."

The tailspin was brief. Staubach was having injury problems again, which hurt the efficiency of the offense. He'd injured a hip and then sprained a thumb on his throwing hand. After the loss to St. Louis Landry tried to add spark to the offense by starting Dorsett against Pittsburgh but Franco Harris ran wild and the Steelers won, 28–13.

Dallas was 8–2 and hosted the Washington Redskins, the only team with a chance to catch the Cowboys in the NFC East. Landry had not beaten a George Allen-coached Redskin team twice in any season, but he already owned a 34–16 victory in Washington that year.

Dallas beat Washington the second time, 14–7. It would end the great Landry-Allen rivalry because George would leave Washington for Los Angeles after the season. He's now out of football after being let go by LA in preseason of 1978, but everybody expects him back soon. He's too good a coach, too fanatical about football, to remain out of the game.

"We were able consistently to beat Dallas because we were in great condition," Allen recently was quoted as saying. Consistently? While Allen was at Washington, Landry's Cowboys held an 8–7 edge, winning four of the last five meetings between the two teams.

Oddly enough, Landry had worked for the Cowboys' organization without a contract for almost two and a half years after signing for three years in 1974. He finally signed a new contract in November, 1977, which called for some $150,000–$170,000 annually to 1981, but Murchison let it be known that Landry, who also owns a percentage of the club's stock, could coach the team as long as he wanted.

"When Clint said I could have the job as long as I wanted, it was a nice statement and I appreciate it," said Landry. "But we still know I've got to be successful in order to stay. In coaching, you win or you don't. You're successful or you're not. There's no use coaching if you're not doing the job.

"This just has been a fine situation for me. There's never been any real problem or conflict within our organization [among Landry, Schramm and Brandt]."

Dallas won its final three games, including a season-ending 14–7 victory over Denver, which played without injured quarterback Craig Morton. Red Miller was saving him for the play-offs.

Dallas hosted the wildcard Chicago Bears, featuring Walter Payton, and coached by Texan Jack Pardee, in the first round of the play-offs. Pardee had said he felt the Bears might have a chance because Dallas would be looking ahead to the NFC title battle against the winner of the Los Angeles–Minnesota game. Charlie Waters intercepted three passes as Dallas destroyed the Bears, 37–7.

Minnesota beat Los Angeles 14–7 in the other play-off game with backup quarterback Bob Lee replacing the injured Fran Tarkenton.

Dallas played the Vikings for the NFC title and a spot in the Super Bowl. Landry was very confident. "I'm not as concerned about our team as I was at this time last year," he said. "Our team is better than it was at this time last year, mainly because of the running game and Tony Dorsett."

The Cowboys beat Minnesota, 23–6, and moved into New Orleans to play Denver, which had toppled Pittsburgh 34–21 and the defending NFL champion Oakland 20–17 for the AFC title.

Six years before Dallas had won a Super Bowl game in New Orleans.

The Cowboys were housed at the same Hilton Inn across from the airport, but Landry brought an almost entirely different team than the one which had captured the NFL title in January of 1972. There were only three holdover starters from that championship club, so Landry became the first coach to bring practically different teams to the Super Bowl. He'd done an amazing rebuilding job with only a slight setback in 1974, the only year Dallas hadn't been in the play-offs since 1966.

Red Miller was confident, saying the Broncos could win, but Landry said, "I knew we were going to win with the 1971 team but I wasn't really certain what we were going to do against Denver. I did know we had an excellent chance because of the good defense we had been playing. I felt to win we had to play great defense and knew we needed to come up with turnovers."

Landry was also truly proud of Craig Morton, who had come over from New York to give Denver enough offensive leadership to go with the Broncos' fine defense. "We think the world of Craig Morton," said Landry. "He was a winner when we had him here and he's come onto a fine team and done an outstanding job, much as Y. A. Tittle did when he went to the New York Giants years ago and Billy Kilmer, when he went to the Redskins. Craig has a lot of talent, is smart and can beat you. You have to put a lot of pressure on him or he'll pick you apart."

Super Bowl XII was played in the gigantic Superdome before 76,400 fans and was billed as a contest between the "cool" of the Cowboys and the "emotion" of the Broncos. Landry later would say it was the highest a team of his had been for a game.

The defense, led by MVP's Randy White and Harvey Martin, simply swamped Morton, who had played so well in play-off victories over Pittsburgh and Oakland. Against a torrid rush he managed to complete just four of fifteen passes, was trapped twice and hurried six other times. Furthermore, he suffered four interceptions.

"We just put too much pressure on him," said Landry. "Craig didn't have much of a chance to show what he could do."

Dallas, leading 13–0, had dominated the first half and, during intermission, Landry reminded his players that the Broncos had had the characteristic all season of making a big play and then surging back. This is exactly what happened as Denver's Rick Upchurch returned a kickoff for a Super Bowl record 67 yards to set up the Broncos' only touchdown. Dallas had a 20–10 lead in the final period but Harvey Martin slammed into Norris Weese, who had replaced the ineffective Morton at quarterback, causing him to cough up the ball to cornerback Aaron Kyle at the Bronco 29.

All week Dallas had worked on a fullback pass by Robert Newhouse. During the game Landry had waited for the right moment to use it. "When Denver lost that fumble, its defense, I felt, would be negative in its thinking," said Landry. "So I thought the time was proper."

Landry called "Brown Right, X-opposite shift, toss 38, halfback lead, fullback pass to Y." On first down from the 29, Staubach lateraled to Newhouse, going to his left. Golden Richards, the split end, started toward cornerback Steve Foley as if to block him. Foley, as had been his tendency, already had come up too fast to play what appeared to be a fullback sweep. He couldn't recover and free safety Bernard Jackson could not get over quickly enough as Newhouse pulled up, then lofted a fine pass to Richards, who took it into his arms and scored with 7:11 remaining. Dallas had put the game away, 27–10.

Dallas joined Green Bay, Miami and Pittsburgh in having won two Super Bowl games. "I think," reflected Landry, "that the ones of us at both games probably felt more satisfaction with the Super Bowl victory in 1972 because people were saying then we couldn't win the Big One. That team had gone through a lot of heartbreak, so it was a great feeling to do it.

"This team doesn't have the experience of that club but, overall, it probably has more top athletes. I felt all along it was possible for this team to do it. It had to put together three outstanding games, two in the play-offs and one in the Super Bowl. It did and that makes us all feel great."

The players had said for some time that they had begun to feel closer to Landry, that he had loosened up. This certainly showed up during a team party held in early June, 1978. Players, coaches, club officials were standing around the swimming pool at a Dallas country club when somebody got the idea to start tossing people into the pool. After the Super Bowl victory in 1972, nobody had had the nerve to push Landry into the shower, as they had Tex Schramm. But this time they did. A bunch of players grabbed him and threw him into the water. He took three players with him. They all came up, wet and smiling. It was a great time for Landry. He had rebuilt his club and was back on top of the NFL.

One of the happiest people after the Super Bowl was Ray Landry, Tom's father. He had gone to the game and Tom had taken him to both the pregame and postgame festivities and, after the Cowboys' victory, he couldn't wait to get back to Mission and tell his friends some of the real inside stories. Ray had gone through a bad period. His wife, Ruth Della, Tom's mother, had died on May 12, 1975, at the age of 76. They had dated while in high school and been married for 55 years and her death left a terribly empty place in his life. He really missed her presence, her quiet dignity, and sometimes he would forget that she was gone and expect to see her.

Some six months after Ruth's death Ray again had begun to do the things he liked to do. He was keeping up with all sports and began to hunt and fish again. One day he was deer hunting when he seemed to lose control and fell. He'd suffered a stroke. It was awfully hard for a while but he was determined to come back, to be able to take care of himself again and he did.

"My goodness," recalled Viola Bourgeois, Ray's sister, "when he got back from New Orleans he was so happy. Just bubbling over and so proud of Tommy and what he had accomplished."

On October 10, 1978, two days after the Dallas Cowboys had brought their record to 4–2 by beating the New York Giants in Texas Stadium, Ray and his brother Arthur, visiting from Oklahoma, were waiting around to watch the World Series when Ray became restless. He told Arthur he was going out to mow the yard. After a few minutes Arthur went out to join him. Suddenly, Ray stopped mowing. He sighed, then fell over backwards. He was dead.

Ray Landry had died just over a month before his eightieth birthday. Tom left to help make arrangements for the funeral, one which the entire town of Mission seemed to attend. A procession went through town, passing the park which had been named after Ray Landry. Relatives and townspeople kept coming up to Tom after the funeral to shake his hand, tell him how proud Ray had been of him. The funeral grounds also were near a school and children waited nearby to get a glimpse of Landry. Tom, Alicia, Tom Jr., Kitty and Lisa were there together, a family. Outside of God, Tom Landry's family always had been the most important thing in his life. It had been the same with Ray Landry.

Photograph courtesy of the *Dallas Morning News*.

Pete Rozelle presents the Field Scovell Award to Tom Landry.

Tom and Alicia Landry with daughter, Lisa.

Danny White, Coach Landry, and Butch Johnson.

Russ Russell photo.

Landry on the sidelines.

Photographs courtesy of *Texas Football Magazine*.

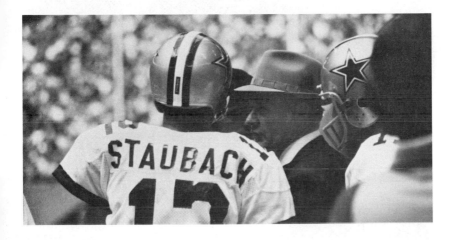

Locker room talk.

Landry is intense both at games and at practice.

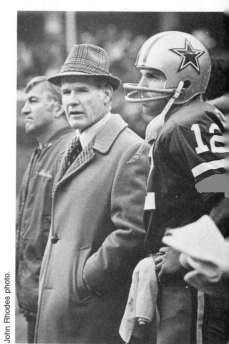

Landry is very cooperative at news conferences.

At the Green Bay Packers game, October 19, 1975.

Landry keeps fit with regular workouts.

Russ Russell photo.

"Here's how you do it!"   Russ Russell photo.

The Landrys and the Murchisons recently hosted a benefit for the

Center for Pastoral Care and Family Counseling in Dallas.

16

THE TOM LANDRY home nestles on an acre and a third of wooded area and is difficult to see from the street, unless you know where you're going and what you're looking for. Actually, it is the best of two worlds. It is very much within the city, a short distance from the heavy traffic flow, and yet the trees buffer the sounds of nine to five and, along with a creek running through the property, help lend a feeling of being out in the country.

Until they bought the house a few years ago, the Landrys had spent most of their years in Dallas in a home in an upper-middle-class North Dallas neighborhood. But when Tom, Jr. and Kitty grew up and moved away and only Lisa remained at home, the Landrys no longer needed a five-bedroom home and began to look around for something more practical. They found the French Colonial in about as secluded an area as you can find and still be in the city, and bought it. The house is some twenty-seven years old, has about the same square footage as the other house, although it isn't concentrated in bedrooms, and their property has three greenhouses, a pool, and ducks often can be found in the pond and creek.

The Landry home fits well in a very affluent section of Dallas in which other large homes also are on tracts of at least an acre. It is a house, a neighborhood suitable for one of the most successful coaches in NFL history, a man who is a minority stockholder and coach of the Dallas Cowboys.

Still it is in Neighborhood, USA, with the daily drama of the gamut from happiness to trauma and soap opera, real and imagined. Yet, the times I have been in Landry's home over the years it has been different from so many others. There has been a great tranquility, not the kind you put on like make-up when the doorbell rings, but a deeper kind. There is control. Things are in place. "I do," Landry has said, "like to see things clean and picked up. So does Alicia."

Tom Landry's home reflects him, as did the former one. Alicia, a child psychology major before she left the University of Texas after her sophomore year to marry Tom, has taken numerous courses in design and interior decorating. She designed and decorated their former house and redecorated their current one. But the house is still Tom because she knows him best, what he wants, how he likes things. Alicia Landry is a

236

beautiful woman who has such strong feelings about pleasing her husband that her philosophy on marriage almost seems to belong to an age long passed. She is happy only if he is happy. She fully understands women's lib, but she also knows what makes her and her husband happy.

Age has been kind to both of them. Once a few years ago when I stopped by, Landry answered the door, and I thought how his physical appearance shamed most men over 35. At 55 he remains trim, in shape, and probably is stronger and in better condition than some players three decades younger. "It's just a form of discipline," he said. "It's very important to me to have discipline so I try to stay in shape. I can't remember when I didn't. If you've done it all your life it just becomes a part of your life, something you always do."

Landry fully understands the limelight and responds in public to the demands of his profession and the call of his religious beliefs. But he does not like to make his home public. He doesn't mind, for instance, if a writer he knows sometimes visits him at home, but he prefers that his home not be written about. A man, even very much in the public eye, must keep something to himself.

Cowboy president-general manager Tex Schramm has worked with Landry for twenty years and, yet, said he had been in Tom's home only a few times. It is amazing that they have gotten along so well so long. Oh, they have disagreed, but each appreciates the other's domain.

When Steve Perkins, who edits the "Cowboy Weekly," a house organ, phoned and asked if he could send a photographer to take pictures in the Landry home, Alicia told him that she wasn't sure because of the cheesecake shots the tabloid ran of the Cowboy Cheerleaders. But she said she would ask Tom. He said no.

Landry had been quoted in a national publication as saying he didn't think the cheerleaders were particularly wholesome-looking on the sidelines and that they distracted from the game. When the organization mounted litigation to stop the pornographic film *Debbie Does Dallas* from being shown in the city because it insinuated that the star was a Cowboy cheerleader, Schramm became worried about Landry's statement.

"What the other side [the one trying to get the picture shown] will say is that even you admit that our cheerleaders are not wholesome, that they are almost pornographic-looking."

"No, no, no, I don't believe that," said Landry. "I didn't mean it that way. I meant wholesome in the context of the way cheerleaders used to be with skirts and sweaters."

Schramm pulled out a tape of the film and when he put it on to illustrate his point, Landry walked out of his office within twenty seconds.

"Tom," Schramm said, "times have changed. Have you been to the beaches lately? What once was considered risqué is now accepted."

"Well," said Landry, "people who feel as I do about religion and Christianity have to deal in absolutes. What is right is right and what is wrong is wrong. Just because times have changed doesn't make something right. Maybe times shouldn't change. I just have a difficult time accepting certain things, such as the way the cheerleaders dress. Sure, I'm aware of what women wear at the beaches. I have a young daughter, you know, and have to contend with modern things myself."

"Tom has his beliefs and sticks by them," Schramm later said. "I know he gets letters from people who don't like the way our cheerleaders look. He'll write them back and say he doesn't condone the way they dress, doesn't believe in it himself, but that the situation is in my domain. Then he'll pass the letters along to me."

Landry was on a benefit show for charity with the Cowboy Cheerleaders but still did not allow pictures of his family to be in issues of the "Insider" along with the cheerleaders.

As the years pass, Landry has become more tolerant of others but has not changed his basic ideals. "I do feel more at ease with myself and others," he said. "I don't know whether it's because I've gotten older or that my faith has improved.

"I think the older you get the more you enjoy life. Certain things don't seem as important as they once did. I think in recent years I've been able to better understand people. Maybe in the early years I didn't appreciate some of the problems people had and didn't accept them in a realistic way. Now, I don't get so hung up on perfection, of people doing things perfectly.

"You look for perfection and you'll be disappointed. I accept the limitations of people better now. I think it goes back to Christianity in my life. I've grown in my faith as I've studied and learned more and it's helped me in my life. Everything is so much more enjoyable as your faith strengthens."

"It seems like since about, oh, 1974 or 1975, Coach Landry appears to be enjoying himself more in regard to the team," said Danny Reeves. "At one time, he seemed very businesslike. But since that time you've been able to joke with him a lot more. He might not always think it's funny but he'll go along with it."

At home you will find Landry wearing a sports shirt, open collar, leisure slacks and shoes and going without the hat that has become a trademark. He will be sitting there with Alicia and you can feel the warmth and understanding between them. When you see him there with her, to say he is cold is like saying, this man is white, this man is black and that is the end of the in-depth description, the character sketch.

"I think the impression of coldness mostly comes across during a game," Landry said. "A coach can't be cheerleader if he's really involved and concentrating the way he has to in order to make the necessary corrections. He can't do it as a pep squad leader. To me it's just like playing golf. Everybody used to say Ben Hogan never would hear people talking when he was walking on a golf course. Distractions can ruin decisions you make on the sidelines. If it's a pass play, I'm trying to read the opposing team's pass defense. A lot of times I won't even see the ball in flight. If it's a running play, I'm looking at the point of attack where the key block is. I have to know whether a play has broken down because of our blocking, or because the other team changed its defense. If you were to see me as a cheerleader, it would mean I was only watching instead of thinking.

"But, sure, at times I'll react to calls or things that happen like other people. I'm also very concerned with players who get hurt. I'd be over there patting them on the back and cheering them on but I'm concentrating on the next play.

"As far as being under control I would say, perhaps, I trained myself to be under control. I've trained myself for a long time to be under control. I know the real secret to success as an athlete is control of yourself and concentration. Those are what make the difference once you get techniques down and training wrapped up. It comes down to the ability to control yourself in stress situations."

"I think," said Alicia, "that a lot of people don't recognize great maturity when they see it. It has bothered me when people would say Tom is cold or doesn't care for his players. That's so untrue. He just has terrific control over his emotions but he feels things just as deeply as anybody.

"He's certainly more outward now than when he first took over the Cowboys. He was the youngest head coach who ever had been in the NFL and he was taking over a new expansion team. It was the most difficult job anybody ever had and took his full concentration. And he did the job, too.

"And Tommy's always been much better with the children than I have because he keeps calm and has a great understanding."

Often, children of successful, well-known parents will be diminished by, or in, their shadows before the children ever really get started in life. The ego or accomplishment of parents not only can cause paranoia in their children but also make small setbacks and failures seem much too large. Sons will try to follow or be pushed into the paths of their fathers, only to find that this was not where their interests lay, not where they really wanted to go.

Tom Landry was very careful none of these things would happen. Landry, certainly, is a very confident man who realizes what he has accomplished, but he is not narcissistic nor has he held his success up before his children, nor allowed anyone else to do so.

Tom Landry, Jr., who has a law degree from the University of Texas and now is in the oil business in Victoria, recalled that his father never pushed him in the direction of football. "I can't recall feeling any pressure either way," he said. "We always were an active family, participating in sports and games and I just liked to play football. Dad would encourage me if I wanted his help and, when I was growing up, he'd play catch with me if I wanted but I just can't remember any pressure at all. When I played I never thought about being his son and living up to anything and I'm sure he had a lot to do with the way I felt. I liked the game but, for me, it was more of a form of recreation, something I enjoyed, rather than something I wanted to be involved with the rest of my life."

He played at St. Mark's Academy in Dallas and accepted a football scholarship at Duke, where he played in the defensive backfield. But at the end of his sophomore year he underwent surgery for the third time on the same knee and doctors, trainers and his coaches advised him to give up the sport.

"I didn't really want to quit playing at that time but, because of my knee problems, it was something I had to do," he said. "No, I never talked to Dad about that decision. I didn't have to."

Tom Landry, Sr. always has said the most important things in his life, in order, are God, his family and then football. When the Cowboys were in New Orleans for the Super Bowl in January 1972, Landry was able to forget the great importance of the game and staged a birthday party for Alicia with all the family in attendance.

"He always has been able to work family occasions into his schedule, no matter how busy he is," said Alicia.

"When I was growing up he was gone a lot," recalled his son, "but we had a pretty normal life when he was at home. He set the highest standards for us but wasn't any big, strict disciplinarian. He never was a great back-slapper either nor a person who carried emotions on his sleeve . . . he wasn't outwardly warm but the warmth was there. I tell you, they just don't make them like him anymore."

Kitty, who is now married to former University of Texas quarterback Eddie Phillips, once said, "When he corrected us, he was usually right and we knew it. There wasn't any big boss stuff." Phillips is in the banking business in Dallas and Kitty still comes by her parents' home each week to visit and also goes jogging with Alicia.

At this writing Lisa, still living at home, has finished two years of junior college and was contemplating attending the University of Texas.

"You try to influence your children to think the way you do in regard to things such as Christian ideals," Landry has said. "Some will lean more to a Christian life than others. You just hope to lay a foundation on which someday, if they've taken another direction, they'll return to the Christian way."

June always has been family vacation time for the Landrys. Over the years they've taken their children to Yellowstone and to the beaches, and the family has fished, played golf and tennis together, gone water-skiing. In recent years, they've still gotten together to go skiing in Colorado.

"Dad, of course," said Tom, Jr., "is just a fine athlete. He does everything well, whether it's golf or skiing."

"Tommy's so good under pressure," said Alicia of her husband. "Well, like in golf, it'll come down to a pressure shot and he'll make it.

"Everybody in the family is a good athlete but me. I like to participate but the times we've all gone skiing in Colorado I've usually been around an instructor while Tommy and the children are off going down those steep slopes.

"I like to play golf, just putter or follow him around. And I enjoy tennis, except I'm near-sighted. I'll toss up the ball to serve and then lose it."

But directly after the season Tom and Alicia usually have gotten away for a few days by themselves.

With the travel, various demands and pressures, professional football hardly seems conducive to a good marriage but, as in most things and situations, it is the people involved who make it work.

"It could have been difficult," said Landry, "if Alicia hadn't been a football fan."

"I love my life," said Alicia. "I love being involved with football. To have a successful marriage it's imperative to have an interest and be involved with your husband's career. It's actually much easier with football because I can be on the scene and share the pleasure as well as the heartaches. A lawyer's or doctor's wife doesn't have that advantage.

"Things are awfully hard for Tommy during the season and we all try to understand that."

During the season Monday, Tuesday and Wednesday are the most difficult days of the week for Landry because he is setting the game plans with his assistants for the offense, defense and specialty teams. On Thursday night after practice Landry tapes his television show and then usually goes out to dinner with Alicia.

"It's difficult to go out to dinner any place where the fans know you," said Landry. "But they're enthusiastic and I understand that."

On Friday Landry comes home for dinner and usually has that night off, although at times he'll spend it in his study looking at films. After a light workout on Saturday mornings when the Cowboys are in town, he'll go home and have, perhaps, his most leisure hours during the season. He'll watch television, read or do nothing at all. Landry likes to read Westerns and also books concerning history, politics and, of course, religion. He also likes Western movies, although he believes they are just not as good as they once were.

When the team goes on the road Alicia usually travels with him on the team charter and they'll usually go out for dinner the night before a game. "By the end of the season I'm exhausted," said Alicia, "but after a week or so I can't wait for it to get started again.

"During the off-season Tommy usually is at home, except for the weekends when he travels for his work with the FCA and things such as that.

"There is nothing at all difficult about being Mrs. Tom Landry. I've never had one person say anything tacky to me or our children. Tommy's the greatest thing going. He's also my best friend and I think I'm his best friend. I just love our life. It's not a nine-to-five humdrum at all.

"One thing I enjoy is the opportunity to meet people that you'd never get to know otherwise. For instance, Billy Graham. Meeting him was a thrill for me. Tommy's a good friend of his. I've gotten to know him fairly well. We've had dinner with him a few times and we took a long automobile ride with him one day, which was really interesting. In fact, my great aunt was one of Billy Graham's teachers when he was studying Bible at Wheaton College."

The Landrys also have been invited to the White House. Alicia said she especially enjoyed talking with Betty Ford a few years ago and attending a dinner for the premier of Israel.

"I look back on our life and wouldn't trade it for anything," she said. "I can remember years in which I don't think we've had a really bad day."

Sometimes I think about how under control a very young man named Tom Landry was as a copilot during missions over Germany in World War II. I think how intelligent he is and how difficult it is to rattle him. Certainly, he makes mistakes but less frequently than anybody I know and usually keeps his head, his cool, when those about him are losing theirs. I think of his attributes and feel he might have been wasted on football, that he should have aimed his life at a bigger stage. I think of so many lesser men who have pushed buttons of war and politics when, perhaps, he could have done so much better, more practically.

"I don't look back on what I've done," he said. "I know this sounds foolish to many people, perhaps ridiculous to non-Christians, but I believe it was God's will that I be what I am—a coach. I put my life in God's hands and believe this is what he wanted me to do, to be. With this in mind I have no hang-ups at all about what I might have done or been. I'm just not one to reflect back on the past very much. When a person does that, he is often affected by what has happened. Therefore, I think of my life as now and the future and don't worry about what might have been, what I might have been. I believe I'm doing what I am supposed to do."

It is not clear what Tom Landry might do when he finally retires from football. He is an honest man and I have told him he should enter politics. He has hinted that he probably would do some kind of religious work. But, of course, it also is not at all clear when he might retire. He has indicated in recent years that he might evaluate his situation in 1980, 1981. But he also has said that this doesn't mean he would retire.

"I feel I'll soon take a look at where I am, what I want to do and see if the incentive is still there to coach," he said. "Right now, it very much is. You know, it's really difficult to get away from this job if your team means something to you. This team means something to me.

"I've always felt I would coach as long as I enjoyed the job, enjoyed working with players. That's the real reward, really, seeing people develop and the things you've planned fall into place, blend. It becomes very exciting. People are the most important aspect of football. To see young people develop and achieve goals transcends everything else in the game."

After the January 1979 Super Bowl loss to Pittsburgh he had said he supposed he and the Cowboys would be remembered in the decade as runners-up. But at another time he had said when asked about himself, "That's for others to evaluate more than me. I've contributed to the technical end of the game I'm sure with the offense and defense we've used through the years. We've been forerunners of the type game now being played. I'm sure I must have had some effect in this area. In other areas, people have to evaluate you as they observe you. Everybody observes the same thing but from a different perspective. In any area, history normally judges a man's success."

Certainly, historians will write that Tom Landry was a very successful coach of a top organization, that he was a great innovator. But, perhaps, they will say that because Green Bay twice edged the Cowboys in the late 1960s, that Vince Lombardi was the coach of the '60s. And, perhaps they will say, although Dallas went to an unprecedented five Super Bowls in the 1970s, that Chuck Noll is the coach of the '70s because the Steelers were the first team to win three Super Bowls. Landry has been so very close to being considered by all as the very best coach of the '60s and '70s and yet he narrowly has missed, often through things beyond his control.

Still, when you leave his home you feel that whatever has happened or will happen, everything will be all right with him, that he does not dwell on the narrow misses of making history. Besides, there is still the 1980s.

A REFLECTION

As I CLOSE this study of Tom Landry, the man and the football legend, I remember a week in early 1968 . . . .

Spanish Cay is in the archipelago that makes up the Bahamas. The waters of the Atlantic, surrounding the small island, seem almost too pure and clear, too blue-green, and the sands are almost white, stretching from the surrounding shore line to a myriad of palm trees covering the interior. Soft breezes seem literally to float over the isle and make you feel as if you're in the middle of one of those movies set in the South Seas. Spanish Cay is the property of Dallas Cowboy majority owner Clint Murchison, Jr., and on it he has had built a landing strip for small craft, a large main house which connects down tree-lined paths to a group of guest rooms that seem like small cottages in themselves, and another nearby house, where those who work for him on the island reside.

It is said that Murchison was looking for a maitre d' when he decided to fly over to Nassau to eat dinner at Blackbeard's, one of the more famous restaurants in the once exotic city where you now can purchase Kentucky Fried Chicken on the corner. Anyway, he very much enjoyed his meal and asked to see the maitre d' and chef. He hired the maitre d' on the spot, to oversee the household at the isle.

I was among the group of media and Cowboy officials, including Tom Landry, who were invited to the island for a few days fishing and escape after the Ice Bowl loss to Green Bay. The isle was so far away, physically and mentally, from football that Landry found it very relaxing, too.

In 1966 I had written some color stories on the Cowboys but hadn't really dealt with Landry on a day-to-day basis until 1967 when I replaced Gary Cartwright, now a free-lance writer living in Austin who has authored a number of books. When that season had ended I'd formed some impressions of Landry but wasn't exactly sure what to think of him. Certainly, he seemed highly intelligent in a football sense, was very cooperative, and I had heard much about his religious convictions. Still, I didn't know what else there was to him. I had spent many years around football coaches who quickly sank when they attempted to talk or relate to anything other than their game.

There were ten of us there but Landry was greatly outnumbered. Five of us were working newspapermen; Tex Schramm had once been sports editor of the Austin *American;* vice president Al Ward had been a sportswriter for the Waco *News-Tribune* and Cowboy public relations director Curt Mosher had left the journalism field to join the Cowboys right before the 1967 season. Only Landry and business manager Tom Hardin had no relationship to sports reporting, either per se or as a skeleton in their closet.

We'd fish during the morning and afternoon and then sit at a huge table and have dinner each evening. When dinner was over, some would play cards, others would read or listen to music or talk. Some people never stop working, really, and would ask Landry questions pertaining to his football team, trying to unlock some secret they'd missed during the season.

One night I found him sitting alone, reading, and invited myself to pull up a chair near him. Once we started talking he would ask me questions about my interests, and we talked about books, movies and somehow got on the subject of the theater. I told him that fall I had seen "The Great White Hope" on Broadway with James Earl Jones and that it had been one of the most moving experiences I'd had. But to my surprise he launched into a very knowledgeable discussion of the Broadway theater and talked about the various shows he'd seen. He said he especially liked "Harvey" and enjoyed watching Mary Martin in various musicals.

"I like music in its place, very much, but just don't enjoy the musicals as much as I do the dramas, either in the theater or the movies," I observed.

"I like some of the musicals," he said. "But some I've seen, I wished they'd move along with the plot. Alicia always liked them. When we were in New York we always went to the Broadway shows. It didn't seem that we missed too many. I didn't particularly care for some of the dramas, the depressing ones. I like to be entertained, not depressed."

We talked for over an hour and for the first time I forgot that he was a football coach and hoped that he forgot I was a writer.

Each day when we'd go fishing the competitive instinct, real or imagined, rose in our blood and so we'd divide into teams, five men going on each of the two boats. We devised a point system for each type of fish we might catch and would tally up each night to see which team won the day's competition. For instance, if you landed a tuna, you got two points, a small grouper, two points, a large grouper, four points, a barracuda, three points, and the marlin we never hooked, 15 points. On each boat were four fishing chairs so, with five fishermen, we rotated. Anytime a guy would land a fish, he'd automatically get up and give his chair to the man who wasn't fishing.

One day I was on the boat with Landry, who insisted he'd rest first and immediately went to a bunk and fell asleep. Every once in a while he'd wake up, check the results, then retire to his bunk to rest or read some paperback Western novel he'd picked up. He finally took a fishing chair and, in less than half an hour, hooked a dolphin. I had been shut out for an hour and a half and said, "Don't get up. I will. I can't catch anything. I'll be sitting here this time tomorrow and nothing'll hit my line."

"You have to think positive," said Landry. "Think positive. Just tell yourself you're going to catch something . . . a marlin." He then retired to the bunk.

"I know you're out there, Moby!" I yelled. "I'll get you if I have to chase you to the ends of the earth!"

"Will you shut up?" growled Frank Luksa. "You're scaring away all the fish in the Atlantic Ocean."

"Now Frank," said Landry from the bunk, "he's just being positive."

Shortly thereafter, something hit my line. I fought and fought and finally brought it in. It was a fish of some unknown origin, about four inches long.

"Well, you got Moby," said Luksa.

"See," said Landry, walking aft, "what happens when you think positive."

That night I initiated a mild political discussion with Landry, beginning something that was to continue on and off for eleven years. Landry is a Republican with conservative leanings, and I am, with some flexibility, a Democrat on the liberal side. But he was very tolerant of my views and, as the night moved along, everyone in the group voiced their opinions. It finally was decided that we'd hold our own impromptu presidential election with some change in format. You did not vote for the candidate of your choice but for the man you felt would become the next President of the United States. Bobby Kennedy won with Nixon drawing three votes.—Kennedy got six votes with one guy voting for Elizabeth Taylor.

Through the years that followed Landry and I often would talk politics prior to the official beginning of his weekly press luncheon in Dallas. There would be a buffet and a long table, branching off into other tables, where radio men, television reporters and newspaper persons would sit to eat. For eleven years Frank Luksa and I sat on either side of Landry at the head table and sometimes would give him a hard time while he was eating, before he stood up to address the media and answer questions.

I learned one thing; Landry is the fastest eater I've ever seen. He would get in line, fill his plate, take his chair and be finished in ten to twelve minutes. The fastest I remember was when he cleaned his plate in five minutes. I found over the years if I didn't beat him through the buffet line, take my seat and get a ten-minute head start, that I couldn't finish my meal before the press conference began.

In 1970 when the Cowboys played in Yankee Stadium the writers were settling down in the press box when policemen came in and started searching typewriter cases, briefcases, under the tables, everywhere. They finally told us there was a bomb scare; somebody had called and said there was a bomb in the press box.

We were getting a little nervous about the prospects when Blackie Sherrod, columnist for the Dallas *Times-Herald,* finished a typically cold and hard New York hot dog and noted, "Don't worry about the bomb, men. I just ate it."

After the game Landry was asked what he'd have done if the press box had blown up during the game. "Hmmm, I suppose we would have observed 30 seconds of silent prayer and then continued play, with enthusiasm," he said.

Seriously, as I look back on the years I covered the Cowboys I believe that Landry treated the media as fairly and honestly as any major news source I've ever known. Certainly, he showed a great deal of restraint and I know we got to him a number of times, especially during the late 1960s when we all were writing that the Cowboys would choke, that they just couldn't win the big one. He hated to read or hear this because he knew the players would read it and, the more they thought about it, the more it would affect them psychologically. But we wrote what had happened, what we felt to be true.

Still, Tom is aware of what is written and has been known to react about it with the players. Former Cowboy defensive end Pat Toomay, in his book, *The Crunch,* recalled two episodes. In 1972 Landry became upset about the way the club was playing and took off his NFL championship ring. He told the team he wasn't going to put it back on until they played like champions. Luksa got wind of this from a player and so did Don Meredith, in town for a television game. Both mentioned it, Luksa in a story and Meredith over the air. This caused Landry to tell the team, "There are signs posted throughout NFL locker rooms that say, 'What you see here, what you hear here, what you say here, stays here.' This applies to us, too. Any player who doesn't have the guts to use his name in an article like that has lost all my respect and doesn't deserve to be on this team."

That same season after the team had performed in a very lackluster way, I wrote in the Dallas *News* that the Cowboys reminded me "of the wishy-washy club of 1968 and 1969." Landry mentioned the article in a team meeting and said something like, "This really bothers me. It hurts me. We're potentially so much better than those teams in the '60s that it isn't funny. Yet, we go out and play like we did . . . ."

During the early years of the Cowboys my predecessor, Gary Cartwright, was prone to say most cynical things about the team, which left itself very open by finding new ways to lose. At a Cowboy Club luncheon, in which Landry answered questions from the audience, he was asked, "Tom, can you tell us how we can get rid of Gary Cartwright?"

"Boy, I tell you Gary has a tough job," said Landry. "You know all of us after losses experience disappointment, are dejected. Gary probably feels the same way we do but he has to sit down at that minute and write his story. He doesn't get to wait around. He has an awfully tough job."

Once a particular writer really had gone after Landry when the team had a 7–1 record and hardly left itself open to criticism. The attacks just seemed to come suddenly, for no logical reason. During the course of a conversation, Landry asked me, using the writer's name. "Is there something wrong?"

"No, not really," I said.

"I don't know . . . he just seems upset or something."

"Actually, he has some personal problems."

"I'm sorry. I hope everything works out all right."

I'm sure Landry feels closer to some newspapermen than he does others but he treats everybody equally, when it comes to news about the club. Because of the Cowboys' vast popularity over the years Landry has remained constantly under scrutiny by the media. He has, I imagine, been criticized more than any winning coach around. But he has remained cooperative and, unlike so many, Landry will not lie to you. Oh, he will stretch things a bit, underplay them or withhold them if he feels it necessary, but he won't lie. You just can't say that about too many.

"He certainly is not beyond getting in little digs at us through the

249

media," said Cliff Harris. "Sometimes you can read things and you know Coach Landry is saying them to try to fire us up, make us more alert."

Before we left Spanish Cay that year some of us got together and decided we should chip in and purchase Murchison a gift for inviting us. We thought and thought . . . what can you buy for a man who has everything? We talked about how nice the guest rooms were, like staying at a fine motel. Motel? The idea came; so we bought Clint a bunch of Gideon Bibles to put in each of his guest rooms.

Whenever I think of Landry, the man, I remember those days on Spanish Cay. I think I got as close to him that week as I ever have—before or since.

Sources

The NFL's Official Encyclopedia of Professional Football, Macmillan, Inc., 1977.

The New York Giants, Dave Klein, Henry Regnery Company, 1973.

There Were Giants in Those Days, Gerald Eskenazi, Grosset & Dunlap, Inc., 1976.

The Crunch, Pat Toomay, W. W. Norton & Company, Inc., 1975.

Dallas Cowboys, Pro or Con, Sam Blair, Doubleday & Company, Inc. 1970.

Next Year's Champion, Steve Perkins, World Publishing Company, 1969.

Cowboy Football Magazine, Editor Dave Campbell.

Lenten Guideposts, Tom Landry, 1971.

Guideposts Magazine, 1970.

Here Come the Texas Longhorns, Lou Maysel, The Stadium Publishing Company, 1970.